HELPFUL,
DEFINITIVE,
COMPLETE

Here is the famous book which tells you
how to be financially successful
in the stock market.

Louis Engel, the author, has been for many
years a partner in one of the country's
top-flight investment firms, where he
specializes in helping people from every
walk of life understand stocks and bonds.

With his wide experience, he writes
with unquestioned authority and a thorough
knowledge of what most people need
to learn about stocks.

Throughout this book, in simple, diamond-clear
language, Mr. Engel makes successful stock
market investment as easy as A. B. C.

IF YOU WANT TO INCREASE
YOUR INCOME, YOU
OWE IT TO YOURSELF TO
READ THIS BOOK!

READ WHAT THE EXPERTS SAY:

New York Times (Burton Crane): "At last there is a book—a two-plus-two-makes-four kind of a book —for incipient investors."

American Banker: "If your reviewer were a banker . . . he would recommend this book without reservation to all potential investors. This book is the first one he has read, written strictly for the layman, in plain everyday English that anybody can understand."

Des Moines Register: "Many books have set out to tell the reader how to get rich, how to 'beat' the market, how to trade, or about various phases of market operations, but this is probably the first book which could hold the interest of either trader or novice."

Christian Science Monitor (Harry C. Kenney): "However, the real importance is in the concise explanation of what it means to invest, how securities are bought and sold, what it costs to buy stocks . . . how one can open an account with a broker, how to find the best in financial advice, and how to read market news."

J. K. Lasser: "Takes the whole story of investing and translates it from the usual financial jargon into words that anybody can understand. And that's a story people ought to know, including a lot of people who already own stocks and bonds."

Financial World: "His book packs authority . . . Your time will not be lost in reading HOW TO BUY STOCKS."

HOW TO BUY STOCKS

BY LOUIS ENGEL

Fourth Edition
REVISED

BANTAM BOOKS · TORONTO · NEW YORK · LONDON

HOW TO BUY STOCKS

*A Bantam Book / published by arrangement with
Little, Brown and Company*

PRINTING HISTORY

Original Little, Brown edition published April 1953

2nd printing	April 1953	9th printing	January 1954
3rd printing	April 1953	10th printing	May 1954
4th printing	April 1953	11th printing	October 1954
5th printing	May 1953	12th printing	April 1955
6th printing	June 1953	13th printing	August 1955
7th printing	August 1953	14th printing	March 1956
8th printing	December 1953	15th printing	June 1956

Little, Brown revised edition published May 1957
Little, Brown third revised edition published January 1962
Little, Brown fourth revised edition published February 1967

Bantam edition published February 1955

2nd printing	February 1955	5th printing	January 1956
3rd printing	March 1955	6th printing	May 1956
4th printing	August 1955	7th printing	September 1956

Bantam revised edition published June 1957

2nd printing	September 1957	5th printing	April 1960
3rd printing	January 1959	6th printing	April 1960
4th printing	August 1959	7th printing	April 1961
8th printing			May 1962

Bantam third revised edition published January 1963

2nd printing	August 1963	5th printing	November 1965
3rd printing	May 1964	6th printing	July 1966
4th printing	November 1964	7th printing	September 1966

Bantam fourth revised edition published July 1967

2nd printing	August 1967	4th printing	February 1968
3rd printing	December 1967	5th printing	August 1968
6th printing			March 1969
7th printing			

To
the memory of
CHARLES E. MERRILL,
*who formed a new philosophy of investing
to fit a new phase of capitalism*

Acknowledgments

SUCH is the process of learning that it is never possible for anyone to say exactly how he acquired any given body of knowledge. And that circumstance I now find somewhat consoling, because in a very real sense this book is not my book, but it is the product of hundreds of different people who over the years have taught me what I have simply written down here.

Obviously, I cannot acknowledge my indebtedness to all these people — many of them I do not even know — and so I must necessarily limit my thanks to those who helped me directly in the preparation and checking of the material in this book.

These include Alger B. Chapman, Jr., Cecil MacCoy, Willard K. Vanderbeck, Stanley West, and F. W. Reiniger of the New York Stock Exchange; John W. Sheehan of the American Stock Exchange; Howard T. Sprow of Brown, Wood, Fuller, Caldwell & Ivey; James H. Lorie and Lawrence Fisher of the University of Chicago; John McKenzie, Russell Morrison, and George Olsen of Standard & Poor's Corporation; Max Fromkin of Fromkin & Fromkin; J. Scott Rattray and Huntly W. F. McKay of the Toronto Stock Exchange; and a score of individuals actively engaged in the securities business — Kenneth R. Williams, Robert L. Stott, Victor B. Cook, Edward A. Pierce, Milija Rubezanin, James E. Thomson, Donald T. Regan, Peter F. McCourt, Cecil C. Burgin, John J. Cahill, Rudolph J. Chval, James D. Corbett, Dwight H. Emanuelson, John F. Ferguson, John A. Fitzgerald, Richard P. Gillette, Calvin Gogolin, Allan D. Gulliver, Gilbert Hammer, Stephen B. Kagan, Arthur L. Kerrigan, George J. Leness, Josiah O. Low, Gillette K. Martin, Michael W. McCarthy, Anthony G. Meyer, Harvey L. Miller, John H. Moller, Samuel Mothner, Joseph C. Quinn, Walter A. Scholl, Julius H. Sedlmayr, Thomas B. Shearman, Robert L. Tebeau, John W. Adams, Jr., and — last but certainly not least — Muriel D. Nutzel, Ann Scourby, Susan Davidson, Elizabeth J. Gibson, Loretta A. Gigante, Loretta D. Hanley, Agnes Rother, Janet K. Low, and Lorraine M. Hanley.

Contents

Foreword

THIS book is based on a very simple premise: that the stock market is going up.

Tomorrow? Next month? Next year?

Maybe yes, maybe no. Maybe the market will be a lot lower then than it is today.

But over any long period of time — 10 years, 20 years, 50 years — this book assumes that the market is bound to go up.

Why?

Because it always has.

Because the market is a measure of the vigor of American business, and unless something drastic happens to America, business is going to go on growing.

Because prices of food and clothing and almost everything else in the country — including stocks — have steadily gone up as the buying power of the dollar has gone down. That's a trend that isn't likely to be reversed.

And so these are the reasons why the author is sold on the value of investing, of buying stocks for the long pull — and not for a quick profit tomorrow.

There's nothing hidden about this prejudice. You'll see it when you read the book. And you will find other prejudices, other opinions, despite an earnest effort to focus this book strictly on facts — the facts about investing that have been obscured all too long by double talk, by financial jargon, and by unnecessary mystery.

Of course it can be said that there are no facts when you get beyond the simple business of adding one and one. That's true. So let's say that here are the facts as the author sees them — and as plainly as he can state them.

He has only one hope: that they will add up to good common sense in your own mind.

LOUIS ENGEL

NOTE: This Foreword was originally written on August 11, 1952. On that day the Dow-Jones industrial average — then as now the most widely accepted measure of the stock market — closed at 280.29. This footnote to the fourth edition is written on October 27, 1966. Today, the Dow-Jones industrial average closed at 809.57.

In the intervening years, the stock market has fluctuated — dramatically so at times, as in 1966, when the Dow-Jones average declined from 995.15 in February to 744.32 in October — but the long-term trend has been unmistakably upward. That performance has served to strengthen my conviction about the value of investing.

Future performance may not be as good as it has been in the past fourteen years — there will even be periods of loss as in 1966 — but there can be no question of the long-term trend, and there need be little fear of any great debacle that would seriously interrupt that trend.

Since this book was last revised five years ago, the winds of change have been blowing with unusual vigor through Wall Street. Already a minor revolution has been wrought in the mechanics of the Street, and before automation runs its course, it is not inconceivable that the computer — by automatically matching buying and selling interests — will usurp some of the trading functions of the New York Stock Exchange and other securities marketplaces.

The other significant change is that which flows from the more aggressive posture assumed by the Securities & Exchange Commission. The resultant reforms, most of them instituted and policed by the industry itself, provide an even greater measure of investor protection.

It is not possible for a book such as this to anticipate all the changes that are bound to come. But, although specific facts and figures cited here may become outdated, nothing can invalidate the book's fundamental thesis that prudent investment in the securities of American business can yield an unmatched return.

                                                              L.E.

A Note
on How to Read This Book

MANY people are afraid to buy stocks because they think investing is a complicated business.

If it were really complicated, more than twenty million Americans wouldn't own stocks, as they do today.

Actually, investing only *sounds* complicated, and that is because it uses a lot of unfamiliar words. The words themselves stand for very simple things.

This book tries to explain the meaning of the technical words by explaining the things they stand for. In other words, each term is explained *in context* as the story of investing unfolds. You won't find a glossary or any long list of definitions anywhere in this book.

In telling the investment story, it begins with the common words in the business — stock, share, capital — and just to be sure that the reader realizes he has encountered such a technical term, the word is italicized the first time it is used. And to be further sure there is no misunderstanding or confusion, no technical term is used until the reader comes logically upon it in the development of the whole thesis.

If the reader has by any chance forgotten the meaning of a particular word, all he has to do is refer to the Index and look back in the book to that page on which the word is first used.

Here, then, is the story of investing told in terms that the author believes everyone can understand — himself included.

CHAPTER 1

What Investment
Means to You

THIS is a book about how to make your money earn more money for you by investing it.

It is not a book about how to make a million in the stock market. If there were any certain way to do that, all the brokers in the world, the men who are supposed to know more than most people about the market, would be millionaires. Needless to say, they're not.

This is a book about investing. Specifically, it's a book about investing in stocks and bonds, which is one way of putting your extra money to work so that in the long run it will earn a good return for you — either in the form of a regular income from dividends or in the form of a profit resulting from growth in value or a combination of both.

Most people, if they have anything left at all after paying their bills, will think first of putting that extra money into a savings bank or into life insurance. Nobody could possibly quarrel with such a prudent course, because these forms of saving or investment are essential if a man is going to protect himself properly against the always unpredictable emergencies of life.

But today millions of people have come to regard *securities* — stocks and bonds in all their varied forms — as another equally good form of investment.

Of course, there's a risk in buying stocks and bonds — and for most people it's a far bigger risk than it needs to be, because they've never taken the time to study securities or find out how to invest in them wisely.

But it should never be forgotten that there's some risk in any form of investment. There's a risk in just having money. Actually, it's a double-barreled risk. The one risk — the risk that you might lose some of your money regardless of what you do with it — is always evident. The other risk is

1

never so apparent. And that's the risk that the money you save today may not buy as much at some future time if prices of food and clothing and almost everything else continue to go up, as indeed they have, more or less steadily, since this country began. The man who simply hoards his extra dollars — puts them in a vault or buries them in the ground — may avoid that first evident risk, the risk of losing any of them, but he can never sidestep the unseen risk, the risk of inflation.

So every decision you make about what to do with your extra money should take into consideration those two kinds of risk — the evident and the unseen.

Naturally, too, you must also consider the return you hope to realize on your money. In most forms of investment the greater the return you try to get, the greater the risk, the *evident* risk, you must be prepared to take.

If you put your money in a savings account, it's almost impossible to lose money because your savings are insured up to $10,000 by the Federal Deposit Insurance Corporation. But most times you have to be willing to accept a return of only 3% or 4% a year, and you have to realize that a savings account provides no protection against the *unseen* risk of inflation. Your money, or capital, won't grow except by the redeposit of the interest you get, and then only slowly.

Life insurance is also virtually 100% safe, thanks to state and federal laws. But there's more sense in buying a standard life insurance policy to protect your family than there is in buying it as an investment. Over a long period of years, the usual life insurance policy may yield a return somewhat better than that of a savings account, but it too fails to protect you against the *unseen* risk. The money you may get on such a policy when you retire is not likely to buy as much as you could have bought with all the money you paid out on premiums over the years.

What else might you do with your money? Well, you might put it into a savings and loan association which makes a business of lending money on home mortgages. Thanks again to government supervision, that kind of investment on your part will be relatively safe as far as the *evident* risk is concerned, but it will probably pay you only about 1% more interest than you would get on a savings account, and it will not protect you against the *unseen* risk of inflation.

You can invest in real estate. And as a general rule real

estate prices are likely to rise if the prices of other things do. So there, you say, you can find protection against that *unseen* risk. Yes, there you can — provided you buy the right piece of property at the right time and at the right figure, and provided you're just as lucky when you sell it. Provided, too, that all the taxes you pay while you own the property don't eat up your potential profit, and provided you cope with all the unpredictable actions of local zoning and assessment boards. Here the *evident* risks are so great, even for those who work full time at buying, developing, managing, and selling properties, that real estate must be classified not as an investment but as a speculation for the average man with only a little extra money.

Finally, you can invest in stocks and bonds. That's what banks do with at least part of the money you deposit with them, in order to earn the interest they pay you and to earn a profit for themselves. The same thing is true of insurance companies. Both kinds of institutions have always invested heavily in bonds, but today they are buying more and more stocks to the limits permitted by the various state laws. Furthermore, commercial banks and trust companies, which are responsible for funds left with them to invest for various beneficiaries, are putting a greater proportion of those funds into stocks.

Why?

Because over the years, the record shows that the average stock has paid a better return and provided a better balance of protection against the evident and unseen risks than any other form of investment.

The stockholders of America are the people who own much of America's business — virtually all its more important business. As that business has grown, stockowners have prospered. As it continues to grow, they will continue to prosper.

Not all of them have prospered all the time. Of course not. But most of them have most of the time. Some have made millions, and some have gone broke, just as some companies have succeeded and some have failed. But over the years, the average investor has earned from 3% to 7% in annual payments on his money. Most important of all, he has seen his stockholdings go up in value as prices generally have risen, and he has thus protected his money against the unseen risk of inflation.

These are the reasons why millions of people are buying

stocks today who never gave them a thought until a few years ago. And uniformly they're finding that it pays to know something about the fundamentals of the business. So . . .

CHAPTER 2

What You Should Know about Common Stocks

THERE'S nothing commonplace about *common stock*. It's the Number 1 security in our system, basic to all corporate business and to our whole free-enterprise system. If you own a *share* of stock in a company, you own part of that company. You and the other shareholders own the company in common.

How does common stock come into being?

Assume for the moment that you've invented a fine new collapsible metal fishing rod. You've got your patents, and you're convinced there is a splendid market for your pocket fishing pole.

You're all ready to begin production, except for that one essential: *capital*. You haven't got the money to rent a small factory, buy the necessary machinery, and hire labor and salesmen. You could get your business under way for $20,000, but you haven't got $20,000. The bank won't lend it to you simply on the strength of your patents, and you can't find an "angel" with that kind of cash to put in your business.

So you decide to form a company and sell shares in the venture. You file the necessary incorporation papers as required by your state law, and the Pocket Pole Company, Incorporated, comes into being.

In setting up that company, you might find twenty men, each of whom was willing to put up an even $1000 of *venture capital*. In that case you'd have to issue and sell only twenty shares of stock at $1000 apiece. Then every man who bought such a share would own 1/20 of the company.

But one man might be willing to put $2000 into your Pocket Pole Company, while another man could only afford to invest $200. So instead of issuing twenty shares of stock at $1000 each, you decide it's better to put a lower price on every share of stock and sell more shares. Such a plan would be more attractive to the people who might be interested in buying the stock, because if they ever had to sell it, they would probably find it easier to dispose of lower-priced shares. After all, more people can spare $10 or $100 than can afford to invest in $1000 units.

So you finally decide to *issue* 2000 shares at $10 apiece. Taken collectively, those shares would represent the common stock issue of the Pocket Pole Company, and the $10 price you set would represent its *par value*.

You sell the 2000 shares at $10 apiece, and by this means you raise the $20,000 capital you need. The Pocket Pole Company is in business. Actually, of course, you might well think of Pocket Pole as *your* business, and when the company was set up, you might bargain with the other stockholders so that you could acquire a stock interest in the company at little or no cost to yourself, but for purposes of simplicity it can be assumed here that you simply buy your stock like any other stockholder.

Every man who owns a share of Pocket Pole stock is a stockholder in the company. He is a share owner, a part owner. How big a part of the company he owns depends on how many shares he buys in relation to the 2000 which are sold or outstanding. If he buys one share, he owns 1/2000 of the company. If he buys twenty shares, he owns 1/100, or 1%, of the company. As evidence of his ownership, a *stock certificate* is issued to each stockholder showing the number of shares he owns.

When the stock is all sold, let's assume the company finds that it has 50 stockholders on its books. Now it would be difficult to operate Pocket Pole if all 50 of them had to be consulted about every major decision — whether to buy this lathe or that one, whether to price the product at $20 or $25.

So the stockholders elect a *board of directors* to oversee the operations of the company. How is the board picked? By the stockholders on the basis of the number of shares of stock each man owns. If there are five men to be elected to the board, each for a set term, the man who owns one share of stock will, as a matter of general practice, be allowed one vote for each of the five vacancies, and the man who owns ten shares will have ten votes for each vacancy.

This five-man board of directors elects its own chairman, and once organized, it is responsible for managing the affairs of the Pocket Pole Company. Since in most instances the board members can't give their full time to the job of running the company, they pick a president to be the actual operating head, and they also name the other major officers. Such officers may or may not be members of the board, but they are responsible to the full board, and periodically — perhaps once a month or once a quarter — the officers report to the board on the progress of the company and their conduct of its affairs.

Then once a year the Pocket Pole Company board of directors will conduct a meeting open to all the stockholders at which the management makes its *annual report* to the owners. Furthermore, the board supplies all stockholders, those present and those absent, with a copy of the report.

If any stockholder is dissatisfied with the way things are going, he can speak his mind at the meeting. He may even make a motion that the board adopt some policy or procedure that he thinks is a better one, and if the motion is in order, it will be submitted to the stockholders for a vote. In most instances, such issues are decided by a simple majority vote with each stockholder being allowed as many votes as he has shares.

If an action that requires a vote of the shareowners is scheduled to come before a meeting, such as the election of new directors, each stockholder is notified, and if he cannot attend the *annual meeting* and vote, he is usually asked to sign a paper that authorizes one or more of the officers or directors to act as his *proxy*, or representative, and vote for him. Sometimes when new directors are to be elected, a dissident group of stockholders will propose a rival slate in opposition to those picked by the management. In such a fight, each camp is likely to solicit signed proxies from the stockholders.

In addition to the regular meetings of the board or the annual meeting of the stockholders, special meetings of either group may be called to deal with special problems.

Why should anybody invest his money in the Pocket Pole Company? Because he thinks it has a good product and one that is likely to make money. If it does, he as a part owner stands to make money. That can happen in two ways: first, through the payment of *dividends*, and secondly, through an increase in the value of Pocket Pole stock.

Let's look at the dividend picture first. Suppose in the first year after paying all bills and taxes the company has *earnings*, or profits, of $2000, or 10%, on its $20,000 *capitalization*, the money that it raised by selling 2000 shares of common stock. That would be a handsome profit for a new company, but not impossible.

It would then be up to the board of directors to decide what to do with that profit. It could pay it all out to the stockholders in dividends, or it could vote to keep every penny of it in the company treasury and use it to buy more machinery to make more pocket poles and earn more profit the following year. Since all stockholders like dividends and all boards of directors know that, Pocket Pole's board might very properly decide on a middle course. It might vote to pay out $1000 in dividends and plow the other $1000 back into the business as *retained earnings*.

Now if the board has $1000 for dividends and 2000 shares of stock outstanding, the dividend per share is going to be $.50. That's what the man with one share of stock gets, while the man with ten shares gets $5, and the man with 100 shares gets $50. For all of them that would represent a 5% return on their investment, regardless of the number of shares they own.

But there's also another intangible return that they would get on their money. Presumably that $1000 which the board decided to retain and plow back into the business will serve to increase the value of every man's share in the company — his *equity* in the company, as it's called in financial lingo.

If an original share of stock in Pocket Pole was fairly valued at $10, each of the 2000 shares might now be considered worth $10.50, since the company has an extra $1000 in addition to the original capital of $20,000.

Already that par value figure of $10 has been made slightly fictitious, and as the years roll by, it will bear no real relation to the value of the stock, if the company continues to earn good money and if the directors continue, year after year, to put a portion of those earnings back into the company. In comparatively few years, the total *assets* of the company — everything it owns: its plant, machinery, and products — might well be doubled without a corresponding increase in its *liabilities* — the sum total of what the company owes. In that case, the *book value* of each share of stock — assets, less liabilities, divided by the number of shares outstanding — would also be increased.

Par value is a term so generally misunderstood and so completely without significance that many companies today either do not set any value on their stock, in which case it is known as *no-par stock*, or they fix the value at $1 or $5, a figure so low that it could not possibly be considered an index of its real value.

Even book value is a term with little real meaning today, although it had a real significance in the last century when *watered stock* was all too often sold to an unsuspecting public. That graphic expression, watered stock, is supposed to have had its origin in the practice of feeding cattle large quantities of salt on their way to market and then giving them a big drink of water just before they went on the weighing scales.

As applied to securities, the phrase describes that kind of company stock which was issued with an inflated value. For instance, an unscrupulous operator might pay only half a million dollars for some company, then issue a million dollars' worth of stock in it. He might sell all that stock to others and pocket a half million profit. Or after he sold half the stock and got his cost back, he might keep the remaining shares and thus own a half interest in the company at no cost to himself. Such stock issues are now virtually nonexistent, thanks to improved business ethics and government regulation.

Most stockholders have come to realize that book value doesn't mean very much. What counts is the earning power of a company and its growth prospects, not the total value of its plants and machinery. The stock of many a big company sells frequently at a price considerably more than its book value — sometimes double or triple the book value. In contrast, other stocks, like those of the railroads, which have gigantic investments in equipment, sell for much less than book value. Book value is frequently thought of as representing what the owner of a share of stock could expect to get if the company were *liquidated* — if it went out of business and sold off all its property. This is often a misconception, because when a company is in liquidation, it can rarely get full value for the property it must dispose of.

So how do you know what a share of stock is worth — Pocket Pole stock or any other?

There's only one answer to that. Bluntly, it's only worth what somebody else is willing to pay for it when you want to sell it.

If the product isn't popular and sales suffer, if the cost of wages and raw materials is too high, if the management is inefficient, Pocket Pole or any other company can fail. And if it goes 'into bankruptcy, your stock can be valueless.

That's the black side of the picture. That's what can happen if the risk you assumed in buying the stock proves to be a bad one.

But if Pocket Pole proves to be a successful company, if it has a consistent record of good earnings, if part of those earnings is paid out regularly in dividends and another part of them wisely used to expand the company — then your stock is likely to be worth more than the $10 you paid for it. Perhaps a good deal more.

And that is the second way in which the stockholder expects to make money on his investment. First, through dividends. Second, through an increase in the value of his stock — or, rather, an increase in the price which somebody else will pay for it. This is known as *price appreciation*.

The price of a stock, like the price of almost everything else in this world, is determined by supply and demand — what one man is willing to pay for a stock and what another one is willing to sell it for, what one man *bids* and another man *asks*. And don't forget that price is not necessarily a reliable guide to good investing. Some people think that a low-priced stock is a good buy because it is cheap and, conversely, that a high-priced stock is expensive. That just isn't so. The stock of one company may sell at a low price simply because it has a large number of shares outstanding — because the whole pie has been cut up into lots and lots of little pieces — while the stock of another equally good company may sell at a high price because it hasn't been cut up into so many pieces and there are relatively fewer shares outstanding. The price of a stock takes on meaning only as you consider it in relation to earnings and dividends per share.

Here, in brief, is the story of common stock — what it is, how it comes into being, what it means to own it.

American Telephone & Telegraph, General Motors, and General Electric may have millions of shares of stock outstanding, and they may even count their shareholders in the millions, but in these giant corporations, each share of stock plays precisely the same kind of role as a share of stock in our Pocket Pole Company, and each stockholder has the same rights, privileges, and responsibilities.

There is only one significant difference between buying a share of Pocket Pole and investing in a share of American Telephone & Telegraph, General Motors, or General Electric.

These big companies have been in business for many years. You know something about them and the reputations they enjoy. You know how good their products or services are. You can examine their financial history, see for yourself how the prices of their stocks have moved over the years and what kind of record they have made as far as earnings and dividends are concerned. And on the basis of such information you can form a more reliable judgment about whether the stocks of these companies are overpriced or underpriced.

In contrast, the man who buys stock in our Pocket Pole Company has nothing to go on other than his own estimate of how good a product the company has and how big its sales are likely to be. There are no bench marks to guide him, no past records on which to base an appraisal of the future.

As a matter of literal truth, the Pocket Pole stockholder cannot properly be called an investor. Most times when a man buys stock in a brand-new company, he isn't investing in it; he's speculating in it. An *investor* is a man who is willing to take a moderate risk with his money for the sake of earning a moderate return, which in the case of common stocks might mean annual dividends averaging about 4% and a growth factor of about the same amount, representing the increase in the value of his holdings over the years. A *speculator* is a man who takes a big risk in the hope of making a big profit as a result of an increase in the price of a stock. An investor usually has his eye on long-term values to be realized over a period of years; a speculator usually hopes to make a profit in a relatively short period of time.

American business needs both kinds of risk takers. Without the speculator, new businesses wouldn't be born, nor would many an old business be tided over a rough spot. Without the investor, a company would not have the capital to carry on, much less grow and expand.

CHAPTER 3

How and Why
New Stock Is Sold

LET's assume that the years are good to our Pocket Pole Company. It continues to grow. The original collapsible fishing pole has proved a best seller, and the company now has a full line of models. Good earnings year after year have enabled the management to put the stock on a regular annual dividend basis. It now pays $1 a year per share — 25¢ a quarter — and in several good years the directors even declared *extra dividends,* one of 25¢ and two of 50¢ a share.

Now the company feels that the time has come when it should expand. It could sell twice as many pocket poles, make twice as much profit, if only it had a bigger factory. So the board of directors decides to expand the plant. That means it will need more machinery, more manpower, and, above all things, more money — a lot more money than it has in the company treasury. Problem: how to get about $40,000.

A bank might advance the money. Maybe two or three banks would each put up part of the loan. But some of the directors don't like the idea of being in hock to the banks. They worry not only about paying interest on the loan every year but also about paying the money back in installments. That kind of steady drain on the company treasury for years ahead could eat into earnings and result in few if any dividends. Furthermore, banks don't usually like to make such long-term loans, and even if they were willing to, they might — to protect their loans — insist on having their representatives sit on the board of directors — and that is a prospect some of the directors don't relish.

Isn't there some other way to raise the money?

Yes, there is.

Maybe the present stockholders would like to put more money into the company. Maybe there are other people who would like to invest in a nice thriving little business like Pocket Pole. There's an idea.

And so the board of directors proposes to the stockholders that they authorize the company to issue 3000 additional shares of stock — 2000 shares to be sold at once, and the remaining 1000 to be held against the day when the company may want to raise more money by selling more stock. Each of the new shares of stock will carry with it the same rights and privileges as an original share.

This proposal is approved by a substantial majority of the stockholders, but not without some disagreement. One stockholder objected to the plan. He thought the company should have two classes of common stock — a *Class A stock* which would consist of the original issue, enjoying full rights and privileges, and a new *Class B stock* on which the same dividends would be paid but which would not carry any voting privileges. In other words, he wanted control of the company kept in the hands of the original stockholders.

The board chairman replied to this suggestion by pointing out that such *classified-stock* setups, A stock and B stock, are no longer popular with investors. True, some companies still have two issues of common stock outstanding, but few companies have followed such a practice on new stock issues in recent years.

Furthermore, the chairman explained that the old stockholders would properly still retain about the same measure of control, since they could be expected to buy most of the new issue anyway. This appeared likely, because it would be offered to them first and on especially favorable terms. This is the usual procedure for companies that have a *new issue* of stock to sell.

In this instance, the board recommended that old stockholders be permitted to buy the new stock at $20 a share — a figure about $2 less than the price at which the original stock was then being bought or sold — while others who might buy any of the new issue that was left over would have to pay whatever the going price might be at the time.

After the stockholders approved the plan, each of them was offered the *right* to subscribe to the new stock in proportion to his present holdings, and this right was clearly set forth in a warrant, or certificate. Every man who owned one of the original 2000 shares was permitted to buy one of the new 2000 shares at $20. And the man with ten old shares could buy ten new ones. The rights had to be exercised within two weeks, for most rights are relatively short-lived, although some are occasionally issued that are good for a period of years, and in the financial community these are not usually called rights but *warrants*.

Some Pocket Pole shareholders, unable or unwilling to purchase additional stock, sold their rights. Often the market in such rights is a brisk one, even when they entitle the holder to buy only a part of a share — a tenth, a fifth, or a quarter of a share of new stock for each old share that he owns.

In the case of Pocket Pole each right was worth $1. Here is the way the value would have been arrived at: If you owned one share of Pocket Pole worth $22 and you exercised your right to buy an additional share at $20, you would then own two shares at an average of $21 apiece, or just $1 less than the going price per share. Hence the right could be figured to have a value of just $1. Actually, some stockholders might sell their rights for a fraction of that, while others might get more than $1 apiece, if the price of Pocket Pole advanced while the rights were still on the market. And, of course, some careless stockholders would ignore their rights, forgetting either to sell or to exercise them.

The standard formula for figuring the value of rights works this way: First take the prevailing market price of the stock (in this case $22) and subtract the subscription price (here $20); divide this difference ($2) by the number of old shares necessary to buy one new share (1) *plus* an additional one (1 plus 1 is 2, and $2 divided by 2 is $1).

When the rights expired, Pocket Pole discovered that all of them had been exercised except for 50 shares of the new issue, and these were readily sold at a price of $22. The company had raised $40,100 of new capital, and now had 4000 shares of common stock outstanding.

Pocket Pole's plan for expanding the plant was put into effect, but because of delays in getting the machinery it needed, it was two years before the new factory was in full operation. That situation raised for the board the awkward problem of how to continue paying dividends to the stockholders. In the first year of the transition period, the board felt obligated to continue paying the customary $1 dividend; but that put a serious dent in the company treasury. The second year the directors decided it would be foolhardy to do that again. They concluded that the only prudent thing they could do was to *pass the dividend* and keep the full year's earnings in the treasury until the new plant was operating efficiently.

But if the company paid no dividend, what would the stockholders say? Omission of the dividend would certainly mean that the price of the stock would go down, for it would be interpreted as a sign of trouble by those who might be interested in buying the stock.

The board found an answer to that problem in the 1000 shares of new stock which had been authorized but not issued. With the approval of the stockholders, it took those 1000 shares and distributed them among the owners of the 4000 outstanding shares on the basis of one-quarter of a share of free stock for every single share which a stockholder owned.

Actually, this *stock dividend* did nothing to improve the lot of any individual stockholder. He was not one penny richer, nor did he actually own any greater proportion of the company. The man who had one share before the stock dividend owned 1/4000 of the company. Now with 1¼ shares out of the 5000 outstanding, he still owned exactly 1/4000.

And yet in terms of future prospects that extra quarter of a share had real potential value. When the company got rolling again, that extra quarter share could represent a real profit and extra dividends, too.

That, happily, is exactly what happened. Pocket Pole prospered. The next year it earned $2 a share, and the directors felt they could prudently restore the old $1 dividend on each share, and to the man who held 1¼ shares that meant a return of $1.25.

CHAPTER 4

What You Should Know
about Preferred Stocks

WITH its new plant and its new machinery, the Pocket Pole Company forged rapidly ahead. Earnings doubled. Then they doubled again. And most of those earnings, by decision of the directors, were reinvested in the business to expand production and improve operations. Dividends were modest. But the company was growing. Now its assets totaled almost $150,000.

Then another problem — and another opportunity — presented itself. The Rapid Reel Company, a well-known competitor owned and operated by a single family, could be acquired for $75,000. It was, the Pocket Pole directors agreed, a good buy at that price, but where could they get the $75,000?

Negotiations with the president of Rapid Reel indicated that he was anxious to retire from business, that he planned to invest whatever he got from the sale of the company so that it would yield him and his family a safe, reasonable income. Further, it was evident that he had a high regard for the management of Pocket Pole and was favorably impressed with the company's prospects. Here was the basis of a deal.

So the directors of Pocket Pole proposed that they take over Rapid Reel as a going concern and merge it into their own. How would they pay for it? By issuing *preferred* stock in the Pocket Pole Company — an issue of 750 shares with a par value of $100 per share — and giving it to the owners of Rapid Reel in exchange for their company.

Like most preferred stock, this issue would assure to the owners a prior claim on all assets of Pocket Pole after all debts had been taken care of, should it ever be necessary to dissolve the company, and the stock would carry a specific dividend payable every year on every share before any dividends could be paid to common-stock holders. To make the deal as attractive as possible for the owners of Rapid Reel, the company was willing to pay a fairly high dividend — $6 on every share, or 6%.

Sometimes such a preferred dividend is not paid in a given year because the company did not earn enough to cover it. But more usually the preferred stock is *cumulative preferred*. Pocket Pole issued cumulative preferred stock. This meant that if Pocket Pole could not pay the $6 dividend in any year, the amount due for that year would accrue to the preferred-stock holders and would be paid the following year or whenever the company had sufficient earnings to pay it. If the company could not make the payments on the preferred for a period of years, they would continue to accrue during all that time and would have to be paid in full before the common-stock holders got as much as a dime in dividend payments.

On the other hand, it was agreed that this would not be an issue of *participating preferred*. This meant that the holders of the preferred would not participate, beyond the stipulated dividend payment, in any of the extra profits the company might earn in good years. Even if earnings were so good that dividends on the common stock were doubled or trebled, the holders of the preferred would still get just their $6 a share and no more. Furthermore, they would have no participation in company affairs and no voting rights except on matters that might adversely affect the rights guaranteed them as preferred-stock holders. They were also guaranteed the right to elect two directors to the board if the company should ever pass, or fail to pay, the preferred dividend for eight consecutive quarters.

Although the terms of this issue might be regarded as fairly typical, there is no such thing as a standard preferred stock. About the only common denominator of all such issues is the guarantee that the owner will be accorded a preferential treatment, ahead of the common-stock holder, in the payment of dividends and in the distribution of any assets that might remain if the company was liquidated. That's why it is called preferred stock, and that's why its price usually doesn't fluctuate, either up or down, as much as the price of the company's common stock.

From that point on, specifications vary widely. Most preferreds have a $100 par value, but some are no-par stocks. Dividends range from 4% up to 6% or 7%, with the higher dividends prevailing in periods when interest rates on borrowed money are high. Most preferreds are *nonparticipating,* but there are many exceptions.

Many preferreds are issued, as Pocket Pole proposed, to acquire another company, but most of them are issued simply to acquire more capital for expansion or improvements at a time when the company's circumstances are such that its stockholders and the public at large might not be willing to invest in more of its common stock.

Cumulative preferreds are by all odds the most common, but there are some *noncumulative* issues on the market — principally those of railroads. Occasionally, on cumulative preferreds, *accrued dividends* pile up in bad years to a point where it becomes impossible for a company to pay them. In such a situation, it may attempt to negotiate a settlement with the preferred holders on the basis of a partial payment. However, some companies have paid off more than $100 a share in accumulated back dividends due on their preferred stock issued at only $100 a share.

Another kind of preferred stock that has become increasingly popular in recent years is the *convertible preferred.* Such a stock carries a provision permitting the owner to convert it into a specified number of shares of common stock. Suppose, for instance, that a company sold a new issue of convertible preferred at a time when its common stock was quoted at $17 or $18 a share; in such a situation, the conversion clause might provide that every share of the new $100 preferred could be exchanged for five shares of the company's common stock at any time in the next five years. Obviously, there would be no advantage to the preferred-stock holders in making such a swap unless the common stock advanced in price to more than $20 a share.

The price of a convertible is apt to fluctuate more than the price of other preferreds because a convertible is always tied to the common stock of a company. This has its good and bad points. If the company is successful and the price of its common stock rises, the holder of a convertible preferred will find that his stock has had a corresponding increase in value, since it can be exchanged for the common. On the other hand, if the common declines, the convertible preferred is apt to suffer too, because one of the features which was counted on to make it attractive has suddenly lost something of its value, and the other features of the issue, such as its dividend rate, may not prove as attractive or substantial as those of orthodox preferreds. Convertibles are always especially popular when stock prices are rising generally.

Most preferreds carry a provision which permits the company to *call in* the issue and pay it off at full value, plus a premium of perhaps 5%. A company will usually exercise this right to call in its preferred stock if it thinks it can replace the outstanding issue with one that carries a lower dividend rate.

From the point of view of the owners of Rapid Reel, the plan which Pocket Pole proposed looked attractive. So they accepted it—after the common-stock holders of Pocket Pole had approved the plan and authorized issuance of 750 shares of 6% cumulative preferred stock in exchange for the Rapid Reel Company.

With this acquisition, Pocket Pole was on its way to becoming big business. And in the next ten years, with booming sales, it strode forward along that path with seven-league boots.

It bought the little Nylon Line Company for cash.

It acquired the Fishing Supplies Corporation by another issue of preferred stock, which it called second-preferred, because it had to recognize the prior claim to assets and earnings that had been granted the owners of Rapid Reel. To make this issue more attractive to the owners of Fishing Supplies, a conversion privilege was included in it; in other words, it was a convertible preferred.

It bought the Sure-Fire Rifle Company by selling an additional issue of common stock and arranging to trade the Sure-Fire stockowners one share of Pocket Pole for every three shares of Sure-Fire that they owned.

Finally, it acquired control of Camping Supplies, Incorporated, on a similar stock-swapping basis.

Now, with a full, well-rounded line of all kinds of fishing, hunting, and camping supplies, backed by an aggressive advertising and merchandising campaign, the company experimented with its own retail outlets. In a few years, these grew into a small chain of 30 sporting-goods stores, known as the Rod & Reel Centers.

Sales multiplied, and so did earnings—up to $10 and $12 a share. Dividends were boosted correspondingly, and with the adoption of a regular $6 annual dividend, Pocket Pole stock was frequently quoted at $120 a share and higher. Stockholders complained that it was too high-priced, that it couldn't be sold easily if they wanted to dispose of their holdings.

So the company decided to *split* the stock on a ten-for-one basis and simultaneously to change its corporate name to Rod & Reel, Incorporated — a much more appropriate name, since most fishermen consider the fishing "pole" passé. Hence it issued new certificates for ten shares of Rod & Reel common stock for every single share of the old Pocket Pole stock. Theoretically, each of the new shares should have been worth about $12, but since stock splits frequently excite unusual investor interest, it wasn't long before the new shares were being bought and sold at prices a dollar or two higher, even though there had been substantially no change in the outlook for the company.

This is the story of Rod & Reel, Inc., formerly Pocket Pole Company, Inc. It is a success story, as it was meant to be, to show the various kinds of stock operations that may mark a company's growth. But for that matter, it is no more of a success story than the real-life stories of General Motors or International Business Machines, Xerox or Polaroid, or any of hundreds of other companies in which the original investors (or speculators) have seen the value of their stockholdings multiplied 10, 20, even 100 times over.

CHAPTER 5

What You Should Know
about Bonds and
Investment Banking

Do you have a lot of money to invest — say $50,000 or
$100,000? Or is there some reason why you should be ex-
traordinarily conservative in your investments?

If so, then you ought to know about *corporate bonds,* the
kind of bond issued by companies like Rod & Reel, Inc.,
and bought principally by *institutional investors* — banks, insurance companies, pension funds, colleges and universities,
and charitable foundations.

If you don't have that much money or some good reason
for being especially conservative, chances are that there are
better investments for you than corporate bonds.

But who can tell when you may get a lot of money? And
anyway, every intelligent investor should know something
about bonds just so he'll have a grasp of the whole securities
business.

The easiest way to understand bonds is to consider the
plight of Rod & Reel's treasurer at a time when the company needed $1,000,000 of new capital — a much greater
sum than any it had ever had to raise before.

It needed that money because over the years it had grown
rather haphazardly, acquiring a manufacturing plant here
and another one there, a warehouse here and some retail
stores there.

Now the whole operation had to be pulled together, made
to function efficiently. An independent firm of engineers had
figured just what economies Rod & Reel could effect by
centralizing most of its manufacturing operations in one big
new plant and modernizing its equipment. In the long run,
the $1,000,000 would unquestionably prove to be money well
spent.

But how to get the money?

As company treasurer, you might first discuss the matter with the officers of your regular bank. They are perfectly willing to supply you from month to month with the credit you need for raw materials, but a million-dollar loan to construct a new plant — well, that is not for them. What you need in the present situation, they suggest, is help from a very special kind of banker, an *investment banker*.

Investment bankers specialize in raising the kind of money that business needs for long-term use, usually in amounts considerably greater than the million Rod & Reel wanted.

Most times when a company wants money, it prefers to get it without any strings attached — without obligating itself to pay any set return on the money. In short, it wants *equity capital,* the kind of money it can get only by selling common stock.

If the company's condition is sound, if its prospects are good, and if the stock market is then very active and healthy, an investment banker may agree to *underwrite* such an issue. That means he will buy all of the new stock himself from the company, and then resell it at a set price per share to individual buyers. As a general rule, this is the only time in the entire life of a stock issue that its price will be fixed — at the time when it is originally issued, either to start a new company or raise new capital. Once the stock is in public hands, its price will be determined solely by how much the buyer will pay and how much the seller wants for the stock he owns.

For the risk that the investment banker assumes, the risk that he may not be able to resell the entire issue that he has bought, he expects to make a profit on each share of the issue.

On small issues, involving only $1,000,000 or $2,000,000, he may be able and willing to carry the whole risk himself, but on most issues he shares the risk with other investment bankers who join with him in forming an *underwriting group* under his management.

When it comes time to sell the issue to the public, the underwriters usually invite other security dealers to join with them in a *selling group,* or *syndicate.*

The costs of underwriting and selling an issue of stock depend primarily on how saleable the underwriting group thinks the issue will be when it is put on the market. Those costs might run anywhere from 3% to 10% of the final selling price, and they are wholly paid by the seller. The buyers get such stock at the announced price, free of all commission cost or other charges. On some issues, such as cheap mining or oil stocks offered at a dollar or two a share, charges might even run as high as 20%, for these *penny stocks* can usually be sold only by costly merchandising effort. A third to a half of the total commission on any new issue might go to those who underwrite it, with the *manager* of the group getting an extra fee for his services, and the balance to those who sell it, but if the issue looks as though it might be "sticky," or hard to sell, the selling commission is likely to be increased and the underwriting commission reduced correspondingly.

Whenever a company wants to raise capital by selling a new securities issue, it may well shop around to see which investment banker will offer the best terms and handle the new issue at the lowest total cost. Once a bid is accepted, the relationship between the company and the underwriter is apt to develop naturally into a close one, and if the company needs to raise additional capital at some future time, it may well expect to get help again from the same underwriter, and it may not even ask for other bids.

However, by law or government regulation, public utilities are generally required to submit any new securities issue to *competitive bidding*. Competitive bids are also compulsory on railroad securities, but the Interstate Commerce Commission, which exercises control in this field, usually exempts the railroads from this requirement.

While most companies might prefer to raise new capital by selling stock, this is not the kind of securities issue which an investment banker is most likely to sanction in the case of a comparatively small company like Rod & Reel. He is more apt to suggest an issue of bonds rather than an issue of stock. Often, in normal years, the aggregate value of new bond issues exceeds the value of new stock issues by three or four to one.

Bonds always represent borrowed money which the company that issues them is obligated to repay. That's why they are called *obligations*. They are a kind of promissory note. When a company sells bonds, it borrows the money from the buyers, and the bonds stand as a formal evidence of that debt. Each bond is an agreement on the part of the company to repay the face value of the bond — usually $1000 — at a specified time and to pay a set annual rate of *interest* from the day it is issued to the day it is redeemed.

The man who buys stock in a company actually buys a part of that company. The man who buys a company's bonds simply lends his money to the company.

The stockholder expects to collect dividends on his stock and thus share in the company's profits. The bondholder expects only to earn a fixed return on his investment in the form of interest payments.

There's one other important difference between stocks and bonds. If a company is successful, the stockholder can hope to make a substantial profit because the price of his stock should go up. The bondholder enjoys no such extravagant hope. No matter how successful a company is, the price of its bonds rarely advances more than a small percentage, and then only if they are considered of unusually good quality with a minimum of risk.

On the other hand, if the bondholder can't expect to gain as much on his capital, neither does he run the risk of losing as much. His investment is much better protected, thanks to the fact that bonds do represent debt, and if a company is dissolved, the debt it owes its bondholders, like any other debt it owes for labor and materials, must be paid before the stockholders, either common or preferred, can get a nickel out of what's left of the company. The claims of bondholders come first, then the preferred-stock holders — and last, the common-stock holders.

It is because the element of risk in bonds is so comparatively slight that they are such a popular form of investment with *institutional investors*. This is the market the investment banker has his eye on when he underwrites a bond issue. Very often, an investor may succeed in selling an entire bond issue to just one or two large institutional customers — a bank, an insurance company, or a pension fund — and not hope to market the issue publicly. This is known as a *private placement*.

Because the institutional market for bonds is such a good market, the underwriting and selling commissions are usually much lower on an issue of bonds than on an issue of stock. Otherwise, the two kinds of securities are issued and sold in much the same way.

From the point of view of any company treasurer, bonds have obvious disadvantages as compared with a stock issue. The interest that must be paid on them represents a fixed charge that has to be met in bad times as well as good times, and the bonds must be paid off when they come due. The stockholder has to be paid only if the company makes money — and even that is not a binding obligation.

On the other hand, if the company is successful, it doesn't mind having to pay 3% or 4% or 5% interest on the money borrowed from bondholders if it can make 10% or 15% profit on that extra capital. Again, bond interest payments are an expense item deducted from a company's earnings before it pays its federal income *tax* on those earnings. In contrast, dividends are paid out of what is left after a company has paid the tax on its earnings. Thus, it actually costs a company less to pay a given amount of money to bondholders than it does to pay the same amount of money to stockholders, because it gets a tax deduction on the one and not on the other.

From the investor's point of view, the best bonds are those that have behind them the strongest assurance that they will be repaid — in full and with the specified interest.

Here the situation is not much different from what it would be if you as an individual sought to get a loan from a bank. If the banker knew you and knew that you would be able to repay the money, he might lend it to you without asking you to put up any collateral, such as your life insurance policies or other property, to guarantee the loan. But if it was a sizable loan, he might even insist that you give him a mortgage on your home.

It's much the same way with companies when they issue bonds. They would prefer to get the money without posting their property as a guarantee that the contract set in the bond will be fulfilled. That, as a matter of fact, is precisely the way the Rod & Reel treasurer felt when the investment banker told him the company would have to *float* a bond issue, not a stock issue.

As long as it had to be bonds, the treasurer proposed that his company issue $1,000,000 of debentures.

A *debenture* is a bond that is backed only by the general credit of the corporation. No specific real estate or property stands as security behind it. It is, in effect, a giant-size I.O.U. Debentures are the most common type of bond issued by big, well-established industrial companies today, and they are being favored increasingly by public utilities. But in the case of Rod & Reel, the investment banker was not disposed to feel that such an issue would be in order, because the company, though successful, was still relatively small and not too well known. He was afraid the debentures wouldn't sell.

The treasurer then asked if a debenture might not be made more attractive by including a convertible provision in it. There are many *convertible bonds* on the market and their terms vary widely, but like convertible preferreds, all of them offer the owner the privilege of converting his bond into a specified number of shares of common stock.

Such a provision may add a certain speculative appeal to the bond — the chance to make an extra profit if the common stock rises — but the typical bond buyer may look askance at such a "sweetener." He knows better than most security buyers that you don't get something for nothing in a security, any more than you do in any other kind of merchandise. A convertible bond may offer the possibility of price appreciation, but its guarantee of safety may not be quite as substantial.

In Rod & Reel's case, the investment banker did not feel that a convertible was feasible, and in the light of his attitude, the treasurer did not even raise the question of whether the company could issue some kind of *income* or *adjustment bond*.

These bonds are a kind of hybrid security, something like a noncumulative preferred stock, since they provide that the interest is to be paid on the bond only as it is earned. If earnings are sufficient to pay only a part of the interest on such bonds, the company must make whatever payment it can to the nearest ½ of 1%; thus on a 5% bond a company might pay only 2½% or 3% or 3½%, depending on its earnings.

There is still another kind of bond, the *collateral-trust bond,* which, like the income bond, used to be more popular than it is today, but Rod & Reel's circumstances were such that this type of security was obviously not suited to them. When a company issues a collateral-trust bond, it deposits securities with a trustee as a guarantee that the bonds will be redeemed and interest paid on them. Usually the securities on deposit are worth at least 25% more than the total value of the bond issue, and they are frequently the securities of subsidiary companies.

As the discussions progressed, it became apparent that the investment banker felt there was only one kind of bond that Rod & Reel could offer, and that was a *first-mortgage bond* — the kind of bond which is secured by a mortgage on all of a company's property, not only on its existing property but sometimes even on all property which it might later acquire.

These bonds are considered to be among the highest-grade security investments, because they offer the investor an undisputed first claim on company earnings and the greatest possible safety. That first mortgage takes absolute precedence over the claims of all other owners of a company's securities, including the holders of debentures, adjustment bonds, or secondary-mortgage bonds that may be issued after a first mortgage has been made.

Having resigned himself to the fact that Rod & Reel would have to mortgage its property, including the new plant which it expected to build, in order to float a $1,000,000 bond issue, the treasurer next took up with the banker the question of what rate of interest the company might have to pay. Here the banker was in no position to supply an answer, because the rate a company has to pay always depends on its credit standing and its earning capacity. And these were the crucial factors on which the banker could not commit himself without a thorough, painstaking investigation of all aspects of the company — the same kind of survey which every investment banker must make, with the help of outside accountants, engineers, and other specialists, before underwriting any new issue of stock for a company.

Bond interest rates vary not only with the health of the company but also with general business conditions. Thus in 1920, AAA bonds — the highest grade there is — paid over 6%, while in 1945, the same grade bonds returned only 2½%. Some bonds of very acceptable quality were paying more than 5% in 1961 and 6% in 1966. Over the years, a rate of 4½% to 5% might be considered more typical.

When money is "tight" — when banks increase the rates they charge on mortgages and loans and increase their interest rates on deposits — bond interest rates usually go up too. If this happens at a time when stock market prices have been going up and dividends, expressed as a percentage of the price, have consequently been going down, as was the case in 1965–1966, a situation develops where the investor can get a better return from bonds than he can from stocks, and he is frequently tempted to shift to the safer investment, especially if he thinks stock prices are likely to sag.

The interest rate of a bond is frequently referred to as the *coupon* rate, because traditionally bonds have appended

to them a number of detachable coupons, one for each six
months of the bond's life. The owner clips each coupon as
it comes due and presents it to the company's paying agent
for payment. Coupons were used because bonds were not
registered on the company's books in the owner's name,
as stock certificates are. Instead, they were the property of
the bearer — whoever had them at a given time — and hence
were called *bearer bonds*. Today, there has been a departure
from this practice. More and more companies are issuing
bonds that are registered in each owner's name, just like
stocks. On some *registered bonds*, coupons are still used for
the payment of interest, but on others the bondholder
gets a check automatically from the company, and this practice is becoming increasingly popular. In time, the phrase
"coupon-clipper" to denote a wealthy individual may vanish
from the language.

Just as crucial as the interest rate of any company issuing
bonds is the question of *maturity* — how long a life the
bonds will have, how soon the company will have to redeem
them or pay them off. In general, the stronger the company,
the longer the maturities. For a company like Rod & Reel,
ten years might be considered the maximum time limit. Furthermore, the company would probably be required to establish a *sinking fund* and pay enough into it every year to
demonstrate that it would ultimately be able to meet its obligations. In view of its building and reorganization plans,
Rod & Reel would probably be allowed a one-year breathing
spell before it had to start putting money into the sinking
fund. Some bonds, known as *serial bonds*, are actually paid
off in year-by-year installments so that the debt is steadily
reduced. Like preferreds, most bonds have call provisions
which permit a company to redeem them before maturity,
if it has the money.

There is a wide variation in how long bond issues run,
but a period of 20 or 30 years is about as common as
any. Curiously, the railroads have issued bonds with the
longest life, and they also have some with about as short a
life as any. Many old rail bonds run for 100 years, and
some have no maturity date; they were issued in perpetuity
— a frank recognition of the fact that no one expects the
rails ever to pay all their debt.

At the other end of the scale, with maturities of only
ten or fifteen years, are the *equipment-trust* obligations. These
bonds are the cheapest method by which railroads can ac-

quire new cars and locomotives; some have carried interest rates under 1½ %. On this kind of bond, the equipment itself stands as the guarantee of repayment.

The maturity of a bond can affect the return you realize on it. You can buy a bond with a 4% coupon rate, but it may *yield* you something less — or something more — than 4%, depending on how much you pay for the bond and what its maturity is. If you pay exactly $1000 for a bond and get $40 interest on it every year, you do realize a 4% yield. But if you pay $1050 for the bond, the $40 annual interest payment obviously represents less than a 4% return on the money you've invested. Furthermore, if you hold the bond until it matures, you will get only $1000 for it on redemption, a loss of $50. If the bond has a twenty-year maturity, that $50 loss would represent, in effect, a reduction of $2.50 a year in your interest payment. Furthermore, over the full twenty years you would have lost the amount of interest that you might have earned on that $50.

The net of it all is that if you pay $1050 for a 4% twenty-year bond, you will realize a yield to maturity of only about 3.65%. Of course, if you buy the bond at a discount instead of a premium — for $950 instead of $1050, for example — you will earn more than 4% on it.

When a company like Rod & Reel has a stock or bond issue to raise new capital, such an issue represents new *financing*. But very often preferred stocks or bonds are issued as part of a *refinancing* operation. Thus, when a company refinances, it may seek to substitute some new bond issue for an outstanding one that it issued many years ago — a process known as *refunding*.

Why should such substitution be made? Because it can be to a company's advantage. As business and investment conditions change, it is frequently worthwhile to call an outstanding issue of bonds or preferred stock on which the company may be paying a high rate of interest. Such an issue can be paid off out of funds raised by the sale of a new issue carrying a lower rate.

CHAPTER 6

How New Issues
Are Regulated

WHENEVER a company like Rod & Reel wants to raise capital by floating a new issue of stocks or bonds, it must comply with the federal law that governs the sale of any such issue offered to the public.

In the boom days of the twenties, many a new stock was sold with few facts and lots of glittering promises. In 1933, Congress changed all that. It enacted a new law, widely known as the *Truth in Securities Act*, and then in 1934, with the passage of the *Securities Exchange Act*, it set up the *Securities & Exchange Commission* to administer both laws.

The S.E.C. requires *full disclosure* of all the pertinent facts about any company before it makes a *public offering* of new stocks or bonds. The company must file a lengthy *registration statement* with the S.E.C. in which it sets forth the data about its financial condition — its assets and its liabilities, what it owns and what it owes. It must also furnish the profit and loss record for the past several years. It must describe all of its outstanding securities and their terms and must usually list all its officers and directors, together with their salaries, bonuses, and stock interests in the company, and it must provide a description of its operations.

If the data appear to be complete and honest, the S.E.C. gives a green light to the new issue. But this does not mean that it passes any judgment whatsoever on the quality of the securities, how good or bad they may be for any investor.

The Securities & Exchange Commission also sees that the information which is filed with it is made available to any possible buyer of the new issue. A company is required to put all the essential facts into a printed *prospectus,* and every security dealer who offers the new stock or bond for sale must give a copy of that prospectus not only to everyone who buys the new issue but to everyone from whom he

even solicits an order. These prospectus regulations are binding for 40 days on all companies whose securities are already publicly owned, but the *Securities Exchange Act of
1964* now provides that the prospectus period shall be length-
ened to 90 days in the case of companies that are offering
their stock to the public for the first time.

The prospectus is usually about 20 to 30 pages long, sometimes even more, but some well-established companies, notably utilities, that can meet certain high standards of financial
responsibility are permitted by the Securities & Exchange
Commission to use a *short-form prospectus* on bond issues,
and in 1966 prospects seemed good that the S.E.C. would
be persuaded to extend the short-form privilege to stock
issues of companies that had a strong financial position and
a record of consistent earnings over a period of years.

During the period when a new issue is under prospectus
regulation, the securities industry is forbidden to disseminate
any public information about the new issue or any other
securities of the issuing company, and the advertising of the
new issue itself is severely restricted. The complete prospectus
or a fairly detailed summary of it can be published, but
barring that, the only other kind of advertising that can be
used is the so-called *"tombstone"* announcement, in which
no information is provided beyond the name of the issue,
its price, its size, and the names of the underwriters and
dealers who have it for sale. And above even this austere
announcement the underwriters usually insert a precautionary
note to the effect that the advertisement is not to be interpreted as an offer to buy or sell the security, since the
offer is made only through the prospectus.

Sometimes you may see a tombstone ad announcing a new
issue and simultaneously stating that the issue has already
been completely sold. You may well wonder why such an
ad appears. The answer is simple. Underwriting houses are
proud of their financing activities, and when they have arranged to sell all of a given issue, they go ahead and publish the new-issue advertisement as a matter of prestige.

Even if a company satisfies all the requirements of the
Securities & Exchange Commission on a new issue, its troubles may not necessarily end there. Most of the states also
have laws governing the registration and sale of new securities. While the requirements of these so-called *"blue sky"
laws* are much like those of the S.E.C., they are sufficiently

varied to cause a company ~ lot of trouble and a good deal of extra expense in filing the necessary forms.

All told, preparing a new issue for sale can be a very expensive undertaking. The bill for preparing the necessary forms and printing a prospectus may run to $15,000 or $20,000, and it can run as high as $100,000. This is the case when a large company brings out a new stock issue and has to offer rights to all its stockholders, for each of them must be supplied with a prospectus. Fees for lawyers and accountants can add a lot more to this bill.

However, the federal law, as well as most state laws, provides an "out" for little companies like Rod & Reel. For instance, if the new issue has a value of not more than $300,000, the company need file only a short registration form with the S.E.C. This is known as a *Regulation A* filing, and companies using it can satisfy the requirements of the law by distributing an abbreviated prospectus or *offering circular,* as it is called. On issues of less than $50,000 it isn't even necessary to prepare a circular. Again, if the new issue can be classified as a *private placement* — usually one that will be offered to fewer than 25 buyers — rather than as a public offering, it doesn't even have to be registered with the S.E.C.

In the case of a small company like Rod & Reel, the investment banker would try to qualify any new issue as a private placement by lining up one or two institutional buyers, perhaps an insurance company or a charitable foundation, before the deal was finally set, and that's why he would insist that the issue be of topflight quality, which in Rod & Reel's case would mean a first-mortgage bond.

While the Securities & Exchange Commission's "full disclosure" rules have undoubtedly done much to protect the investor, it is probably also true that they are more exacting than they have to be, and this may deter some companies from trying to raise new money for expansion. Again, the prohibition on disseminating *any* information about a company while its new issue is under prospectus regulation can work unnecessary hardship on investors who have an understandable interest in that company's other securities. The intent of the rule — to prohibit promotion of the new issue — is good, but the application is sometimes unduly restrictive.

Furthermore, it has been argued that the individual investor doesn't really benefit as he should from the protection that the prospectus regulations provide. Most individuals who buy a new issue — and their number is few compared with those who buy securities already on the market — rarely examine the prospectus or understand it if they do. As a matter of fact, if the buyer knows that the Securities & Exchange Commission cleared the issue, he is apt to believe that the commission has endorsed it — and anything that is good enough for the S.E.C. is good enough for him.

Nothing, of course, could be further from the truth. Full disclosure can protect against fraud. It can't guarantee a profit or protect against loss. *Caveat emptor* — "Let the buyer beware" — is still the rule of the market, and it applies with particular force to new, unseasoned issues. This is especially true, for example, regarding the low-priced oil and uranium shares which were unloaded on the public a few years ago. Many of these stocks were not worth the paper they were printed on, but the S.E.C. often lacked the necessary power to deal with the promoters behind them. Needless to say, many new issues of these worthless penny stocks avail themselves of the "small-issue" or Regulation A exemption.

CHAPTER 7

What You Should Know about Government and Municipal Bonds

THE *government bond* poses an interesting paradox. Here is the one security about which more people know something than they do about any other. And yet here is the one security which is fully understood by probably fewer people than any other.

An estimated 85,000,000 Americans learned what it meant to lend their money on a bond, with the promise of repayment and the assurance of interest, during World War II when they bought the famous Series E bonds, and there are still other millions whose education in investments has been initiated by buying these savings bonds since the war.

But only the big institutional buyers of government bonds, plus a comparative handful of dealers, who regularly buy and sell hundreds of millions of these securities for a profit measured in fractions of 1%, really understand the government bond market and know how it can be affected by subtle shifts in the credit and money policies of our own government or another government half the world away.

There are dozens and dozens of different government issues, carrying different coupon rates, different maturities, different call provisions.

Some are issued for very short periods of time. These are *Treasury bills* with maturities as short as 91 days, *certificates* ranging up to a year, and *notes* that may run up to five years. On the short-term issues, interest rates usually range around 2% or 3% but have gone as high as 5%, and during World War II the government pegged the interest rates on bills at a low ⅜ of 1%.

In contrast, *Treasury bonds* have maturities in excess of five years and range up to 32 years. By law, the Treasury may not issue bonds with an interest rate of more than 4¼%, but in periods when money is tight and interest rates on other forms of investment are substantially higher, *Treasuries* may sell in the open market at a discount, and the investor who buys a bond at less than par may well realize a yield in excess of 4¼% if held to maturity. In recent years, maturity rates on long-term bonds have generally ranged between 4% and 4¾%. The 4¼% interest-rate ceiling does, of course, restrict the Treasury in the issuance of new bonds during a period of tight money.

While Treasuries may sell at a discount in the open market when competitive interest rates are high, it is equally true that they are apt to sell at a premium — a price above par — and return a lower maturity yield when interest rates are generally low. These bonds, representing the great bulk of the federal debt, are always freely traded in the market at prices which change only slightly from day to day, rarely as much as a quarter or a half point. As a matter of fact, price spreads in this market are usually so close that the minimum price fluctuation on government bonds is only 1/32 of a point — occasionally even 1/64 — as compared with 1/8 of a point on stocks.

Regularly traded by the same dealers and on much the same basis as the government bonds are those bonds issued by various government agencies, such as the Federal Home Loan Banks and the Federal Land Banks.

And there are other government bonds which are not traded in any market, bonds that can be bought only from the government and sold back to the government at set prices, bonds that never suffer any fluctuations in market price. These are the *savings bonds* — Series E and Series H — and they can be bought at virtually any bank. No commission is charged; they are handled free as a patriotic service.

When the savings bonds were first introduced during World War II, the maximum yield that you could get was 2.9%. You paid $75 for an E bond, and then ten years later you could cash it in for $100, thus realizing an average annual return of 2.9%. If you cashed it in earlier, you got less on your investment. As interest rates increased in later years, the government was forced to liberalize the return on its savings bonds, and it accomplished this objective by shortening the maturity from ten years to nine years and eight months, then to eight years and eleven months, to seven years and nine months, and finally in 1966 to seven years. These changes resulted in boosting the yield from the original 2.9% to 4.15% if held to maturity.

All along the line, the Treasury also made similar changes in its Series H bonds. Unlike E bonds, which are sold at a discount ($75 for a $100 bond, for instance), H bonds are sold at their full face value, and the government sends the buyer an interest payment every half year, smaller payments in the early years, larger payments as the bonds approach maturity. Whereas E bonds come in denominations as small as $25, the smallest H bond is $500.

Despite all the differences between various issues, government bonds have one common characteristic: they are regarded as the safest investments in the world.

What security lies behind them? The pledged word of the Government of the United States. Just that. Nothing else. As long as that word is believed and accepted — as it must be by all Americans, since we *are* the government in the last analysis — government bonds, if held to maturity, offer the best protection you can find against the risk of losing any of your capital.

But because their prices do not rise in an inflation, they offer poor protection against the risk that your dollars will lose something of their purchasing power if prices generally go up. People who paid $75 for an E bond in 1956 got $103.32 back in 1966, but it would buy only about $86 worth of goods in terms of 1956 prices. Like the federal government, states, cities, and other units of local government, such as school districts and housing authorities, need capital — to build schools, roads, hospitals, and sewers, and to carry on the many other public projects which are their responsibility. So they too issue bonds, and these are called *municipal bonds*.

Unlike the federal government, which underwrites its own bonds, these local units of government go to the investment bankers for their money, just as a corporation does, and the banker underwrites municipal bond issues in very much the way that corporate bonds are underwritten and sold.

There are tens of thousands of municipal bond issues on the market. Interest rates on municipals in 1965 averaged about 3½%, but rates have been as high as 5% in the depression and as low as 1½% shortly after World War II. Most municipals are serial bonds; some are paid off in only a year, and some run for as many as 50 years.

No one but an expert can hope to know all about the different characteristics, the different qualities, of municipal

COMPARATIVE YIELDS IN DIFFERENT INCOME BRACKETS

Comparative net yields from
taxable vs. tax-exempt securities
Based on tax rates in effect July 1966

to equal these tax-free yields from municipal bonds you would have to get returns in taxable dividends shown below

If you're married and your taxable income is—	If you're single and your taxable income is—	2½%	2¾%	3%	3¼%	3½%	3¾%	4%	4¼%	4½%	5%	5½%	5¾%	6%
$24,000—$28,000	$12,000—$14,000	3.91	4.30	4.69	5.08	5.47	5.86	6.25	6.64	7.03	7.81	8.59	8.98	9.38
28,000—32,000	14,000—16,000	4.10	4.51	4.92	5.33	5.74	6.15	6.56	6.97	7.38	8.20	9.02	9.43	9.84
32,000—36,000	16,000—18,000	4.31	4.74	5.17	5.60	6.03	6.46	6.90	7.33	7.76	8.62	9.48	9.91	10.34
36,000—40,000	18,000—20,000	4.55	5.00	5.45	5.91	6.36	6.82	7.27	7.73	8.18	9.09	10.00	10.45	10.91
40,000—44,000	20,000—22,000	4.81	5.29	5.77	6.25	6.73	7.21	7.69	8.17	8.65	9.62	10.58	11.06	11.54
44,000—52,000	22,000—26,000	5.00	5.50	6.00	6.50	7.00	7.50	8.00	8.50	9.00	10.00	11.00	11.50	12.00
52,000—64,000	26,000—32,000	5.32	5.85	6.38	6.91	7.45	7.98	8.51	9.04	9.57	10.64	11.70	12.23	12.77
64,000—76,000	32,000—38,000	5.56	6.11	6.67	7.22	7.78	8.33	8.89	9.44	10.00	11.11	12.22	12.78	13.33
76,000—88,000	38,000—44,000	5.95	6.55	7.14	7.74	8.33	8.93	9.52	10.12	10.71	11.90	13.10	13.69	14.29
88,000—100,000	44,000—50,000	6.25	6.87	7.50	8.12	8.75	9.37	10.00	10.62	11.25	12.50	13.75	14.38	15.00
100,000—120,000	50,000—60,000	6.58	7.24	7.89	8.55	9.21	9.87	10.53	11.18	11.84	13.16	14.47	15.13	15.79
120,000—140,000	60,000—70,000	6.94	7.64	8.33	9.03	9.72	10.42	11.11	11.81	12.50	13.89	15.28	15.97	16.67
140,000—160,000	70,000—80,000	7.35	8.09	8.82	9.56	10.29	11.03	11.76	12.50	13.24	14.71	16.18	16.91	17.65
160,000—180,000	80,000—90,000	7.81	8.59	9.37	10.16	10.94	11.72	12.50	13.28	14.06	15.62	17.19	17.97	18.75
180,000—200,000	90,000—100,000	8.06	8.87	9.68	10.48	11.29	12.10	12.90	13.71	14.52	16.13	17.74	18.55	19.35

bonds, but in the main they offer the investor a good degree of safety, and consequently their prices are more stable than those of stocks, almost as stable as those of government bonds, as a matter of fact. They are "safe" because the word of any unit of government, like the word of the federal government, can generally be accepted. Then too, in most municipal bonds, the money that is raised from specific taxes is pledged to the payment of interest on the bonds and to the repayment of the loan over a period of years. In the case of bonds issued to finance municipal power or water systems or state toll roads, the revenues collected from these projects are pledged to the meeting of the interest and repayment obligations set in such bonds, and that is why they are called *revenue bonds*.

Municipal bonds are bought by banks, fire and casualty insurance companies, estates, and many individuals. They have special appeal for the man in a high-income bracket because he doesn't have to pay a federal tax on the interest he gets from a municipal bond, as he must on the dividends which he gets as a stockholder or on the interest payments he collects from corporate bonds or most government bonds. Characteristically, income from such bonds is also exempt from state taxes in those states where they are issued.

It is this feature of tax exemption which has made municipal bonds increasingly attractive to investors in the upper income tax brackets. As the demand for the bonds has increased, cities and states have been able to issue bonds at lower interest rates.

Under the tax laws, at least as they existed in 1966, a single man earning around $50,000 a year could get the same net return on a tax-exempt municipal bond yielding 3% as he could on a stock that paid a dividend twice as large, and, comparatively speaking, he took no risk.

On p. 37, a table shows just what return an individual at various income levels would have to earn on stocks or other taxable investments in order to retain after taxes as much as he could realize from tax-exempt municipal bonds with coupons ranging from 3% to 6%. These figures are based on tax rates as they existed in 1966.

CHAPTER 8

How Stocks
Are Bought and Sold

THE stocks of the biggest and best-known corporations in America are bought and sold on the *New York Stock Exchange*. In World War II days, the average daily trading volume was less than a million shares, but in 1965 an average of more than six million shares a day changed hands on the exchange, and in 1966, with volume running 50% ahead of that rate, ten-million-share days were not uncommon. And ten million shares are likely to be worth more than a half billion dollars in the aggregate.

That much money has a lot of glamour about it. It builds its own folklore. As a consequence, the stock exchange has become one of the most publicized institutions in the world, the very symbol of American capitalism.

But somehow that publicity has got in the way of public understanding, so much so that the stock exchange could almost be described as the business nobody knows — the business nobody knows but everybody talks about.

A lot of people, probably most people, think the stock exchange sells stock. It doesn't. It doesn't own any, doesn't sell any, doesn't buy any. If stocks lose $5,000,000 in value, the exchange doesn't get five cents of it. It is simply a marketplace where thousands of people buy and sell stocks every day, through their agents, the *brokers*.

Nor does the stock exchange have anything to do with fixing the price at which any of those stocks is bought and sold. The prices are arrived at in a two-way auction system: the buyer competes with other buyers for the lowest price, and the seller competes with other sellers for the highest price. Hence, the stock exchange can boast that it's the freest free market in the world, the one in which there is the least impediment to the free interplay of supply and demand.

When the buyer with the highest bid and the seller with

the lowest offering price conclude a transaction, each can
know that he got the best price he could at that moment.
As buyer or seller, you may not be wholly satisfied, but
you can't blame the stock exchange any more than you can
blame the weatherman if it's too hot or too cold for you.

Perhaps you've heard that the stock market is "rigged,"
that big operators drive prices up or hammer them down
to suit themselves and make a profit at the little fellow's
expense. Yes, there are some classic stories like that, and
they were true, especially in the last century and even as
recently as the nineteen twenties, when big market operators
resorted to all kinds of questionable devices to *manipulate*
stock prices to their own advantage.

But today there are laws, stringent laws, to prevent price
manipulation, and they are vigorously enforced by the Securities & Exchange Commission. The abuses of the twenties,
which were blamed in part for the great market crash of
1929, brought the Securities & Exchange Commission into
being in 1934, and thirty years later, after an exhaustive
study of the securities business, the commission got from
Congress a substantial grant of additional power to help it
in its work of policing the markets. This was the Securities
Exchange Act of 1964.

In addition to the new law the Securities & Exchange Commission now has modern science working on its side. In
1966, the commission got a computer, which makes possible
instantaneous surveillance of stock market actions and mul-
tiplies many times the effectiveness of the men who for years
have kept their eyes glued to the stock ticker, looking for
suspicious price jiggles — anything which might suggest that
the freedom of the market was being tampered with.

Actually, the commission leaves much of the regulatory
work in the hands of the exchange. Its rules, which are
generally designed to prevent unfair trading practice and protect the individual investor, were tightened when the exchange was reorganized in the thirties, and they were tightened still further in many areas as a result of the Securities
& Exchange Commission's market study and its drive for
another grant of power from Congress in 1964.

Today, there is probably no business in the world that
operates under more stringent regulation or with a stricter
self-imposed code of ethics than the New York Stock Exchange.

When the original securities law was first enacted, Congress even undertook to protect the buyer of securities (and the seller too) against himself — against his own greed and rashness. Before 1934, you could buy securities with only a small down payment, or *margin*. Typically it was 20%. Often it was less. And an occasional customer even "bought" securities 100% on credit — without putting up a dime. That's how a few people made a fortune on a shoestring, but it's also how more of them brought disaster on themselves and thousands of others in the 1929 crash.

Nowadays, the *Federal Reserve Board* decides what the minimum down payment shall be, and its decision is binding on everybody. The board changes the figure from time to time. Since 1934, it has ranged from as low as 40% of the purchase price up to 100%, and when the 100% rule prevailed, that meant there was no credit at all; the buyer had to pay in full for his stocks.

This power alone — the power of the Reserve Board to say what the minimum margin shall be — guarantees that there will never be another market crash quite like 1929. Stock prices are bound to go down from time to time, and down sharply. Indeed, in 1937–1938, despite the regulatory powers of the federal government, they dropped about 50% in just eight months; and in 1962 there was a decline of more than 25%; and in 1966 a drop exceeding 20%. But it can still be said that the market can never crash as spectacularly as it did in 1929, when it began the big slide down to the 1932 low, a drop that saw stocks lose on the average almost 90% of their value.

That can't happen again, because under the Reserve Board's margin regulation, prices can never be as overinflated as they were when people bought hundreds of millions of stocks by putting up only a small fraction of that amount in cash.

One noteworthy result of all the regulations that have been imposed on the market has been a change in the character of the market itself. It has become more of an investor's market, less of a speculator's market. Of course, speculators still buy and sell stocks in the hope of making a profit, and this function is not only legitimate but useful and desirable in the main, because it helps provide a continuous and liquid market. It helps stabilize prices, thus permitting the investor to buy and sell more readily and at fairer prices.

Nevertheless, more of the people who buy stocks today are doing so for the sake of earning a good return on their money over the long pull. They are not *"in-and-outers,"* people trading for a small profit on every market move. Generally, they hold their stocks for years and years. They're investors — people who want to be part owners of those biggest and best-known corporations.

All told, on the New York Stock Exchange, the stocks of more than 1200 of these companies have been *listed*, which means that they have been accepted for trading there. Collectively, these listed companies employ about a quarter of all workers and account for almost a third of the total assets of all corporations in the United States. As far as earnings and dividend payments are concerned, they account for considerably more than half of the national total.

To qualify for listing on the exchange a company has to meet certain requirements, which have become more exacting over the years. In 1965, when the exchange raised its standards for the fourth time in seven years, these were the principal qualifications a company had to meet if it wished to have its securities traded there:

(1) A minimum of 2000 shareholders of whom at least 1700 must own at least 100 shares apiece.

(2) A minimum of 1,000,000 shares outstanding, of which at least 700,000 must be owned by the public, not by the company itself.

(3) A market value for its publicy owned shares of at least $12,000,000.

(4) Annual earnings of at least $2,000,000 before taxes and $1,200,000 after taxes.

Most of the listed companies exceed these regulations by a wide margin. The biggest of the companies, American Telephone & Telegraph, had 2,840,500 shareholders who owned 530 million shares worth over $32 billion at the end of 1965. The second largest company, General Motors, had 1,313,000 shareholders with 287 million shares worth $30 billion.

Not all companies prosper, of course, and that's why the exchange has a set of minimum standards that a company must meet in order to keep its stock listed there. It will be *delisted* unless it has at least 800 shareholders, of whom 700 must own at least 100 shares; unless publicly owned shares total at least 300,000 with a market value of $2.5 million; and unless its net earnings for the last three years average at least $400,000. A dozen or more companies are likely to be delisted in any given year.

All listed companies must agree to publish quarterly reports on their financial condition, as certified by the independent accountants. In the old days, only annual reports were required, and some companies were admitted on these terms. Nevertheless, almost all listed companies now report quarterly.

A company must agree not to issue any additional shares without exchange approval, and it must have a *registrar* in New York City to see that no more shares of stock are issued than a company has authority to sell. It must also have a *transfer agent* who keeps an exact record of all stockholders, their names, addresses, and number of shares owned.

The companies whose stocks and bonds are traded on the exchange have nothing to say about its operation. The brokers run their own show, although the paid president must be a man who has no connection with the securities business and the 33-man *Board of Governors* must contain three public members who have no identification with the securities business.

For years, the Securities & Exchange Commission has felt that the interests of the public shareowners were not adequately represented on the board, that it was dominated by professionals, who work on the floor of the exchange, as distinct from members who buy and sell for the public. Consequently, in 1966, the exchange decided to rotate the office of board chairman, with the office filled one year by a professional, the following year by a public broker — an arrangement that may not wholly satisfy the S.E.C.

Legally, the exchange isn't a corporation or even a partnership. It's nothing but a voluntary association of individual members whose number totals 1366. It is the "private club" aspect of the exchange about which the S.E.C. occasionally frets.

The business of trading in stocks in New York goes back to the early eighteenth century, when merchants and auctioneers used to congregate at the foot of Wall Street to buy and sell not only stocks but wheat, tobacco, and other commodities, including slaves.

In 1792, two dozen merchants who used to meet daily under a buttonwood tree on Wall Street and trade various stocks agreed from then on to deal only with each other and to charge their customers a fixed commission. Thus began the New York Stock Exchange.

How do you become a member of this association today? If you are approved by the exchange's Board of Governors, you buy a *seat*. Since nobody but a postman is on his feet more continuously than a broker, that is one of the classic misnomers of our language. It had its origin in the leisurely days of 1793 when the new association took up quarters in the Tontine Coffee House and the members could be seated while they transacted business.

What does a seat cost? That depends on how good business is on the exchange. In 1929, three different seats were sold at $625,000 each, an all-time high. Later the number of seats was increased 25%, so no one of them afterwards was worth quite as much, but it is hard to believe they could ever fall again to the low they hit in 1942, when one was sold for $17,000, which is less than the amount regularly given as a gift to the family of a member on his death out of the exchange's Gratuity Fund, supported by all the members. In recent years, seats have recovered some of their former value, and in 1966 they commanded a price of $250,000.

A handful of the seats — only 34 in 1966, as contrasted with more than a hundred some years ago — are owned by men who aren't really brokers at all. They are *floor traders,* men who buy and sell stocks wholly for themselves. Because they pay no commissions, by virtue of their membership in the exchange, they are able to make money by moving in and out of the market, trying to make a quarter of a point profit here, an eighth of a point there — usually in the most active stocks.

In its extensive study of the market, which supplied the groundwork for the 1964 Act, the Securities & Exchange Commission took the position that floor traders performed no useful economic function and that they should be phased out of existence. This the exchange has strongly resisted. Nevertheless, it did come up with a set of new rules to govern traders' activities. These provide that 60% of a trader's transactions must be of a "stabilizing" nature. To qualify as "stabilizing," a purchase can be made only when the price on the preceding sale has dropped, and a sale can be made only when the price on the preceding sale was up. Other rules are designed to make sure that the traders, who now account for less than 1% of total volume, enjoy no advantage over the public. All members do enjoy some slight advantage over the public since they are entitled to place *off-floor orders* — usually phoned from their offices or anywhere outside the exchange — at commission rates that are only about a fifth of what the public pays.

Most of the other brokers on the floor earn their living by executing buy or sell orders for the public, either directly or indirectly. In 1966, there were 651 *member firms* represented on the exchange, of which 499 were partnerships and 152 were corporations, and these firms owned a total of 1138 seats for the partners or voting stockholders who act for them on the floor. In 1966, these brokerage firms operated 3701 offices in 903 cities throughout the United States and 183 offices in 25 foreign countries. In still other cities they are represented by correspondents — over 13,000 of them. Usually these *correspondents* are local security dealers or banks that have wire connections to some member firm.

At least a million miles of private telephone and teletype wires keep all the offices of these brokerage firms, the so-called *wire houses,* in almost instantaneous touch with the exchange, and as a result the man who has his office next door to the exchange has no advantage over the man who lives 3000 miles away.

CHAPTER 9

What It Costs
to Buy Stocks

SINCE the New York Stock Exchange began, the brokers who are members have charged minimum *commissions* on the orders that they execute to buy or sell stocks for others.

How much are these commissions?

They vary with the price of the stock and the number of shares bought. But on almost any purchase or sale, the commission is a great deal less than you probably imagine. Most people think in terms of the 5% commission that a real estate broker usually charges on the sale of property. In contrast, the commission charged on stocks averages out to about 1% on all orders executed on the New York Stock Exchange over a period of a year.

Here is the basic schedule of rates made effective March 30, 1959:

On a purchase or sale amounting to $100.00 or less: as mutually agreed, usually 6%.

On a purchase or sale between $100 and $399.99: 2% plus $3.

On a purchase or sale between $400 and $2399.99: 1% plus $7.

On a purchase or sale between $2400 and $4999.99: ½% plus $19.

On a purchase or sale amounting to $5000 or more: 1/10% plus $39.

These rates apply on the purchase or sale of 100 shares of a given stock. If you buy or sell a multiple of 100 shares, say 300, figure the commission for 100 shares and multiply by three. You can, of course, buy or sell fewer than 100 shares, but if you do, your transaction costs will be slightly higher at every level than the commission charge on 100-share orders.

Regardless of the dollar amount involved in a 100-share

transaction, the standard commission is usually not less than $6 and never more than $75.

There is also a standard commission for corporate bonds traded on the New York Stock Exchange. The usual charge is $2.50 per bond.

Since only members of the exchange can execute orders there, other securities dealers must turn over all regular commission orders for listed securities to some member for execution. This means that if you give an order to a non-member, such as a bank or local securities dealer, you may have to pay an additional fee.

Over the years, commission rates have been increased from time to time, largely at the urging of the smaller member firms that find themselves unable to contend with rising costs as efficiently as the big, highly automated wire houses. The last such proposal came a cropper, however. As recommended by a special committee of the exchange, the proposal was a package deal that would have increased minimum commissions by $1.00 on each transaction over $100, forced members to make mandatory *service charges* for rendering monthly statements to their customers on their accounts, and offered *volume discounts* ranging from 30% on orders in excess of 3000 shares up to 50% on orders involving more than 100,000 shares.

Although the proposal died, partly because of opposition to one part of the package or another and partly because rising volume brought prosperity to all brokers, the exchange community knows it has not heard the last of the volume discount idea. The reason is simple. There is no law that says listed stocks have to be traded on the exchange — any stockholder can sell his shares directly to anybody else he likes, if he arranges for the proper transfer — and in recent years many large institutions have been circumventing the exchange because they feel they can get a better price on a large block of stock or incur less cost by private trades arranged through large security houses that are not members of the exchange — the so-called *"third market."* One way to keep this business on the exchange might be to offer volume discounts. But before taking such drastic action, the exchange will want to see what results flow from the change that it made in its own rule (*Rule 394*), which until 1966 required members to execute all orders to buy or sell listed stocks on the floor of the exchange and only there. This rule, aimed at barring *split commissions,* was amended in

1966 under pressure from the Securities & Exchange Commission to permit member firms to buy or sell outside the exchange if such deals with nonmembers would result in more advantageous trades for the customer than the member firm could get on the floor of the exchange. The amended rule imposes many restrictions on such trading off the exchange — nonmembers, for instance, must meet various high standards in order to establish their acceptability as buyers or sellers — but it was expected that the change would permit many member firms, especially the bigger ones, to earn at least one commission on big-block transactions that otherwise might have been concluded entirely within the third market.

Although the commission schedule is usually a matter of controversy only within the securities business, an investor in Chicago decided to make it his business in 1965 and instituted a suit alleging that the New York Stock Exchange violated the *antitrust laws* by enforcing a uniform schedule of commissions. Never has the exchange been so concerned about a legal action as by the *Kaplan case,* an action that seemed destined to be fought all the way to the Supreme Court.

What worries the exchange is that there is precedent for the argument that the exchange is subject to the antitrust laws, despite the fact that its almost every act is supervised or regulated by a government agency — the S.E.C. This precedent was established in 1963 in the *Silver case* when the U.S. Supreme Court held that the exchange had violated the antitrust laws in ordering several member firms to terminate their wire connections with a nonmember security firm in Dallas. In 1966, it appeared that the only way the exchange could get out of its antitrust troubles was to persuade Congress to pass an act specifically exempting it, but the exchange well knew that it couldn't hope to accomplish that objective without the support of the S.E.C., and it might have to pay a price for that support — the price of still greater subjection to S.E.C. control. But to keep its uniform commission schedule — to prevent rate-cutting or price competition — the exchange was willing to pay almost any price.

In addition to paying a commission on every transaction, a security shareowner must also pay a *transfer tax* whenever he sells a stock on the exchange. (There is no tax on purchases.) The transfer tax has long been levied by New York State, and in recent years — at least until 1966 — the tax rate had ranged from one cent a share on stocks selling under $5.00 up to four cents a share on stocks selling at $20 or more. So small a tax — small, even though it did net New York $100 million in 1965 — presented no serious problem, until New York City's Mayor Lindsay in 1966 proposed a 50% increase in the tax on the understanding that he would get it back in state aid to his hard-pressed city. That is when the exchange threatened to move across the Hudson River to New Jersey or at least establish an auxiliary trading floor there to handle large-block transactions. The tax issue was finally compromised with a boost of only 25% so that transfer fees now range from 1¼ ¢ to 5¢ on every share sold, but the idea of establishing an auxiliary floor in some tax-free state is one that may not die. After all, a tax of even 5¢ a share on a 100,000-share sale is $5000.

In addition to the transfer tax, a small fee is levied on all stock sales to cover the costs incurred by the Securities & Exchange Commission in its regulatory work. It amounts to only 1¢ on every $500 worth of stock — or any fraction of $500.

Most large brokerage firms are headquartered in New York City, and are consequently subject to the city's special business tax. For years that was a gross receipts tax, which initially was only 2/10 of 1% but rose steadily over the years to a level of 1½% on all commission income. In 1966, this tax was supplanted by a new business income tax which would be levied on all sources of a broker's income and result in a still heavier tax load. This city tax cannot be passed along to the buyer or seller of securities, but it does represent a significant item in the broker's cost of doing business and does make any proposal for an increase in commission rates look more attractive to many.

CHAPTER 10

How
the Stock Exchange Works

WHAT actually happens on the New York Stock Exchange when a broker gets an order to buy or sell stock? How is the transaction completed with another broker so that both buyer and seller are assured of the best price possible at that moment?

Consider first the physical layout of the stock exchange. It is a big building at the corner of Wall and Broad streets in New York City. The trading room looks somewhat like an armory, with a high ceiling and a *trading floor* about half the size of a football field.

All around the edge of the trading floor are *"telephone booths,"* as they are traditionally called, although today they might as appropriately be called teletype booths. These booths bear no resemblance to any other phone booths you have ever seen. They are open at both ends, and along the two sides there are spaces at which a dozen or more clerks, representing various brokers, can work. At each clerk's space, there is a narrow shelf at which he stands and does his paper work and above the shelf there is a bank of telephones connecting him with his home office. These phones were once the nerve ends of the entire stock exchange business, for it was through them that all public orders to buy or sell stocks came to the floor of the exchange. The phones are still used, but as part of its modernization program, the exchange has permitted most large brokerage firms to install teletype equipment in or near the telephone booths so that they can receive orders direct from their branch offices. This eliminates the necessity for relaying orders by phone from the home office to the floor clerk, and since teletype orders are printed, the possibility of error is also reduced.

Spaced at regular intervals on the trading floor are eighteen *trading posts,* twelve on the main trading floor and six in the "garage" or annex. Each trading post, or station, is a horseshoe-shaped counter, occupying about 100 square feet of floor space. Behind the counter, inside the post or station, there is room for a dozen other clerks and for several paid employees of the exchange.

All buying and selling is done around the outside of the trading post. About 75 different stocks are bought and sold at each post at different positions around the perimeter, a half dozen or so at each position.

Little placards on a board above the counter show just which stocks are sold at each position, and below each placard is a price indicator showing the last price at which a transaction in that stock took place and whether this price represented an increase or decrease from the last different price — a plus sign or *up tick* if it represented an increase, a minus sign or *down tick* for a decrease.

When an order is received at the headquarters office of any brokerage firm in New York City, it is phoned over to a clerk in that firm's telephone booth on the exchange floor (unless, of course, the order comes direct to the floor by teletype). Some firms have booth space for only one or two clerks, while one big wire house has about 40 spaces in nine booths. When the clerk gets the order over the phone, he writes it out in a kind of shorthand and hands it to his *floor broker* to execute, because only members can trade on the floor. If the broker is not at the booth, the clerk can summon him simply by pushing a button. Every broker has a number, and when the clerk pushes the button, the broker's number is flashed on a large *annunciator board* at each end of the trading room. If the clerk knows his broker is busy with other orders, he employs the services of a so-called *"two-dollar broker."*

There are more than 100 of these men who own their own seats on the exchange and make their living by transacting business for the wire houses. The two-dollar broker got his name in the days when he received that fee for every order he executed. Nowadays he is compensated on a sliding scale which ranges from 50¢ to $4.00 per 100-share order executed. In the average case, he makes about $3 on every order he handles. This is called a *floor give-up commission,* for the obvious reason that the broker who is responsible for the order gives up a part of his commission to the broker who actually executes the order. The commission is commonly called *floor brokerage.*

Let's assume that with the passage of years, Rod & Reel, Inc., has grown to the point where its stock is listed on the New York Stock Exchange, and that the order which the clerk gives his broker is a *market order* to buy 100 shares of Rod & Reel. A market order is one that a broker must execute as soon as he can at the best price he can get. As soon as the broker has the written order in his hand he walks — no running is permitted on the floor — over to the trading post where Rod & Reel is traded and where he knows he will find any other brokers who might have orders to buy or sell Rod & Reel.

As he approaches the post, he looks at the price indicator and notes that the last sale of Rod & Reel took place at 18¾, which means $18.75 a share. However, some broker may now be willing to sell it for less than that price, and so as he enters the *"crowd"* of other brokers at the trading position — two, three, or more of them — he simply asks, "How's Reel?" He doesn't disclose whether he wants to buy or sell; he just asks the question. Another broker may answer "Eighteen and three-eighths to eighteen and three-quarters," or simply, "Three-eighths, three-quarters." This means that 18⅜ is the best bid, the most any broker is then willing to pay, and 18¾ is the best offer, the lowest anyone will sell for.

Our broker will try to get the stock cheaper if he can; so he waits a few seconds for other offers. Finally he decides to tip his hand and make a bid. So he says, "One-half for one hundred," by which he means that he will pay $18.50 a share for 100 shares.

If he gets no response, he may raise his bid by ⅛ of a point. This is the minimum fluctuation in the price of most stocks. So he announces, "Five-eighths for one hundred." At this point, perhaps, the first broker, who was offering the stock at 18¾, may have decided that he can't get that price. Or another broker, who may have entered the crowd later, will decide to accept this bid of 18⅝. If either one of them decides to "hit" the bid, he says, "Sold," and the transaction is concluded, simply on the basis of that spoken word. Conversely, if a broker decides to accept an offering price announced in the course of an auction, he simply says, "I'll take it." No written memoranda are exchanged by the brokers.

The rules of the New York Stock Exchange provide that all bids to buy and all offers to sell must be made by open outcry. No secret transactions are permitted on the floor of the exchange. Furthermore, a broker cannot conclude transactions between his own customers without presenting their orders to buy or sell on the floor. For instance, the broker may have a market order to buy 100 shares of Rod & Reel and another market order to sell 100. He can't just *"cross"* these orders privately and effect a transfer of the stock between his two customers. He must send both orders to the floor, where the appropriate bids and offers must be made. Only in very rare cases are off-the-market crosses permitted, and even in these cases, both buyer and seller must know that the cross is being made, and the stock exchange must grant permission.

No broker is permitted to execute any orders except during the official trading hours of the exchange. These are from 10 A.M. to 3:30 P.M., New York time, Monday through Friday, excepting holidays.

As soon as a transaction such as the Rod & Reel purchase at 18⅝ is completed, the broker who bought the stock and the broker who sold it make their own records of the transaction. A report is phoned back to their offices so that the buyer and seller may each be advised that the transaction has been concluded and what the price was. Brokerage firms with teletype order service direct to the floor simply send the information from the floor back to the originating office.

After the market closes, the two brokerage firms involved in the transaction will arrange for the actual transfer of the stock and the payment of the amount due. Actually these two firms might have concluded many transactions with each other in the course of the day, and, in turn, each of them might have dealt with dozens of other brokers.

All settlements between member firms are arranged through the *Stock Clearing Corporation* in such fashion that the physical exchange of cash or securities is reduced to an absolute minimum. To illustrate: a firm may have sold 1100 shares of Rod & Reel for its customers on a given day and bought only 1000 shares. The transfer of 1000 shares from its customers who sold the stock to the customers who bought that same number of shares is purely an internal bookkeeping problem for the firm to settle. But it would still owe some other broker 100 shares, and to settle this matter, it gives the clearing corporation 100 shares, which the corporation in turn will give to another broker who bought 100 shares more than he sold. Time was when the brokers who owed shares at the end of the day would deliver the actual certificates to the clearing corporation, where other brokers to whom shares were due would pick them up. Now, all member firms keep a supply of all stocks at the clearing corporation, and the transfer of shares between brokers is accomplished simply by debiting or crediting each broker's account. Dollar balances — the net amounts owed by brokers and the net amounts due them — are settled in the same fashion.

To return to our Rod & Reel order, after the sale took place at 18⅝, one of the four or five *floor reporters,* paid employees of the exchange who stand outside each trading post, would see that the price indicator on the post was changed — from 18¾ to 18⅝. And since this sale was below the preceding sale, he would be sure that a minus sign showed beside the price figure.

For unnumbered years, he would then write a report of the sale — the name of the stock, the number of shares involved, and the price — and hand it to a page boy, who would take it to the pneumatic tubes that lead directly from each post to the ticker room. There a notation of the sale would be typed onto the *ticker tape,* and it would be carried by wire to the *tickers* in every broker's office throughout the country.

That was the procedure for reporting a sale and making the announcement on the tape until 1966, but that year the exchange, prodded by the S.E.C., began to catch up with modern technology. That year it installed the first *optical card-scanning* devices at two trading posts which made it possible to eliminate the floor reporter's handwritten slip. All the reporter now has to do is draw pencil lines through coded boxes on a preprinted card and insert the card in the scanner. The machine automatically "reads" from the card the name of the stock, the price, and the share volume involved in the transaction. So successful was this experiment that the exchange moved as rapidly as the availability of equipment permitted to install similar scanning devices at all other posts so that by the end of 1966 it expected to have a completely automatic system in which the scanning machines at all 18 posts would feed transaction data into a computer, and the computer would itself "drive" the ticker tape without the involvement of any human beings.

With this first step toward *automation* of floor operations, some brokers began to wonder if the day might come when

computers would take over virtually the entire trading function and render both them and the exchange itself obsolete.
After all, they had seen what a revolution computers had
wrought in just a few short years in the accounting, bookkeeping, traffic, and even research departments of their home
offices.

On the tape the name of every stock appears only as
initials or a combination of letters, such as C for Chrysler
Corporation, CP for Canadian Pacific and CRR for Carrier
Corporation. The single-letter symbols are, of course, the most
highly prized and the best known. Thus A stands for Anaconda, F for Ford, J for Standard Oil (New Jersey), T
for American Telephone & Telegraph, and probably the best
known of them all, X for U.S. Steel.

Rod & Reel might have the symbol RAR, in which case
the sale of 100 shares at 18⅝ would appear on the tape
simply as:

RAR

18⅝

If 200 shares instead of 100 shares had changed hands, the
transaction would be noted this way:

RAR

2s 18⅝

If 1000 shares had been involved, it would appear on
the tape this way:

RAR

1000s 18⅝

When sales volume is so heavy that the ticker, which can
print 900 characters a minute — almost the limit of readabil-
ity — falls as much as one minute behind, the price information is abbreviated to the last digit plus a fraction,
except when that digit is a zero, as in 20 or 30. If the
ticker was late, our sale at 18⅝ would appear as:

RAR

8⅝

It is assumed that people who are following the stock

closely on the ticker will be able to supply the missing first digit. If the stock were to go up to 20 or above, this price would be noted in full, such as 20⅛, on the first such sale.

The ticker doesn't usually fall as much as five minutes behind the market, except on big-volume days — 10 million shares or thereabouts — but sometimes this does happen. In such situations, to keep traders abreast of the market action, the exchange resorts to *flash* printing, and at half-minute intervals it flashes the latest prices of 30 key stocks representing a variety of industries on the tape. These up-to-the-second price announcements are always preceded by the word "Flash," and no volume figure is given. Whenever the tape recovers lost time, it returns to usual routines.

When most people think of buying or selling stock, they think of doing it on the basis of a market order, one to be executed as soon as possible after it reaches the floor and at the best price then prevailing. Actually, an individual very often wants to buy or sell a stock only if it can be done at a certain price or better. Thus, you might want to buy 100 shares of Rod & Reel only if you didn't have to pay more than 18½. You could place an order to this effect with your broker. It's called a *limit order,* and you can tell him whether it's good for a day, a week, or a month, or "good till canceled."

The stock will be bought for you only if it can be bought at 18½ or less. Perhaps when the order is actually executed, your broker will be able to get the stock at 18¼. On the other hand, the stock may actually drop to 18½, and your order won't have been filled. That's because other orders to buy at 18½ were placed ahead of yours, and the supply of the stock offered at that price was exhausted before your order was reached. In that kind of situation, if you asked your broker why your order wasn't executed, he would tell you that there was *"stock ahead."*

Limit orders can also be used in selling stock. Thus, if you owned Rod & Reel stock, you might be willing to sell it, but only if you could get $19 for it — $19 or more. You could place a sell-limit order to that effect with your broker. Sometimes, you might like to place a day limit order to buy or sell at a specified price, but you would still like to have your order executed that day even if the stock didn't quite reach the price level you set. You could accomplish that by having the order marked for *execution "at the close"* regardless of the market level.

There's still another kind of suspended order, and that is known as the *stop order*.

Suppose you had bought Rod & Reel at 12 or 13, and the stock had risen to a level where you had a nice profit — perhaps to 19 or 20. You might want to protect that profit in case the market dropped sharply, and you could do so by instructing your broker to sell the stock if it declined to, let's say, 18. This would be a stop order, and your broker would see that it was executed if Rod & Reel ever fell as low as 18. Whenever it hit that mark, your stop order would become a market order to be executed at the best price then possible. Again, because other people might have placed orders ahead of yours to sell at the $18 figure, the price might slip to 17¾ or 17½ before your order could be executed.

Occasionally, the exchange will exercise its authority to prohibit stop orders in individual stocks, but such action is taken only when the stock has followed a very volatile pattern of price movements and when the exchange fears that the execution of stop orders would trigger a sharp sell-off.

In theory these fixed-price orders, both limit orders and stop orders, look pretty attractive as a means of controlling your profit or losses. In practice, however, they don't work as well for the average investor as you might think. To have any real utility, a limit order has to be fairly close to the prevailing market price. For instance, if Rod & Reel is selling at 18½, there might not be much point in placing an order to buy it at 16 or even 17. And if you place a limit order at 18, you might just as well buy it outright at 18½. If you don't, you might never get another chance to buy it so cheaply. The price might rise to 19 or 20, and go right on up. The same logic applies in reverse when it comes to selling stock.

In short, decisions to buy or sell that turn on getting an extra fraction of a point profit are not apt to be sound decisions for the average investor.

CHAPTER 11

How a Market Is Made

WHENEVER you place an order with a broker, he is responsible for seeing that it is executed at the best price possible, the best as far as your interests are concerned. Often this would require him to spend far more time on your order than he can afford to spare if he is to see that all his other duties are also properly executed. Thus, for instance, if you were to place a limit order to buy Rod & Reel at 18 or better when the stock was selling at 18½, you could hardly expect your broker to spend all his time keeping an eye on Rod & Reel, waiting to see if it dropped to 18.

In a case like that, he would turn your order over to another broker who, as his agent, would watch the stock for you and execute the order if he could. This agent would be the *specialist* in Rod & Reel stock.

A specialist is a broker who has elected to confine his activities to a particular group of stocks sold at one spot around the perimeter of a trading post. He never moves away from that spot; he is always there to accept orders from other brokers and, for a give-up commission, to assume responsibility for their execution.

All told, there are about 350 specialists, representing some 90 specialist firms, who handle the stocks of the more than 1200 companies listed on the exchange. Some big specialist firms may handle as many as three or four dozen stocks, and some have only a few. In some active stocks, like General Motors or U.S. Steel, there are as many as three specialists, each competing with the others.

No broker can operate as a specialist except with the approval of the stock exchange, and he must be a man of substantial means, for every specialist firm is required to have enough capital to buy as many as 2000 shares of every stock in which it specializes. In the case of a stock priced at $50 a share, the specialist would need capital of one hundred thousand dollars, just to handle that one stock.

True, specialists can make financing arrangements to meet as much as 75% of their capital requirements, but even so, big specialist firms that handle dozens of stocks must have many millions of their own money.

A specialist must not only function as an agent for other brokers, executing the orders that they leave with him, but must also be willing to buy and sell for his own account those stocks in which he specializes. In fact, this is his primary responsibility if he fulfills the obligation imposed upon him by the exchange to maintain a "fair and orderly market." When a specialist executes orders for other brokers, he is himself operating as a broker. For technically that is what the word broker means — a man who acts as an agent for others. But when a specialist buys or sells for his own account, he is acting as a *dealer*. That is the whole distinction between a broker and a securities dealer. A broker simply bargains *for* you; a dealer bargains *with* you and acts as a principal in the transaction. He sells securities to you that he owns himself or buys such securities from you at an agreed price.

When a commission broker comes to the trading post with an order to sell a stock and there are no other brokers with buy orders for that stock at the post, the specialist will make a bid for the stock himself. Similarly, when a broker wants to buy a stock and there are no other sellers, the specialist will offer it for sale himself. Normally, about 15% of stock exchange volume results from this kind of buying and selling by specialists for their own accounts.

On each of the stocks in which he specializes, the specialist keeps a book, and in this *specialist's book* are entered all the limit or stop orders that other brokers have given him for execution whenever possible — orders that cannot be executed at the time because they are "away from the market" or not in line with prevailing prices. If a specialist gets two or more orders to buy a stock at the same price — or to sell it at the same price — he enters them in his book in the order in which he receives them. Those that are received first are executed first, whenever the price auction permits, regardless of all other conditions or circumstances.

Thus, if your order for Rod & Reel at 18 was the first one in the specialist's book, and if the stock was offered at that price, your order would be filled first. Even if he wanted to, the specialist couldn't buy the stock for his own account at 18 until your order and all others in his book at that price were executed.

Whenever the last sale of Rod & Reel was made at 18½, the specialist's book might typically show one or two limit orders to buy at 18⅜, one or two others at 18¼, and perhaps three or four at 18, since most customers place limit orders in round figures rather than fractions. On the sell side, his book might show a couple of orders to sell at 18⅝, a few at 18¾, and several at 19 or higher. On either the buy or sell side, these might be either limit orders or stop orders, and would be so marked in his book.

In that situation, if a broker came to the trading post with a market order to buy Rod & Reel and there were no other brokers there with stock to sell, his query "How's Reel?" would be answered by the specialist. The specialist would reply, "Three-eighths, five-eighths," meaning 18⅜ bid and 18⅝ offered, since 18⅜ was the highest buy order and 18⅝ the lowest sell order that he then had in his book. This would be the *bid-and-asked* quotation as of then.

Since a specialist's primary responsibility is to see that there is no violent fluctuation in the price of any stock he handles, he usually undertakes to see that the difference between the bid and the asked price is only ¼ of a point or so, although it might be more on high-priced issues.

Because specialists are generally faithful to their obligation of maintaining orderly markets, well over 90% of all transactions on the exchange take place at prices which show a fluctuation of ¼ or less from the next previous transaction. Whenever there is a more than normal gap between bid-and-asked quotations, the specialist, under the rules of the exchange, is expected to do something about it. Specifically, to narrow the gap he is expected to make appropriate bids or offers of his own — to buy or sell the stock as necessary for his own account.

Furthermore, if one of his stocks is moving rapidly up or rapidly down, he is expected to *stabilize* the market in that stock. If there is heavy pressure of sell orders which pushes the price down, he is expected to buy the stock for his own account. Conversely, if buy orders are pushing the price up too rapidly, he is expected to sell the stock from his own inventory. He may even be forced to sell stock he doesn't have, and if he does, he can only hope that somewhere along the line he will be able to buy an offsetting amount of the stock at a lower price because he knows he will have to make good the stock he has sold to other brokers.

The obligation to maintain a fair and orderly market can indeed impose fearsome responsibilities on a specialist. Important news developments can drastically affect a company's prospects and result in a sudden torrent of buy or sell orders. Sometimes such a development will delay the opening of a stock for half an hour or more after trading is supposed to begin at 10 A.M.; sometimes it will force suspension of trading for a period of time. In such situations, the specialist will consult with floor officials and one or two governors of the exchange, and they will decide what constitutes a fair price quotation, and when trading in the stock begins again, that's the price at which the specialist is obligated to buy or sell.

A classic illustration of the kind of a dilemma that frequently confronts specialists is that which resulted from the news break in early 1964 that Lockheed had developed the A-11, a jet plane whose performance, in the words of President Johnson, far exceeded that "of any other aircraft in the world today." The President made that announcement on a Friday, and Lockheed had closed that day at 38. What price would it open at Monday? That morning the Lockheed specialist was confronted with market orders to buy 30,000 shares, and in his book, he had offsetting sell orders that totaled only 17,000 shares — 13,000 less than were needed. Floor traders were willing to sell 3200 shares, and the specialist had 5600 in his inventory. As for the remaining 4200 shares, the specialist had no choice but to sell shares he didn't have in the hopes of being able to cover his shortage by buying 4200 shares later in the day at a reasonable price.

After conferring with the governors, the specialist set an opening price of 40¾ — $2.75 above Friday's close — and trading opened on a block of 30,000 shares at that price. Lockheed closed that day at 40⅜, after 299 individual transactions valued at some 5½ million dollars, but the most significant thing is that the specialist ran such an orderly market that no one of those transactions took place at a price that varied more than ⅛ or ¼ from the preceding transaction.

In addition to stabilizing the market and being willing to buy or sell when there are no brokers with offsetting orders, the specialist performs another important service, which is called *"stopping a stock."*

Suppose your broker came to the trading post with your market order for Rod & Reel when the best offering price in the specialist's book was 18⅝ and when there were no other brokers there with better offers. Anxious to get a lower price for you if possible, and yet not wanting to miss the market if it went up, your broker would ask the specialist to "stop" 100 shares for him at 18⅝. If another broker came up then and offered Rod & Reel at 18½, the specialist would buy it for your broker and earn a commission. On the other hand, if the stock was not offered at a lower price but sold again the next time at 18⅝, the specialist would execute your buy order at that figure. He could not execute your order at more than 18⅝, for when he was asked to stop the stock, he agreed that 18⅝ would be the maximum price your broker would have to pay. He'd try to buy it cheaper if he could, but 18⅝ would be the top price.

In his function as an agent for other brokers — by stopping stock for them or by executing limit or stop orders — the specialist accounts for about half of any average day's trading volume.

After every sale a wholly new auction starts. Thus, if a transaction in Rod & Reel had just been concluded at 18⅝, other brokers in the crowd who might be trying to buy 100 shares apiece would immediately restate their bids, probably the same bid — 18½. If there was no order on the specialist's book that had a clearly established time priority, these simultaneous bids would have parity, and if a broker then came up and offered the stock at 18½, the brokers who wanted to buy at that price would settle the matter as to which one would get the stock by tossing a coin.

The brokers who lost out might then report to their customers that they had "matched and lost." Customers who get such a report often wonder why they never win. The answer is that the broker never reports when he matches and wins; the customer simply gets the stock.

In the case of simultaneous bids, if one broker has an order for 200 shares while the others are trying to buy only 100 shares apiece, the larger order takes precedence if the seller offers a block that big or bigger. If the seller offers 200 shares, the broker who wants 200 will get them all. If the seller has 300 shares, the broker who wants 200 will get his first, and the others will have to match for the remaining 100.

Very often, before placing a market order, a customer

wants to have a pretty exact idea of what he might have to pay. To accommodate such a customer, the floor broker will try to "get the *market and the size*." This means that he will ask the specialist for the current bid-and-asked prices and for the size of the orders at these prices. The specialist will tell only the highest bid and the lowest offer, such as on Rod & Reel. "Three-eighths, five-eighths," or 18⅜ bid, offered at 18⅝. He is not permitted to reveal any of the lower bids or higher offering prices shown on his book. As far as the size of the orders is concerned, he might say, "One hundred either way," by which he would mean that he has 100 shares to buy at 18⅜ and 100 to sell at 18⅝. If he had 100 to buy and 500 to sell, he would say, "Three-eighths, five-eighths, one and five."

The specialist is not required to divulge the size of the orders on his book if he feels that it would not be in the best interests of the buyers or sellers.

Bid-and-asked prices — but not size — can be obtained by brokers who are far away from the floor by calling the exchange's *Voice-Answer-Back Quotation Service*. By dialing code numbers for individual stocks, member firms that subscribe to the service are connected to the exchange's computer, which responds by reading back information that has been stored in its memory core and prerecorded in a simple 126-word vocabulary. The information includes not only the bid-and-asked quotation, but also the high, low, and last sale price, plus volume information. The service, which can handle 300 calls simultaneously, supplies some 8,500,000 quotes a year.

Because the specialist's book gives him a feel of the market that no other broker or investor can possibly have and because he not only can but *must* buy and sell for his own account to maintain an orderly market, he is obviously in a position to affect the trend of prices in a very important way. To be sure that the specialist does not abuse his privileged position or manipulate prices in any way to his personal advantage, the exchange has circumscribed his operations with a set of highly technical rules, which have become steadily more stringent over the years. The most recent tightening up of specialist rules came as a result of the S.E.C.'s exhaustive study of security markets, culminating in the Securities Exchange Act of 1964. As a matter of fact, the whole study was touched off by a scandal involving two specialists on the American Stock Exchange, second in importance to the New York Stock Exchange, who were found guilty of price manipulation and who were forced out of the securities business by revocation of their S.E.C. registration license.

Despite the fact that various surveys, including the S.E.C.'s own, have not turned up any evidence of wrong-doing by specialists on the New York Stock Exchange and have even demonstrated what a useful service they render, the S.E.C. continues to regard their operations with grave suspicion, and there is no doubt of the fact that those operations will be kept under much closer surveillance by both the exchange and the S.E.C., now that both bodies are equipped with computers which make possible closer surveillance of price movements on individual transactions.

Whenever the hue and cry is raised that specialists ought not to be allowed to trade for their own accounts, that their functions should be restricted to running the book and executing orders for other brokers, specialists ask what would have happened to the stock market if they had not been able and willing to step into the breach at the time of President Eisenhower's heart attack in 1955 or the day when President Kennedy was assassinated in 1963.

On Monday, September 26, 1955, when the market opened, after the news of Eisenhower's heart attack had broken over the weekend, sell orders far outnumbered buy orders. It was virtually impossible to open trading in any stock. The sell orders would have depressed prices beyond all reasonable levels before buying sentiment could be generated. The specialists met the challenge. They bought steadily for their own accounts at prices only moderately below the levels that had prevailed at Friday's close. All told, one quarter of the stock purchases that day were made for specialists' own accounts — 1,759,360 shares with an estimated market value of $80,000,000. Eisenhower's recovery enabled the specialists as a group to work off the stock they bought without loss — indeed, with profit — but when they took the risk, they did not know whether or not they would be wiped out.

On November 22, 1963, the performance of the specialists was equally noteworthy. The story can be summarized in terms of what happened to 25 key stocks between 1:40 P.M., when news of President Kennedy's assassination hit the exchange floor, and 2:07 P.M., when the exchange was closed down by the governors. At 1:40 P.M. specialists in these 25 issues held 126,000 shares worth over $7,000,000 in their own inventories, but when panic selling engulfed the floor, the specialists stepped in to buy, risking their own personal solvency. In the following 27 minutes, 570,000 shares of these 25 stocks were traded on the floor, and of this total, the specialists bought more than 144,000, increasing their inventories to almost 230,000 shares, then worth $12,348,000. And it should be noted that the floor traders also helped stabilize the market in these stocks, buying 31,000 shares on balance. True, again, the specialists sustained no loss, thanks to a rapid market recovery, but that's something they couldn't count on when they took their big gamble.

The S.E.C. contends that specialists have not always behaved in such exemplary fashion in other big breaks, notably May 1962, but then perhaps no one can be a hero all the time.

CHAPTER 12

How
Large Blocks of Stock
Are Handled

In his role as a market-maker, buying and selling for his own account, the specialist very often performs a notably useful service in helping brokers dispose of sizable blocks of stock — 1000 shares, 5000 shares, even 10,000 shares or more.

Suppose you had a block to sell. Your broker might first attempt to find the other side of the market, to see if he could develop buying interest in the stock among his other customers, especially among institutions that regularly buy or sell in sizable quantities. If your broker was successful, he would *cross* the orders on the floor by offering the block either at the last sale price or between the bid-and-asked quotation and simultaneously bidding for the block at the same price.

If your broker was not successful in finding matching buy orders, he would be confronted with the problem of how to dispose of the stock on the floor. And it is a problem. If the block is simply dumped on the market, that very action might depress the price, and your broker would end up getting less than fair value for you. On the other hand, if he fed the stock out, 100 shares at a time, he might fare no better. In a falling market, he might fare even worse.

Time was when a broker in that situation could turn the order over to the specialist to execute on a *"not-held"* basis. On this basis the specialist would be free to exercise his own best judgment about when and how to sell the stock. He might, for instance, hold the order back in the expectation that prices would rise, but if instead they dropped before he executed the order — if other orders were filled

66

at higher prices than he finally realized on all or part of his not-held order — he was at least assured that the broker for whom he was acting would "not hold him to the tape," that is, would not hold him responsible for failing to sell at those better intervening prices.

For some years now, the S.E.C. has insisted, however, that specialists cannot accept not-held orders, and this makes the handling of them difficult for the broker. One thing he can do is ask the customer to change his order into a limit order, and the broker can then turn it over to the specialist to execute as best he can above the minimum.

Usually, when a broker has a large block to sell, he will take the problem right to the specialist and enlist his help. After all, the specialist is as interested as your broker is in disposing of your block with the least possible impact on his market. The specialist might, for instance, know some floor traders who would be interested in buying all or part of the block. Or the specialist might be willing to buy it outright for his own account, thus assuming the entire risk that he would be able to sell it at a profit.

Frequently, a bank, insurance company, pension fund, charitable foundation, or other large owner of securities will want to sell a block of stock so large that it cannot be handled in the normal routines of the stock exchange. Such blocks might range in size from as little as 4000 or 5000 shares of a high-priced, relatively inactive stock to hundreds of thousands, even millions, of shares of some stock with a broader market. This is the kind of problem that can be solved only by employing precisely the same underwriting and marketing techniques used to sell an entirely new issue of stock.

As a matter of fact, the most common device for moving such a large block is known as a *secondary distribution* (as distinguished from a new issue or primary distribution). A secondary distribution, like a new issue, can be handled either by a member firm of the New York Stock Exchange or a securities dealer who is not a member, and it will usually involve the participation of both members and nonmembers.

If the block is a listed stock, an announcement of the impending offering is made on the exchange ticker on the day of the sale, and the actual offering to the public generally takes place after the close of the market. This advance publicity that a sizable block of stock is hanging over the market can, of course, have an untoward effect on the price of the stock during the day's trading. Actually, if the exchange community is in any way concerned about the overhanging block, the price may already have drifted downwards for a day or two, because news of the impending secondary gets around as soon as the broker or dealer who is handling the sale sets about organizing his underwriting group.

The underwriters participating in the secondary buy the block outright from the seller and assume the risk of re-selling it to the public, often inviting other brokers and dealers to join them in the selling group. The underwriters charge the seller a *gross spread*, which typically will amount to three or four times the normal commission rate, although it can range from as little as two commissions to as much as six commissions. This spread covers the manager's fee, the underwriting commission, and the selling *concession*, which normally runs from a third to a half of the gross spread.

The price at which the block is offered in a secondary distribution that involves a listed stock is usually the price at which that stock is sold in the last transaction on the floor that day, although it might be either lower or higher depending on the attractiveness of the offering.

If you had no particular desire to buy a given stock at the close of the market, you may wonder how you could be interested in buying that same stock at the same price just a little later the same day. The answer is simple: To induce you to buy, the underwriters offer the stock on a commission-free basis, no matter how many shares you buy. The seller pays all the costs, and that's why the gross spread is so big.

On a secondary distribution the underwriting group usually undertakes to stabilize the market with S.E.C. sanction, just as they do on an original underwriting. Obviously, it would not be possible for them to sell their stock at the price fixed in their agreement with the seller if the same stock was being offered in the open market at substantially lower prices — prices that more than offset the commission saving to the buyer. In such cases, the underwriters would have to buy up the stock offered at the lower price and add it to their own block. If large quantities of the stock appear at considerably lower prices, they may have to give up their *price stabilization* efforts, withdraw the block, and wait for a better market, a happier day.

By all odds the largest secondary in history was the distribution on May 3, 1966, of Howard Hughes's holdings in TWA — a block of 6,584,937 shares of stock in that airline. Merrill Lynch, Pierce, Fenner & Smith Inc., the world's largest brokerage firm, handled the deal and headed the group of 410 underwriters, who offered the stock at the May 2 closing price of $86 a share. The entire offering, worth $566,304,582, was sold in half an hour. Only one underwriting deal has ever exceeded the TWA distribution, and that was the original public offering of stock in the Ford Motor Company in 1956. This was handled by seven securities firms operating as *joint managers,* and it had a gross value of $657,900,000.

A second technique for distributing a large block of stock is the *special offering.* A special is handled the same way as a secondary, except that participation is limited exclusively to members of the New York Stock Exchange and takes place on the floor of the exchange during regular trading hours. In recent years, the special offering has fallen into general disuse, as a third technique — the *exchange distribution* — has gained in popularity.

An exchange distribution is usually handled by a single brokerage firm, and the block is disposed of wholly by its own sales organization. Occasionally, but only rarely, two or more firms will join forces in such an offering. When a broker undertakes an exchange distribution, he usually does so on a *"best efforts" basis.* This means that he makes no absolute guarantee of the price, nor does he commit himself to selling the entire block. (Occasionally, even secondaries are handled on a "best efforts" rather than an underwriting basis.)

An exchange distribution is, in effect, nothing but a giant cross. The seller gives the broker what amounts to a market order, and the broker's salesmen then seek to develop buying interest among their customers on the assumption that the stock will be available at or near the price then prevailing on the exchange. When the sales organization has developed buy orders which in the aggregate match the size of the block, the broker checks the seller a last time to be sure he is satisfied with the price then prevailing, and if he is, the floor broker will then offer the block on the exchange and simultaneously bid for it, usually at the last sale price or at a price between the bid-and-asked quotations.

The entire operation may take only an hour or two, although if the issue is sticky, a day or two may be required to develop the necessary buying interest. Occasionally, the broker may even decide that he can't swing the deal at all and cancel all negotiations, or he may find that he will be able to move only part of the block, but such developments are uncommon.

One problem the broker doesn't have to worry about on an exchange distribution is the problem of price stabilization. He has his selling worries before the block comes to the market, and once the cross is effected, he is off the hook. He doesn't have to support the market for the stock in order to complete the sale.

There are two chief advantages to an exchange distribution from the seller's point of view. Since there is no public announcement of the offering and since the entire transaction is usually handled within a single broker's organization, there is little likelihood that news of the impending block sale will depress the price of the stock before the offering is made, as often happens with secondaries or specials. Again, since there is no need to organize an underwriting syndicate or a selling group, the cost to the seller is lower — characteristically, one or two commissions less than he would have to pay on either a secondary or a special. The buyers, of course, get their stock without paying any commissions, since all costs are borne by the seller.

Before a member firm can complete a secondary, a special, or an exchange distribution, it must obtain the approval of the exchange authorities, but this is generally almost automatic.

Banks, insurance companies, and other institutions are more apt to encounter a serious problem in selling a large block of securities than they are in buying one, but institutional business has grown so rapidly in recent years — it accounts for a quarter or more of New York Stock Exchange volume — that it is sometimes also difficult for these big purchasers to acquire the stock they want at a fair price and without disturbing the market. To meet this situation, the stock exchange in 1956 also established a mechanism known as the *exchange acquisition*, which works exactly like the exchange distribution, except in reverse. The broker who handles such a transaction solicits sell orders from his customers at a net price, free of all commission, until he accumulates shares equal to the buyer's order, and the buyer usually pays at least a double commission.

The exchange acquisition has never proved popular —

there was only one in ten years — and it isn't hard to see why. It's one thing for a broker to ask a customer if he wants to buy a stock commission-free; it's another — and more awkward — thing to ask him if he wants to sell a stock commission-free. The customer is immediately suspicious. Why, he asks himself, should his broker want him to sell that stock, particularly if it is one the broker recommended that he buy in the first place?

CHAPTER 13

How Small Orders
Are Handled

ALL stocks bought and sold on the stock exchange are
traded in units of 100 shares, with the exception of a few
inactive stocks. The 100-share unit is known as a *round lot*.

But what if you want to buy or sell just ten shares of our
hypothetical Rod & Reel Company? The answer is that you
can do it, and your order will be executed at exactly the
same price as if it were a round lot, although when you
buy an *odd lot*, anything from one to 99 shares, you will
pay an extra fee for the services of the *odd-lot broker*
who does nothing but handle these small orders.

This extra charge is offset to some extent by the lower
commission rate that the exchange has set on odd-lot orders.
At every level in the rate schedule (page 46), odd-lot commissions are $2 less than round-lot commissions on transac-
tions involving the same dollar amount. The minimum commission on all orders, round-lot and odd-lot, is usually $6,
but above that minimum, no odd-lot commissions can be
charged greater than $1.50 a share or $75 on a single
order. These maximums have been set to protect the customer who may want to buy only a few shares of a very
high-priced stock, one selling perhaps at $400 or $500.

The question of just how much the odd-lot customer
should pay the odd-lot broker for his service — indeed, the
whole question of whether his service might not be provided far more efficiently than it has been — was one of
the key questions raised by the S.E.C. in its study of the
securities markets, which led to the Securities Exchange Act
of 1964.

To understand the S.E.C.'s concern about the odd-lot
broker it is necessary to understand just how he has traditionally operated.

There are two odd-lot brokers — Carlisle & Jacquelin and

DeCoppet & Doremus — and for years they have enjoyed a virtual monopoly, handling 99% of all the odd-lot orders that reach the floor of the exchange. As a matter of fact, these two odd-lot houses aren't brokers at all; they are security dealers. If you buy 10 shares of Rod & Reel, one or the other of the odd-lot houses will supply your broker with the 10 shares from his own inventory. If you sell 10 shares, the odd-lot house will buy it from your broker and put it in inventory. If you order 10 shares of Rod & Reel and the odd-lot broker doesn't have it in his inventory, he must buy a round lot of the stock, sell you your ten shares, and put the other 90 shares in inventory — an inventory which in the aggregate can run to many millions of dollars.

Under the rules of the exchange, the odd-lot broker must fill your market order for any stock at whatever price prevails on the *next* round-lot transaction after your order reaches the trading post. For this service, the odd-lot broker for many years charged a fee of 12½¢ on every share of stock bought or sold below $40 a share, and 25¢ on every share of a stock selling at $40 or above. In effect, this meant that on stocks under $40, the odd-lot customer paid ⅛ above the market price when he bought and got ⅛ less than the market price when he sold. On stocks above $40 he paid ¼ more and sold at ¼ less. In June 1966, the S.E.C. finally forced the exchange and the odd-lot houses to raise the "break point" from $40 to $55, but that didn't end the commission's concern about the whole odd-lot picture.

The odd-lot broker not only executes market orders but also handles limit orders. These do pose an additional problem. Since he buys stocks for you either ⅛ or ¼ above the actual market price and sells for you at ⅛ or ¼ below the market, he does not execute a limit order unless the price is such that it covers his fee. Thus, if you place a limit order to buy an odd lot of Rod & Reel at 18½ or lower, he will not execute the order for you until the round-lot market price drops to 18⅜ or below. A limit order to sell at 18½ will not be executed until the stock reaches 18⅝. If the stock was selling over $55, the differential would be ¼ instead of ⅛. Like round-lot customers, the odd-lot investor can mark his limit order for execution at the close regardless of price.

Stop orders on odd lots are executed whenever the stock hits the specified price. If you place a stop order to sell Rod & Reel at 18½, it will become a market order for execution as soon as feasible whenever the stock hits that price. However, if it is executed at 18½, you will net only 18⅜ on the sale because your broker will deduct the odd-lot differential of ⅛ of a point.

If you want to be sure of buying a particular stock without waiting for the next round-lot transaction, you can instruct your broker to have your order executed at whatever offering price prevails when that order reaches the trading post. If you want to sell, you can instruct him to sell at the prevailing bid.

To assure the odd-lot buyer the same price as the round-lot buyer, each of the big odd-lot houses has two brokers at every trading post. These men, over 100 of them, are not mere employees of the two firms. They are partners of those firms and regular members of the exchange or they are individuals who own their own seats and represent the odd-lot houses on the floor.

The odd-lot firms do not deal with the public, only with other members, so that in effect they are brokers' brokers. Consequently, your market order for ten shares of Rod & Reel must be placed through a regular member firm. When your order reaches your broker's booth on the floor, it is marked for handling by either DeCoppet & Doremus or Carlisle & Jacquelin. (Most wire houses try to split their odd-lot business between the two houses.)

The clerk in the booth then sends the order by pneumatic tube — there are 35 miles of such tubes in the exchange — direct to the trading post on which Rod & Reel is sold. A page boy stamps the time at which the order is received and gives it to the odd-lot broker handling business at that post for whichever odd-lot house this order is marked. The broker goes at once to the position at which Rod & Reel is sold, and when the next round lot of Rod & Reel is traded by other round-lot brokers, the price arrived at in that transaction becomes the price at which you buy your ten shares. You get all the benefits of having participated in that auction.

After the sale, the odd-lot broker makes a report of the transaction, time-stamps the report, and sends it back by pneumatic tube to your own broker's booth.

You might ask why the odd-lot house doesn't simply set its price on the basis of the next Rod & Reel sale reported on the ticker? The answer is that the odd-lot houses guarantee that they give the small investor the actual market price — the price that is made in the next round-lot auction after his order. That actual price and the price shown on the ticker may be quite different, partly because of delays in getting prices on the tape, partly because the tape sometimes runs late.

Arguments occasionally arise because of that very difference in prices, and that's why odd-lot orders are time-stamped as they arrive at the trading post and again as they leave. Further, back in their headquarters the odd-lot brokers have a clerk for each of the eighteen trading posts on the floor, and each of those clerks does nothing but watch a special *deleter tape* which shows nothing but the trades executed at the post he is watching; all others are deleted. And that tape is also time-stamped every minute. Hence, the odd-lot firms are well prepared to answer any complaint from an odd-lot customer or his broker that his order was not executed at the proper price.

How important is the odd-lot buyer in the total exchange picture? One answer to that question is to say that he is both more important and less important than he used to be. With the great growth in the number of shareholders since the early 1950's, he has become numerically much more important, and yet collectively he accounts for a steadily decreasing percentage of the volume of total shares traded. In 1929 and 1930, the little man accounted for almost 20% of the volume, but in the forties and fifties, the odd-lot trading declined to about 15% or 16%, and in the big-volume years of 1963 through 1965, it dropped to little more than 13%. Of course, because he buys in so much smaller units, he accounts for a much greater proportion of total transactions. Of all orders executed for the public, about 40% are for odd-lotters.

One reason why odd-lot volume as a percentage of the whole has shrunk steadily is that since World War II many popular stocks have been split on a two-for-one, five-for-one, or even a ten-for-one basis; and with the consequent lowering of the per-share price of such stocks, many small customers have found themselves able to buy in the more economical 100-share units. Hence, they have graduated into the round-lot end of the business.

No matter how important the odd-lot buyer may be in the total volume picture, there are so many millions of him that the S.E.C. has been deeply concerned about him and his welfare. Specifically, it has been most concerned about what he has to pay for the service he gets.

In its critique of the odd-lot business, the commission took the position that the odd-lot customer should only have to pay the actual costs of handling his order, plus a reasonable profit allowance to the odd-lot firms. To the S.E.C. this meant a sliding scale of differentials, perhaps beginning at 1/32 of a point on very low-priced stocks and ranging up through 1/16 and 1/8 to a maximum of 1/4 on very high-priced stocks. Or better yet, a flat percentage differential based on the dollar value of the transaction rather than the price of the stock.

On the argument that any such drastic change would only confuse the odd-lot customer, the odd-lot brokers, backed by the exchange, argued for a simpler solution. They proposed raising the *"break point"* from $40 a share to $55 so that more odd-lot customers would be able to trade at the 1/8 differential instead of 1/4, and they sold this compromise to the S.E.C. in June 1966. But since half of all odd-lot transactions involve stocks selling at less than $40 and since customers trading in these stocks would reap no benefit simply from raising the break point, it could be assumed that the commission was not wholly satisfied.

Further to placate the S.E.C. the exchange said at the same time that all member firms would have to show the exact odd-lot differential on customers' confirmations.

It seemed certain that the commission would insist on still other basic reforms in the odd-lot business, for it had made plain its opinion that it considered the traditional system highly inefficient. It used the term "featherbedding" in describing the archaic system which it said was designed only to preserve the jobs of the highly paid odd-lot brokers who account for 10% of the members of the exchange. There can be little doubt in these days of automation and computers that a considerably improved and more economical system could be devised for handling odd-lot orders. Nor in mid-1966 was there much doubt that the odd-lot houses and the exchange authorities would ultimately come up with such a system, vested job interests notwithstanding.

Competition alone might speed the day, for the big wire houses, skilled in the techniques of automation and anxious both to serve their customers better and to turn an extra penny or two for themselves, are sometimes inclined to wonder by what divine right the two odd-lot firms are permitted to divide the very lucrative melon just between themselves. Why, they wonder, shouldn't they handle some of the business?

CHAPTER 14

How the Monthly Investment
Plan Works

UNTIL January 1954, the smallest amount of stock that anyone could buy was one share. In that month, however,
member firms of the New York Stock Exchange initiated
the Monthly Investment Plan — commonly known as M.I.P.
— under which it is possible to buy a fractional share of
stock, a fraction figured out to the fourth decimal point.
The plan wasn't formulated, of course, for that reason —
just to permit an investor to buy part of a share. It was
designed to permit people to invest a set sum of money
every month — or every quarter, if they preferred — and
to acquire for that money full or fractional shares of any
stock listed on the New York Stock Exchange, except those
sold in ten-share units.

By this method of systematic saving and systematic investing, a person would thus be able to acquire a worthwhile interest in the stock of some company on a regular
budget basis. He would not have to wait to become an investor until he had acquired several hundred dollars, enough
to buy five or ten shares of some stock.

The Monthly Investment Plan, in short, is geared to the
tempo of life today, since most American families are used
to settling their bills and making their installment payments
on a monthly budget basis.

M.I.P. is a method of buying stock by the dollar's worth,
regardless of how the price may change from month to
month, just as you buy $2.00 or $3.00 worth of gasoline,
regardless of what the per-gallon price is.

Under this plan, the buyer signs a "contract" — it is actually nothing more than a declaration of intent — with a
member firm of the exchange, under which he agrees to accumulate shares of a particular stock listed on the exchange
and to invest a regular sum of money — anything in ex-

cess of $40 — every month or every quarter toward the purchase of that stock.

Since M.I.P. contracts can be canceled by the buyer at any time and are so drawn that the buyer can skip payments without penalty, they are in no sense of the word binding or obligatory.

Here's how the plan works: Suppose you want to buy shares in Rod & Reel at the rate of $50 a month. Out of each payment the broker gets his standard commission, and with the balance the odd-lot dealer buys whatever number of full and fractional shares he can for you, at whatever odd-lot price prevails at the opening of the market the day after each payment is received; fractional shares are computed to the fourth decimal place.

Thus, if the broker got your $50 payment on a Monday and Rod & Reel opened Tuesday morning at 18⅜, he would buy you 2.5497 shares. Only $47.17 would have been applied to the purchase of the stock, because the brokerage commission on transactions of less than $100 is 6%, or $2.83 in this case. Furthermore, you would have paid 18½ for Rod & Reel, because the odd-lot house from which the stock was bought collects its regular ⅛ of a point over the market on a stock selling at Rod & Reel's price.

When the buyer closes out his M.I.P. contract, he gets a stock certificate for whatever full shares he has purchased, and any fractional share that may remain is sold at the prevailing price and the proceeds remitted to the buyer. Some brokers charge $1 for a stock certificate in an amount less than 50 shares, but other brokers will supply full-share certificates at any time without charge.

Dividends become due and payable on all shares, including fractional shares, from the moment any shares are bought; and these dividends, as they are received by the broker and credited to the customer's account, are automatically applied to the purchase of additional shares. This is one of M.I.P.'s unique features, for only under this plan can the investor automatically reinvest the dividends he collects on any of 1200 stocks on the New York Stock Exchange.

Because commissions are proportionately less on purchases of more than $100, many M.I.P. customers let their funds accumulate for three months and buy on the more economical quarterly basis.

Buying stocks in small units is expensive — expensive for the broker and expensive for the customer, but M.I.P. does have the advantage of helping investors establish regular habits of thrift. Then, too, consistent buying of the same stock provides protection for the small buyer in the event of a decline in price. If he continues buying in the same dollar amount while the price declines, the average cost of all the shares he owns will be reduced, and if the market rises again, he stands to make a tidy profit. Of course, if he discontinues buying in a downtrend and sells out when the value of his accumulated shares is less than their purchase cost, he will incur a loss.

At the end of 1965, there were 166,000 plans in operation, 42,000 of them having been opened that year. The reason why 1965 was a particularly lush year is that this was the year in which several brokers began pushing M.I.P. as a means by which listed companies — and some unlisted ones too — could initiate employee stock purchase plans on a voluntary, payroll-deduction basis. Hundreds of companies have now joined forces with brokers to promote such plans, and tens of thousands of their employees are now becoming stockholders in their companies for the first time. There is nothing new, of course, about company-sponsored stock purchase plans, but the M.I.P. angle is new and attractive to many managements because the broker carries the onus of selling the plan, and management feels less responsible for the price action of its stock. The plan is attractive to the employee because he acquires his stock commission-free; the company picks up the commission tab. Again the employee escapes payment of virtually all the odd-lot differential on the stock he acquires, since the company purchases the stock for all the employee accounts monthly in a single block and hence acquires virtually all the stock at the cheaper round-lot rate.

If it were not for these corporate stock purchase plans, the Monthly Investment Plan could not claim much of a record of success in the first dozen years of its existence. At least three or four times as many plans had been opened — and closed — over the years as were in operation at the end of 1965.

Some M.I.P. investors had become regular customers, since they had learned that they could accumulate their money themselves and buy an occasional odd lot at a lower commission cost. But others — many others — had simply fallen by the wayside. They had found it easy to drop out of

M.I.P. because there was no compulsion, actual or implied, to keep up their payments.

Reasons for M.I.P.'s disappointing performance are not hard to find. Since M.I.P. began, the market has been extraordinarily active, and brokers' sales representatives have been too busy attending to their regular customers to undertake much missionary work on behalf of M.I.P. It is no overstatement to say that M.I.P. was never sold by the brokers; it was bought by the customers.

There is a second explanation for the disinclination of brokers' sales representatives to push M.I.P. Many of them feel that it is not right to exact the highest commission (6%) from the investor who characteristically is least able to pay it. But the blunt fact of the matter is that these small accounts are costly to put on the books and to handle afterwards — far more costly in relation to the return the broker gets than regular accounts. Furthermore, it can be argued that the high commission cost is justified because America is used to paying a price to learn thrift. Consider the fact that the bank depositor who joins a Christmas Club gets no interest on his savings. Consider the high carrying charges which are levied on the buyer to finance all installment purchases. The pay-as-you-go man is used to paying both as he goes and as he comes.

CHAPTER 15

Other Exchanges—
Here and in Canada

ALTHOUGH they differ somewhat in rules, regulations, and operating mechanics, the other fifteen stock exchanges in the United States function fundamentally in much the same way as the New York Stock Exchange.

All told, the securities of some 3000 corporations are listed on the organized exchanges, but on the basis of the dollar value of all stocks traded, about 83% of the business is done on the New York Stock Exchange — the *Big Board,* as it is called — with little more than one-third of the total listings.

In recent years, these other exchanges have been steadily increasing their volume at the expense of the New York Stock Exchange, but the Big Board has always enjoyed such dominance that the business it has lost to other exchanges is little more than a flea bite. Nonetheless, it complains volubly.

The second biggest exchange is the *American Stock Exchange,* which until 1953 was known as the *New York Curb Exchange.* With about 1000 listed stocks, this exchange normally handles about a quarter to a third as much share volume as the New York Stock Exchange, but because the average price of its shares is also only a quarter to a third of the average of Big Board shares, it accounts for only 8% or 9% of the total dollar value of all stock transactions. Rightly or wrongly, the American Stock Exchange is regarded as a kind of prep school for the New York Stock Exchange. Many important companies like General Motors and Montgomery Ward and the various Standard Oil companies had their start on the old curb exchange.

But there are many other well-known companies, such as Hormel, Horn & Hardart, Lerner Stores, Mack Truck, Mead Johnson, Northeast Airlines, and Stop & Shop which remain

faithful to the American Stock Exchange and have made
no attempt to get their securities listed on the Big Board,
even when the requirements for listing there have been less
exacting.

The New York Curb Exchange got its name from the
fact that it actually began as a curbstone market, first on
Wall and Hanover streets in New York City and later on
Broad Street. It remained an outdoor market until 1921,
when it finally moved indoors, thus depriving the city of
one of its most colorful spectacles. Most of the trading was
done by hand signals, and orders were relayed to the brokers
by shouts and whistles from clerks perched on the window-
sills of their offices in adjoining buildings. Even in its spacious
new building, far more modern than the New York Stock
Exchange, orders are relayed from the clerks at their phones
to floor brokers by hand signals.

Included among the 650 members of the American Stock
Exchange are, of course, all of the nation's major brokerage
firms. With increased activity in recent years, seat prices
have risen steadily — to a level of $120,000 in May 1966.
The all-time high of $254,000 was reached in 1929, the all-
time low of $650 in 1942.

In general, the American Stock Exchange functions in very
much the same way as the Big Board, with one notable exception. There are no odd-lot brokers on the floor of the
American Stock Exchange. Odd-lot orders are filled by the
specialists. Because the average price per share is so much
lower on the American Stock Exchange, a greater proportion of its traders buy and sell in round lots rather than
odd lots. The odd-lot differential is the same on both exchanges, and so are the commission rates.

Although it was a price-manipulation scandal involving
two specialists on the American Stock Exchange that touched
off the whole S.E.C. investigation of the market and led to
the Securities Exchange Act of 1964, it can fairly be said
that this exchange moved more rapidly than the Big Board
did to put its house in order and conform to S.E.C. standards of self-regulation. The reforms were pushed through
by the new administration which the American Exchange installed in 1963 as part of its complete reorganization program.

It can also be said that the American Stock Exchange
moved more rapidly than the New York Stock Exchange to
automate its procedures and to maximize computer applica-

tions in the conduct of business — including a stock-watch technique to spot unusual trading patterns for prompt study by the staff. The American Exchange also installed electronic equipment to speed reports of transactions from the floor to the ticker before the Big Board did.

The third biggest United States Exchange, the *Midwest Stock Exchange,* came into being in 1949, when the Chicago Stock Exchange undertook to effect a consolidation of its activities with those of other exchanges in Cleveland, St. Louis, and Minneapolis-St. Paul. Volume on the Midwest Stock Exchange is only about 3% of what it is on the Big Board.

Other regional exchanges include the Pacific Coast Stock Exchange, which is located in both Los Angeles and San Francisco, the Philadelphia-Baltimore Stock Exchange, and those in Boston, Cincinnati, Detroit, Pittsburgh, Salt Lake City, and Spokane. Also included are the Chicago Board of Trade, which is generally known as the nation's primary commodity market, and the relatively new National Stock Exchange, organized in New York in 1962 by another commodity exchange, the New York Mercantile Exchange. All these exchanges are registered with the Securities & Exchange Commission, which means in effect that the commission has approved their rules and regulations as being adequate for the discipline of any member who violates his public trust. The exchanges in Colorado Springs, Richmond, and Honolulu are exempt from regulation because they are so small.

The *regional exchanges* were organized originally to provide a marketplace for the stocks of local companies, but as these companies grew and acquired national reputations, many of them wanted their securities on an exchange in New York City, the nation's biggest money market. And so, naturally, did the Big Board. As it succeeded in luring many issues to New York, the regional exchanges languished.

But in recent years, the regional exchanges have managed to turn the tables on the Big Board. They have begun to trade in the same securities that are listed on the New York Stock Exchange, and in 1965 the business they did in these stocks amounted to more than 85% of their total business. Furthermore, it's a business that is growing every day.

To get this business in Big Board stocks, the regional exchanges have induced some of the big companies to list their securities on one or more of the local exchanges as well as on the New York Stock Exchange, and if a company hasn't wanted to go to the expense of *dual listing* the regional exchanges have simply made their own arrangements to trade in those securities without formal listing. Such arrangements must be approved by the Securities & Exchange Commission.

This trend has grown so that about half of all the Big Board stocks are now also traded on one or more regional exchanges, and in the main, these are the most popular stocks, stocks that account for over 80% of Big Board volume. The American Stock Exchange has not shared in this bonanza, because under S.E.C. rules a stock cannot be traded on two exchanges in the same city.

The reason for the great growth of trading in Big Board stocks on the regional exchanges isn't hard to find. It all traces back to Rule 394 of the New York Stock Exchange, the rule that forbids a member firm to split commissions with a nonmember. When a big securities dealer who did not belong to the exchange had a sizable block of some Big Board stock to buy or sell, he often arranged to have the order executed on a regional exchange by a member firm, which had developed the other side of the order — a purchase to match the dealer's sell order or a sale to match his buy order. The dealer and the member firm split the commission, and everybody was happy — everybody except the officials of the New York Stock Exchange. (The seller, incidentally, is likely to be especially pleased since he avoids payment of the New York State transfer tax.) In 1965, some 1500 blocks of Big Board stocks, involving over 11,000,000 shares, were crossed on the regional exchanges, and the number of such crosses was steadily increasing. With the 1966 amendment to Rule 394, permitting member firms to deal with nonmembers under certain specified conditions, it seemed likely that some of the regional exchange business in Big Board stocks might dry up, but it will never wholly disappear. For one thing, the amended Rule 394 still imposes such onerous restrictions on off-board trades that many dealers and many member firms will still find it easier to do business on the regional exchanges.

When a Big Board stock is traded on a regional exchange, the price is generally determined by the last price shown on the New York Stock Exchange ticker. There is no auction. The specialist who handles such a stock simply bases his bid-and-offering quotations on the last New York ticker price and buys or sells either round or odd lots. On odd lots, he will charge just what is charged on the Big Board, including the differential of either ⅛ or ¼ of a point. Thus, the buyer pays just what he would if his order were handled on the New York Stock Exchange. Nothing annoys the New York Stock Exchange more, because it feels that these local brokers are making a profit out of an auction operation to which they make no contribution. Local brokers retort that they are broadening the market and offering a tax saving on sales.

Except on crosses where sizable commissions are involved, New York Stock Exchange member firms will normally execute orders for Big Board stocks in the New York market even though they are dually listed. Of course, if a broker gets an order for a Big Board stock after that exchange is closed for the day and if it can still be executed on some other exchange, such as the Pacific Coast Exchange, which is still open because of the time difference, he will execute it there if the customer wishes. This situation sometimes permits a man to make an advantageous trade if a big piece of news breaks after the close of the New York market.

The most important new competition that faces the New York Stock Exchange today comes not from the regional exchanges in the United States, but from the exchanges north of the border, where the big boom after World War II stimulated worldwide interest in the ownership of Canadian stocks.

Of the six Canadian exchanges, by far the largest is the Toronto Stock Exchange, which does about 80% of the share trading and two-thirds of the dollar volume of the Canadian total. In some years, the Toronto Stock Exchange has passed even the New York Stock Exchange in share trading (though not approaching it in dollar value), but generally it stands about third or fourth in dollar value of stocks traded on all the United States and Canadian exchanges. In 1965, the dollar value of all stocks traded on the Toronto exchange came to $3.2 billion against almost $73 billion for the New York Stock Exchange.

The other Canadian exchanges are the Montreal Stock Exchange, Canadian Stock Exchange (Montreal), Vancouver Stock Exchange, and Calgary Stock Exchange. Interest in oil and mining shares runs especially high in western Canada, while industrial shares are still the prime attraction on the more staid markets in Montreal, which used to dominate the Canadian securities scene until the boom gave Toronto its chance to take over the leadership. The Toronto Stock Exchange boasts the most modern plant and the best mechanical facilities of any exchange in the world, facilities that have enabled it to handle a volume exceeding 29,000,000 shares a day without undue strain.

Many of the common stocks listed on the Toronto and Montreal exchanges are on a dividend-paying basis, but the typical buyer of Canadian stocks — or "shares," as he usually calls them — isn't so much interested in dividends. He buys common stocks because he wants to share in the dynamic growth of the country and its industry, and he expects his shares to pay him a handsome profit over the years ahead as a result of an increase in price.

In the main, stocks are traded on the Canadian exchange very much as they are in the United States, but there are several significant differences.

For one thing, floor trading is not restricted exclusively to member brokers. Thus, on the Toronto exchange, every member is permitted to appoint as many as five "attorneys" to execute orders for him.

Again, there is no formal system of specialists who make markets in various stocks by buying or selling them for their own accounts such as there is on the New York Stock Exchange.

There are also significant differences in the units of trading. Thus, on the Toronto exchange, oil and mining stocks selling at less than $1 a share — the so-called "penny stocks" — are traded in units of 500 shares, and if the price is $1 or more, the trading unit is 100 shares. On industrial stocks — principally the shares of manufacturing or distributing companies — still different units of trading are employed. On such stocks selling at less than $25 a share, the unit is 100 shares; between $25 and $100, it is 25 shares; and if the price is over $100, it is 10 shares. All of these different units are known as *board lots* rather than round lots.

Odd lots can also be bought or sold on Canadian exchanges, but they are not handled by special odd-lot brokers as they are on the New York Stock Exchange, and the price of an odd lot is not automatically determined by the price that prevails on the next board-lot trade. Each odd-lot order is the subject of separate bargaining between two or more brokers on the floor. In general, orders for 5, 10, or 20 shares of a stock are handled expeditiously, but the man who wants to buy some irregular number of shares — 3, 13, 23 — may encounter some difficulty.

As a matter of general practice, the odd-lot buyer of industrial shares on the Toronto exchange is apt to have to pay about ⅛ or ½ more per share than he would on a board-lot order, while on oil or mining shares, the extra costs will vary from a few cents a share on stocks selling under $1 to as much as 10¢ or 15¢ on stocks selling over $1.

Canada does not have a national agency like our own S.E.C. to police and regulate the securities business, but every province has its own securities commission, and the house-cleaning job which the S.E.C. has been doing or forcing the industry to do here has found its reflection in Canada, particularly in Ontario. Public criticism and government investigation have led the Toronto exchange to tighten lax procedures and to initiate significant reforms. The most important of these are the establishment of a market surveillance department to ferret out price manipulation and the adoption of a disclosure policy to compel listed companies to give shareholders bad news as well as good and to make full information available to the public, not just to "insiders."

Meanwhile, the Ontario Securities Commission continues to try to catch up with the high-pressure operators who have been peddling questionable oil and mining stock south of the border by mail and by phone ever since the speculative boom got under way in Canada twenty years ago.

Many of these *"boiler shop"* operations have revolved around uranium or other mining projects which often existed only in the promoter's mind. Oil-drilling ventures have had something of a play from these touts, too.

Typically, the promoter offers the unsuspecting prospect a chance to buy shares in a new mining or oil company at a bargain price, less than the announced offering price on the new issue, and he is assured that they can be resold any time at the full price or better. "Engineers' reports" are given the prospect to convince him that the properties to be worked by the company have rich and promising deposits; in the usual case those properties adjoin some fabulously productive mine or well already in existence. Very often whether the company actually proceeds with its venture depends on how many suckers the promoter finds; and if he succeeds in raising adequate capital, you can be sure that he and the company's officers have cut themselves into a substantial ownership interest of the company at virtually no cost to themselves.

It is a good idea to check carefully with some established broker before signing up for a block of stock in the Pipe Dream Mine. Don't worry about missing the chance of a lifetime. If the stock is worth buying at all, it will probably be just as good a buy a couple of days from now as it is today.

CHAPTER 16

How the
"Over-the-Counter"
Market Works

IF you can buy stocks and bonds of only about 3000 companies on the registered stock exchanges, where, you may ask, can you buy or sell the securities of the tens and tens of thousands of other companies that exist in this country?

Where, for instance, would you have bought the stock of the Rod & Reel Company in the days when it was growing up and before it could ever hope to be listed on any exchange?

The answer is that you would have bought it in the over-the-counter market, and that's where you buy or sell all the other *unlisted* securities today — nearly 50,000 of them. Actually, this market isn't a place; it's a way of doing business, a way of buying or selling securities other than on a stock exchange. Buying interest is matched with selling interest not on a trading floor but through a massive network of telephone and teletype wires that link together thousands of securities firms here and abroad.

The over-the-counter market is difficult to define or describe because transactions that take place in this market have few if any common characteristics. You might, for instance, conclude a purchase or sale with a security dealer who operated a one-man shop in some small town, or you might deal with the largest broker in the world headquartered in Wall Street.

You might buy a highly speculative $2.00 stock in some little-known company, or you might make a highly conservative investment in a blue chip security with more than a century of seasoning behind it.

You might buy a security that the dealer himself owns, or

you might buy a security that he acquires for you to fill your order.

You might pay a commission, or you might pay a flat price.

All of these transactions would have about them just one common denominator: the price you would pay if you were buying or the price you would get if you were selling would not be a price that was arrived at by an auction system, as on an exchange; it would be a price arrived at by negotiation — negotiation between dealer and dealer, negotiation between dealer and customer.

Whenever prices are negotiated, there is room for the knowledgeable to take advantage of the unknowledgeable. There is room for sharp practice, even for outright chicanery. It is not surprising therefore that a substantial part of the Securities Exchange Act of 1964 was aimed by the Securities & Exchange Commission at tighter regulation of the over-the-counter market, for the commission has long been concerned about abuses in the field. Nor is it surprising, as a result of the enactment of that law and the promulgation of various regulations under it, that the over-the-counter market finds itself today a business-in-transition, a business less susceptible of simple description than ever before.

Probably the most common kind of over-the-counter transaction is the kind you would have entered into if you had bought Rod & Reel common stock at a time before the company had grown to a point where its shares were acceptable for trading on an exchange.

Suppose you had gone to your securities dealer and placed an order to buy 50 shares — any number you like because over-the-counter securities aren't sold in round lots and odd lots. Now, let's assume that the dealer doesn't have Rod & Reel himself and hence cannot sell the stock to you out of the inventory of stocks that he does carry. So he calls another dealer who does have some and asks the price. He may check two or three other dealers to see if he can get a better price.

Let's say the best price anyone quotes him is 18½, or $18.50 a share. That is the *inside price* to him, the price one dealer quotes another; often it is called the *dealer price* or *wholesale price*. It's not the price at which he'll sell to you. That price, the *outside price*, may be 19 or even more.

Whatever the price, it will be a *net price* to you — all you have to pay. You won't be charged a commission. The price is all-inclusive. Of course, instead of a commission, the dealer makes a profit. Often the profit is larger than the commission would be if you bought a stock selling at the same price on the New York Stock Exchange, and the net result is that you pay more.

Thus, if the dealer quoted you a price of 19, you would pay him a total of $950. In contrast, your total cost for 50 shares of a stock selling at 18½ on the New York Stock Exchange would be $945.50 — a total comprised of $925 for the stock itself, plus ⅛ of a point or $6.25 for the odd-lot differential and a standard commission of $14.25. But this, of course, is something the dealer may not point out to you. Instead, he may even make a point of the fact that your purchase is "absolutely commission-free," as though he were giving you something for nothing.

If you are selling at net instead of buying at net, the dealer will follow much the same procedure. He will check other dealers and perhaps discover that the best price anyone will pay is 18¼. He might then offer to pay you 18 or 17⅞, and that again would be a net price. You wouldn't have to pay a commission.

Perhaps after he bought the stock from you, your dealer might decide not to sell it to the other dealer who had bid 18¼ for it. Perhaps he thinks he can make a bigger profit on it if he holds it himself. There may have been three or four other people who have come to him lately and expressed an interest in Rod & Reel Company. He might be able to sell it to one of them at 19 and make a much larger trading profit for himself. Or the stock might even go higher in a little while. He has looked into the Rod & Reel situation himself, and prospects appear good. Maybe the dividend will be increased. Maybe in a few months he will be able to sell the 50 shares at 20 or 21 or better.

For any or all of these reasons, the dealer might decide to keep the stock himself. If he does, he is said to *"take a position"* in the stock. If he buys and sells it regularly himself, he is said to *"make a market"* in that stock, very much as a specialist does on the New York Stock Exchange.

Once a dealer makes a market in a stock, he is expected to be willing to buy it or sell it at any time and to announce the prices at which he is willing to trade it.

These prices will, naturally, be of two kinds. There will be the inside, or wholesale, prices for other dealers — perhaps 18¼ bid, offered at 18½ — and the outside, or retail, prices for his customers, which might be 18 bid, offered at 19¼.

Price ranges such as these are the kind that might prevail on a stock that was fairly active. If the stock was inactive, there might be a considerably wider spread, on both the inside and outside markets, between what a dealer would be willing to pay for a stock and what he would ask for it if he was selling it.

Thus, if Rod & Reel was not well known, his risk in taking a position in that stock would be greater. He might have only occasional buying inquiries, and perhaps the only way he could ever move it would be to go out and sell it aggressively himself.

On such a stock, the dealer might quote an inside market with a spread of a full point or more between the buying and selling price. As for the outside, or retail, prices, he'd be tempted to charge whatever the traffic would bear. He would buy it as cheap as he could and sell it as dear as he could.

Remember, when you buy a stock from a dealer on a net price basis, you are negotiating or bargaining with him. You are asking, "How much will I have to pay?" And the dealer, in effect, is asking "How much will you pay me?" He is not acting as your agent, trying to buy or sell something for you at the best price possible; instead he deals with you as a *principal* in the trade. He doesn't collect a commission; he tries to make a profit.

That's the way a net trade works. But not all over-the-counter transactions take place on a net price basis.

Thus your dealer might prefer to handle your order for 50 shares of Rod & Reel on an *agency basis,* in which case he would charge you the inside price, plus a standard commission. This is likely to be the case if you are dealing not with a local security dealer but with one of the branch offices of a member firm of the New York Stock Exchange. The over-the-counter business of such firms is handled by a separate *trading department* located in the headquarters office, but their representatives in branch offices handle orders for both stock exchange and unlisted business. And their trading departments will act both as principal and agents, handling some stocks in which they make markets on a net price basis and buying or selling others for their customers on a commission basis.

When an over-the-counter stock is bought on an agency basis, a member firm generally will take the best inside price it can find and add to the total cost of the purchase the exact commission that it would receive on the same number of shares selling at the same price on the New York Stock Exchange. A sell order would be handled the same way, with the broker deducting his standard commission from the total price of the sale.

Some brokers and dealers — a comparative handful — are willing to handle over-the-counter business on an agency basis but are not equally willing to adhere to the New York Stock Exchange commission schedule. They feel they are entitled to ask higher commissions because they are used to making so much larger profits when they trade on a net price basis.

Whenever you buy an over-the-counter stock, two questions are apt to bother you. (1) How do you know your dealer got the lowest possible inside price, and (2) How do you know the price he quotes you is a fair one?

The *National Quotation Bureau* goes a long way toward providing a reassuring answer to the first question, and the Securities & Exchange Commission has taken a giant stride under the Securities Exchange Act of 1964 toward answering the second.

Every day the National Quotation Bureau, a privately owned price-reporting service, publishes in its *"pink sheets"* the inside prices on 8300 over-the-counter stocks and 2000 bonds. These are the prices at which hundreds or thousands of different dealers announce their willingness to buy or sell various securities in trades between dealers.

Any dealer who wants to have his prices quoted supplies them every afternoon to the bureau. The quotation sheets are mimeographed overnight and published the next morning in three different editions — Eastern, Western, and Pacific Coast. Since any dealer who has an important position in a stock wants to stimulate inquiries about it from other dealers, the pink sheets, subscribed to by almost every important dealer in the country, render a valuable service.

In its study of the over-the-counter market, which preceded the Securities Exchange Act of 1964, the S.E.C. gave the National Quotation Bureau a reasonably clean bill of health, but it is keeping a watchful eye on the service so that it will not be abused by dealers. The S.E.C. wants to be sure that every dealer stands behind the prices he announces in the pink sheets and that they are not used to give a false illusion of value or market activity. If a dealer announces a price he is willing to pay for a given stock, he may get away with a refusal to buy one day, on the ground that the market has moved away from his bid, but if he publishes the same price the next day, he has to take stock offered to him at that price or run the risk that an official complaint will be lodged against him.

When the 1964 act was passed, the S.E.C. made it clear that it felt automation was in order, and a committee of dealers went to work to see how high-speed computers, hooked up to quote machines, could be used to identify market-makers, insure firmness of quotes, and provide up-to-date price information more efficiently than the present system does.

Meanwhile, in 1966, one member firm — Merrill Lynch, Pierce, Fenner & Smith Inc. — introduced to the over-the-counter market its own automated quote system and simultaneously announced a pricing policy which virtually guaranteed that the customer would never pay more than a standard commission, no matter whether his order was executed on a net price or commission basis. The firm's automated system enables its representatives in 170 offices to obtain instantaneously from the trading department the inside quote on any of the 500 stocks in which the firm makes a market — just by pressing four buttons on a desk-model quote machine. When the quote is flashed back on the machine's viewing screen, the representative can immediately execute the customer's order to buy or sell anything up to 100 shares on a net price basis simply by adding or subtracting the equivalent of a New York Stock Exchange commission to the inside quote. Although orders for other stocks in which the firm does not make a market cannot be executed on the spot, the same policy prevails: all agency orders are executed at the best dealer price, plus or minus the standard commission.

Perhaps the single most dramatic reform which the S.E.C. brought about after the 1964 law was enacted is the publication in the newspapers of more accurate and dependable quotations on over-the-counter stocks. Prior to that action, bid-and-asked quotations of a somewhat fictional nature were supplied to newspapers by the *National Association of Securities Dealers*, a quasi-government agency which represents 3700 dealers but which is also vested with authority by the S.E.C. to censure, fine, suspend, or expel members that do not abide by regulations. (From 1939 through 1965, about 430 firms had been expelled and thereby lost their right to participate in any underwritings.)

Over-the-counter quotes were not — and are not today — actual prices. They have always been only indications of the price range within which the customer might expect to trade. Prior to 1966, quotes on the bid or buy side furnished by the National Association of Securities Dealers were always reasonably accurate, but the asked or offering quotes were almost always inflated by 4% or 5%, sometimes even more. Thus a stock offered at 21 might actually have been available at 20 — and the customer who paid 20½ would have been delighted at the bargain he thought he got.

The Securities & Exchange Commission took a dim view of this practice, and after a bitter fight with many smaller dealers in the industry the commission forced the publication daily of more realistic quotes. On 1300 stocks that are considered to have a national market — stocks like Anheuser-Busch, Dun & Bradstreet, Kaiser Steel, or Eli Lilly — the S.E.C. in 1965 insisted on the publication of accurate inside dealer quotes, both bid and asked. Then in 1966, after a study by an outside marketing consultant had demonstrated that the requirement had not worked undue hardship on the dealers, the N.A.S.D. decided to extend its honest pricing rule to some 2500 stocks that are considered to have regional markets. As a result, virtually all prices for over-the-counter stocks that are published in newspapers are honest, actual quotes, not inflated on either side.

One issue between the Securities & Exchange Commission and the industry that was still unresolved two years after the passage of the 1964 act was the so-called *riskless transaction*. Suppose you place an order for a given over-the-counter stock in which your dealer does not make a market. He might find that the best inside market is 39 bid, offered at 40, but he sells it to you at a net price of $42, having marked it up the full 5% — a markup long accepted as the maximum that a dealer can charge on a net trade, unless special circumstances justify an even greater margin. The S.E.C. has contended that such riskless transactions are unfair to the customer, and that the least the dealer should be compelled to do is disclose the markup on the customer's confirmation.

Neither the Securities & Exchange Commission nor the National Association of Securities Dealers objects to a dealer's taking a 5% markup, or even a larger profit, if the dealer really earns it, as he often does in trying to buy or sell a little-known security.

Suppose you were in New York and wanted to dispose of some stock you owned in a little lumber company out in Oregon, a company that was virtually unknown outside its home town. Your dealer might not be able to get a bid from any other dealer in New York, where most of them are congregated. He might then try his luck in Chicago or San Francisco or Portland by calling or teletyping dealers in those cities. Ultimately, to promote a bid, preferably more than one, he might wire or phone local banks in the area to see if they knew of any possible buyers. He might even phone the company itself to see if it wanted to buy any of its own stock. For such special service the dealer is obviously entitled to a special extra profit.

In addition to the publication of the inside quotes, many other reforms have flowed from the enactment of the 1964 law. The next most important of these is the requirement that companies whose stocks are sold over-the-counter (except insurance companies, which are regulated by state insurance commissions) must make annual reports to the Securities & Exchange Commission and their shareholders if they have assets in excess of $1,000,000 and more than 500 stockholders. It is estimated that this provision affects at least 3000 companies.

Other significant new regulations include requirements that guarantee the character and competence of all dealers and their sales representatives, provision for the regular inspection of all dealer organizations by the N.A.S.D. to assure compliance with all rules and regulations and fair dealing with all customers, controls to assure the honesty of all advertising and sales literature, authority to proceed against any individual as well as any firm guilty of unfair dealings, and provisions to suspend trading for ten days in any over-the-counter security. This is a power that the S.E.C. can use to control the so-called "hot issues," which frequently in the over-the-counter market can skyrocket in price in a relatively short time and then plummet back to their starting point, or lower, just as rapidly, often without any provable manipulation.

In summary, the Securities & Exchange Commission can today exercise essentially the same power over the over-the-counter market and unlisted companies that it has long wielded over the exchanges and the listed companies.

Despite this improved climate of regulation, the phrase "over-the-counter" will probably continue to suggest to many investors the kind of shenanigans associated with the phrase "under-the-counter." The unfortunate label — which goes back to colonial times when the few securities that existed were often traded by a merchant, just like other merchandise, right over his store counter — will not die, despite concerted efforts to substitute other terms, such as unlisted or *off-board* or *off-exchange*.

Because of the vast size and formlessness of the over-the-counter market, it embraces many kinds of securities and many types of trading operations that fail to square with the characteristic picture which has been presented so far.

In the first place, not all of the securities sold over the counter are unlisted. Many stocks listed on the New York, American, and regional exchanges are frequently sold in private trades at a negotiated price instead of by auction on the exchange. The market on the smaller exchanges for some of these stocks is more fictional than real. Days and weeks may pass without a single trade in the security, and there may be a wide gap, maybe three or four points, between the bid-and-asked prices on such a stock. In a case like that, the buyer or seller, particularly of a sizable block, can very often get a better price in a private trade on the "third market" than he can by exposing his bid or offer on the exchange.

Even stocks listed on the New York Stock Exchange are not immune to competition from big over-the-counter dealers, who will often offer a better price on a large block of some stock than the owner, usually an institution, might be able to realize if it were offered on the exchange floor with the consequent risk that the very size of the block might depress the stock's price under the exchange's auction system. Furthermore, once a price is agreed on in an over-the-counter deal, the seller knows precisely what he will get, and he doesn't have to expose himself to the vagaries of the marketplace; there's no guesswork. It was this situation which led the exchange to relax its Rule 394 and permit members to do business with nonmembers under certain specified conditions.

In the second place, our characteristic picture is not wholly accurate, because a big part of over-the-counter trading doesn't involve stocks at all. It involves bonds. Virtually all government bonds traded in the open market are sold over-the-counter either by banks or by a few large independent dealers. The New York Stock Exchange business in government bonds represents only a tiny fraction of 1% of such business handled over-the-counter. All municipal bonds and the great bulk of corporate bonds are similarly traded over-the-counter.

Finally, while the over-the-counter market is the place where all new companies first offer their securities to the public and where the securities are sold of many companies whose financial health may not be exactly robust, it is also the market where you can find stocks of the most impeccable quality. While the Chase Manhattan Bank deserted this market for the Big Board a few years ago, the stocks of virtually every other bank are still sold over-the-counter, and some of them, incidentally, are stocks that boast records of continuous dividend payment going back over 180 years — half a century more than the New York Stock Exchange can claim for any of its issues. Not only bank stocks but all life insurance company stocks and almost all fire and casualty insurance stocks are traded in the over-the-counter market.

And if you are interested in the shares of some of the great industrial foreign companies, located in England, Germany, Japan, or elsewhere, you can have your choice of hundreds in the over-the-counter market, while only a comparative handful are available on the exchanges. You can buy an interest in these foreign companies by buying *American Depositary Receipts* — or *A.D.R.'s,* as they are more commonly known. These certificates, which are traded just like stocks, are the evidence that a certain number of shares in some specified foreign company have been deposited to the owner's credit in the foreign office of a United States bank or one of its correspondent banks abroad.

The over-the-counter market is indeed Everyman's Market, for it offers securities that suit any investor's purse and any man's speculative or investment preference. But the chief attractiveness of the market will always lie in the prospect that one may find there the stock of some young company that will turn out to be another Xerox or IBM. And the prospect is not an empty one. In 1965, the over-the-counter market counted some 350 stocks with price increases exceeding 100% — half a dozen times as many as the New York Stock Exchange could boast.

CHAPTER 17

Investing—
or What's a Broker For?

SUPPOSE you decide that the time has come for you to put some of your extra savings into securities. What do you do next? How do you go about buying stocks or bonds?

You might go to your local banker and ask him how to proceed. He'll know several investment firms in your general community and probably at least one man in each of them. But don't forget that the banker is actually in competition with those security houses for your savings. He may buy government bonds or other securities from them himself, but the typical banker outside the big-city banks is quite apt to look with a jaundiced eye on *your* buying securities. He would rather see you add to your savings account or employ your money in other ways through his bank — in a local business, in real estate, or in mortgages, for example.

Again, don't forget that most bankers are extremely conservative. It's their business to be. When it comes to investing the bank's own money, they have been legally compelled to confine those investments largely to government and other high-grade bonds. They may have little familiarity with stocks and understandable misgivings about them. They don't realize that the individual's investment problem is apt to differ considerably from a bank's problem.

And what is true of a banker is apt to be true of a lawyer too. He's likely to be almost as conservative, because he thinks of investments principally in his role as a trustee, a man legally responsible for the administration of an estate.

So where else might you turn for help if you want to buy securities?

The answer to that is: a broker, because he's obviously the man best qualified to help you with your investment problem. That's his whole business. If you don't know the name of a broker, one of your friends or associates surely does. And if you don't want to ask, look in the financial section of your daily newspaper. You'll find brokers' advertisements there. Study those advertisements for a while; decide which firm seems to have the kind of policy you like and the service you need. Then visit the firm. You don't need a letter of introduction.

But can you trust brokers' advertising? After all, advertising is special pleading, notoriously given to overstatement, exaggeration, and excessive claims. That may be generally true, but nevertheless, it is a matter of fact that you can place much greater confidence in brokers' advertising than you can in the advertising for virtually any other product or service. What is true of their advertising is equally true of all their sales promotion literature because under the rules of the New York Stock Exchange all forms of communication with the public by member firms must be approved by the exchange before publication. Furthermore, almost all member firms submit their advertising and their sales literature to the scrutiny of their own legal counsel as well as the exchange.

In its censorship work for more than a quarter century, the exchange has adhered to the general standards of truthfulness and good taste, and in judging the acceptability of any advertisement or report, the exchange has concerned itself not only with what was said but what was omitted and should have been said.

In the early sixties when the S.E.C.'s study of the securities industry pointed the need for many reforms, the exchange tightened up its regulation of advertising and all other forms of communication, spelling out its standards in meticulous detail. Specifically forbidden is language that is promissory or flamboyant or contains unwarranted superlatives; opinions not clearly labeled as such; forecasts or predictions not stated as estimates or opinions; recommendations that cannot be substantiated as reasonable; boasts about the success of past recommendations unless they meet a set of exacting requirements; and any evasion of a broker's responsibility to disclose any special interest he might have in any given security he recommends.

Shortly after the exchange adopted its standards, the National Association of Securities Dealers adopted roughly similar regulations which apply to all over-the-counter dealers in that association.

Yes, you are justified in placing greater faith in the advertising of the securities business today than almost any other advertising you are likely to encounter in newspapers, magazines, radio, or television.

Lots of people still shy away from the broker for a variety of reasons. Some of them feel embarrassed about the amount of money they have to invest. Maybe they have only $500 to put into stocks, perhaps only $40 or $50 a month, and they figure a broker wouldn't be interested.

Maybe some brokers wouldn't be, but the big wire houses are spending millions of dollars in advertising every year to tell the smaller investor that they definitely are interested in him and in helping him invest his money wisely. So is the New York Stock Exchange.

And still people hesitate. Perhaps they think of the broker as a somewhat forbidding individual who gives his time only to Very Important People, people who are well-heeled and travel in the right social circles. That's not true. There's nothing exclusive about the brokerage business today. No spats or striped pants. The club rules are all changed, and coffee and hamburgers are more popular items on the club menu than champagne and caviar.

Another thing that stops a lot of people is the jargon that brokers talk. You know that there's nothing mysterious about words like "debenture" or "cumulative preferred" or "stock dividend." True, they're specialized words, because they apply to very specialized things, but there's nothin: difficu! to understand about either the words or the things they stand for, if you take the trouble to learn them.

Finally, some people don't want to go to a broker because, frankly, they distrust him. They're afraid of being sold a bill of goods, a block of stock i · some worthless company. That happened back in the twenties. Nobody can deny it. Maybe it happened to people you know — your father, your uncle, some member of your family.

Can it happen today? Yes, it *can* happen because no law or regulation has ever been devised that will put every crook and swindler in our society behind bars. Occasionally — very, very occasionally — you may still encounter one of those gyp artists in the securities business intent on unloading some stock on you and other unsuspecting investors so he can run the price up and then sell out his own holdings at a fat profit, leaving you to hold the bag when the price subsequently plummets.

Occasionally — but again, very occasionally — you might

be sold such a stock at a highly inflated price by a thoroughly honest but somewhat naïve and irresponsible broker who has been taken in by the propaganda that the gyp artist always seeks to spread. The S.E.C. and the exchange are constantly on the alert to track down and scotch such false and misleading *tips* or *rumors,* for their circulation is a clear-cut form of illegal price manipulation, but, alas, brokers — like all human beings — can fall prey to propaganda that promises an easy dollar, a quick profit.

A broker may logically and legitimately try to sell you on the idea of buying stocks, because he believes in investing, but unless his firm is involved in an underwriting of a stock or the sale of a large block, he hasn't any selfish reason to try to sell you any particular stock on the New York Stock Exchange, because his only return is the standard commission. As far as that commission is concerned, there is no difference between what he makes if you put a given amount of money into one stock or the other. So as far as self-interest is concerned, it doesn't matter to him which you buy.

Of course, when you buy stocks on a net basis — over-the-counter stocks — there is more of a chance that you can be sold something the dealer has an interest in unloading at a profit. But that doesn't happen too often. Few businesses are as competitive as the American securities business today, with every broker and dealer in the country anxious to get customers and keep them for a good many years to come. In that kind of situation there's not much room for the second-story operator who plays fast and loose with the customer's best interests.

Credit the Securities & Exchange Commission, if you wish. Or credit the stock exchange's own housecleaning. Or credit the moral influence of a healthy competition.

But credit also the fact that the men in the securities business are, in the vast majority of cases, men of conscience and probity, responsible to a standard of ethics as high as prevails in any business you can name.

What it all comes down to is this: The safest way to begin investing is to choose some listed stock through a member firm of the New York Stock Exchange and study that stock, the company behind it, before you buy.

If there's no member firm near you, you can write to one and buy by mail. Or you can order the stock through virtually any bank or security dealer in the country, although

you may have to pay an additional handling charge. Such
a charge is wholly legitimate.

But if the securities dealer tries to dissuade you from
buying a listed stock, if he tries to switch you into Wildcat
common or some other dubious stock, you had better check
with another house.

To help protect investors against the high-pressure, "fast-
buck" peddlers of dubious stocks, the S.E.C., with the co-
operation of industry trade groups and the Better Business
Bureau, has issued an investor's guide which makes these
ten recommendations to all investors:

1. Think before buying.
2. Deal only with a securities firm which you know.
3. Be skeptical of securities offered over the telephone from
   any firm or salesman you do not know.
4. Guard against all high-pressure sales.
5. Beware of promises of quick, spectacular price rises.
6. Be sure you understand the risk of loss as well as the prospect of gain.
7. Get the facts. Do not buy on tips or rumors.
8. Request the person offering securities over the phone to
   mail you written information about the corporation, its
   operations, net profit, management, financial position, and
   future prospects, and save all such information for future
   reference.
9. If you do not understand the written information, consult
   a person who does.
10. Give at least as much thought when purchasing securities
    as you would when acquiring any valuable property.

CHAPTER 18

How You Do Business
with a Broker

LET's assume you finally make up your mind to buy some stock, like General Motors or General Electric, and you go to a broker, a member firm of the New York Stock Exchange, to place your order.

What's likely to happen? What's a broker's office like? What do you say and what do you do? How does he operate?

A lot of people go in and out of a broker's office all the time, people who want to look at the ticker tape and see how some particular stock is doing, and people who just like to watch the passing show or want to take refuge from rain, snow, or heat. So if nobody pays any attention to you when you walk in, don't feel that you're being neglected. Just walk up to the first person who looks as though he works there and tell him you would like to talk to somebody about buying some stock. That will get action fast.

Maybe that person will take you to the manager, who in turn will introduce you to a *registered representative* with whom you can discuss your problem in more detail. Maybe you'll skip the manager and be referred directly to some registered representative.

What's a registered representative? In the twenties he was called a *customer's man*. That's not a title in favor any more, because the customer's man got a bad reputation as a fast-work artist with a glib line when it came to selling bonds to old college chums or clubhouse cronies. Today's registered representatives bear little resemblance to that character.

Again, the old customer's man used to "play the market" a good deal himself. Most brokers now are happy to see their employees invest in securities, but they frown on too much "in and out" trading by a registered representative for his own account. And they can keep close tab on that

because of a New York Stock Exchange rule which generally
forbids any employee of a brokerage firm to buy or sell
securities except through the firm for which he works.

Many a customer refers to the registered representative as
"my broker." Actually, of course, he isn't. He is an employee
of the brokerage firm, and he simply represents the firm's
floor broker, who will actually execute your orders on the
exchange. That's why he's called a representative. The "registered" part of his title means that he has been licensed by
the S.E.C. and approved by the exchange as a man of good
character and one who is thoroughly informed about the
operations of the securities business. In fact, he has had to
pass a searching examination in the subject administered by
the New York Stock Exchange. (The National Association of
Securities Dealers gives the same kind of examination to representatives of nonmember dealers.)

Registered representatives — also called *customer's brokers*
or *account executives* by some firms — come in all kinds and
qualities. Some are young, and some are old. Some are Democrats — yes, Democrats — and some are Republicans. Some
have been in the business for years, and some are comparative newcomers.

These newcomers deserve a special word, because their en-
trance into the field is itself an evidence of how the business has changed. From the time of the depression to the
end of World War II, only a handful of college graduates
went into Wall Street. They looked for greener pastures —
the big corporations.

But nowadays the securities business is getting its share of
the topnotch men — and women too — from every graduating
class. Many an old customer's man coasted for years on his
reputation as an all-star halfback. His successor's career is
apt to be based much more solidly on a record of real scho-
lastic achievement, plus extracurricular leadership. Often, he
will have taken work at some university's graduate school of
business.

Again, the customer's man of yesteryear rarely bothered
to acquire any formal training in the business; he just picked
it up as he went along. The present-day registered representative has usually put in a much more painstaking apprentice-
ship. More often than not, he will have attended some firm's
training school, plugging away eight hours a day for several
months at basic lessons in accounting, economics, security
analysis, and investment account management.

The registered representative is the man you deal with when you do business with a brokerage firm. He is usually assigned to you by the manager of the office, and if at any time you find his service less than satisfactory, all you have to do is ask the manager to be assigned another man.

And if you don't like the brokerage firm itself, try another. There are hundreds of them, some big and some little, some offering a wide variety of special services and facilities, and a few with little more than a desk and a telephone.

All of them can buy and sell securities for you, and all of them will execute your orders faithfully; they won't "bucket" them. A *bucket-shop* operator is a man who accepts your order to buy a stock at the market — and your money — but he doesn't execute the order; instead he pockets your money and gambles on his ability to buy the stock for you sometime later at a lower price and make a profit for himself on your order. He reverses the method on a sell order. Needless to say, all such operations are thoroughly illegal, and today they are virtually nonexistent, thanks to the vigilance of the Securities & Exchange Commission and the stock exchange.

You can talk to your registered representative with complete candor, because whatever you tell him about your affairs will be held in strict confidence. A broker never reveals who his customers are, much less anything about their circumstances.

The more you tell him about your finances — your income, your expenses, your savings, your insurance, and whatever other obligations, like mortgage or tuition payments, you may have to meet — the better will he be able to help you map out an investment program suited to your needs.

It is a part of his job to see that you get information or counsel whenever you need it. Don't be embarrassed about asking him the simplest kind of question about investing — about a company, about some financial term, or about the ticker, the *quote board*, or the desk-model *quote machines*, which are the focal points of interest in every brokerage office.

The tape offers a free show and a fascinating one. Some board watchers have been coming into the same broker's office, sitting in the same chair, every day for years, just for that show. Rarely do they buy or sell, and they constitute a real problem to the broker. They take up space for which he pays substantial rent; they contribute few commissions;

and they often make it difficult for the cash customer to fight his way through to the desk of his own registered representative.

The tape itself is no longer what it was in the days when conquering Channel swimmers rode up Broadway through paper snowstorms. If tape is used at all, it isn't even paper any more. It's made of cellophane, and it is often projected on a treated silk screen by a movie machine. As the stock symbols and price figures march across this eight-foot Translux screen, moving from right to left, everybody in the board room can see as many as six or eight of the last reports on sales. This is the widely used system developed by *Teleregister*, now a part of Bunker-Ramo Corporation, but there is another kind of ticker screen, known as the *Lectrascan*, which doesn't use tape at all. In this system, developed by Ultronic Systems Corporation, exchange transactions pass through the system's computer and are projected in orange-colored, neon-lighted characters against a black screen. The transactions are reported in normal reading sequence (from left to right), and the symbols and prices do not move across the screen. Each one is simply replaced — in place — by a later transaction.

Many brokers project both New York Stock Exchange and American Stock Exchange transactions as well as prices on some commodity markets.

The old glass-domed ticker with its paper tape is now virtually obsolete — so much so that weeks before New York City is due to stage one of its traditional Broadway parades, the city fathers ask owners of the old-fashioned tickers to save their old tape, and this is then distributed by a city department to top-floor tenants in the buildings along Broadway so that it can be showered down on whatever conquering hero has earned this deluxe demonstration.

In addition to the ticker, virtually all brokers also have a *quote board,* or stock board, on which the prices are posted for a number of leading stocks, sometimes only 30 or 40 stocks and sometimes hundreds. For some stocks the board will show the full range — yesterday's closing price, today's opening, the highest and lowest prices today, and the price on the last reported sale.

For some stocks only the last price is shown. On those boards operated by Teleregister, whenever there is a sale in any stock which is "boarded," the little figures automatically click over to show the latest price information for that stock.

All fractional prices are quoted in eighths, so that a price of 26 4 means 26 4/8 or 26½.

A similar kind of board, called a *Quotron,* offers the same kind of information on stock prices, either full range or last sale, but its developer, Scantlin Electronics, Inc., boasts that its larger numbers are easier to read and that the board operates more quietly.

All three services, Teleregister, Ultronics, and Scantlin, provide other valuable market information for board display — the popular market averages, data on the volume of trading, number of issues both up and down, information on the most active stocks, etc.

The computer-operated desk-model unit, offered by all three systems, is the most significant development of recent years in the whole field of price and quotation service. With any of these machines, the individual registered representative simply by pressing a few keys can get instantly the latest bid-and-asked quotation and full-range price data on every stock listed on the New York and American Stock Exchanges, plus some regional and Canadian exchanges, as well as comparable data on many commodity markets.

A wide variety of other securities information, either projected on a small screen or printed on tape, is instantaneously available through some or all of these systems — the dividend rate for any stock, its earnings for the past several quarters, present price as a multiple of its earnings, stocks with new yearly highs or lows, the most active stocks of the day, etc. So useful and comprehensive is the service of these desk-model units that some brokers have dispensed completely with the public display board.

Ultimately, all these systems are certain to provide over-the-counter quotes as soon as the National Association of Securities Dealers has computerized a quotation service throughout its far-flung domain.

In those sections of the country where the electric board service is not available or in those offices where the broker's business doesn't warrant the expense of such an elaborate installation, the old-fashioned *chalk board* continues in use. Employees known as *board markers* take sections of the tape as it comes from the ticker and chalk up the latest prices.

If you want to know the latest price and the day's range on a popular stock like U.S. Steel, all you have to do is phone your representative. He can look at the board or his electronic desk unit and give you complete information. Or he can get the latest bid-and-asked quotations for you in a minute or two through the exchange's mechanized quote service by phoning or wiring.

And if you want to have a pretty good idea of what you might have to pay for a stock before you buy, don't hesitate to ask for a quote. After all, in a typical year, brokers may ask the Quotation Bureau of the New York Stock Exchange alone for as many as 23,000,000 quotes.

One more call won't hurt.

CHAPTER 19

How You Open
an Account

EVERY new customer of a brokerage firm must open an *account* with that firm before he can either buy or sell securities.

Opening a *cash account* with a brokerage firm is very much like opening a charge account at a department store. It simply involves establishing your credit so that the broker is sure you can pay for whatever securities you order, if funds to cover such purchase have not been deposited in the account.

This is important, because when you place a market order for a stock, neither you nor the broker can know to the exact penny just what you will have to pay. You may know that the last sale took place at 18½ a share, but when your order is executed, even a few minutes later, the price may have gone up or down by an eighth of a point, a quarter of a point, even more. So when the purchase is made, the broker assumes the responsibility of paying for the stock and sends you a bill, a bill that you are supposed to pay in four business days because your broker must settle his account within that time.

Because no one can know just when an *open order* — a limit order or a stop order — may be executed and because the customer may be away from his home or office at the time of execution, brokers can in their own judgment extend the payment date to seven business days after the transaction, but if payment is not received then, a further extension can only be granted by the exchange because a technical violation of the Federal Reserve Board's *Regulation T,* governing all matters of credit on stock transactions, will have occurred.

In the case of a Monthly Investment Plan account, the broker has no credit problem, because the customer makes his monthly or quarterly payment in advance of the purchase.

If your first transaction with a brokerage firm involves the sale of some stock that you already own, instead of a purchase, you will still be asked to open an account, because the brokerage firm must still comply with the stock exchange rule which compels every broker "to learn the essential facts" about his customers as a protection against fraud or other illegal practices. For one thing, the routine of opening an account provides the broker with some assurance that the securities you offer for sale are really yours.

A bearer bond, for instance, can be sold by anybody who holds it, and it might easily be a stolen certificate. Even a registered bond or a stock with your own name on it presents a problem to the broker. It may be made out in the name of John Smith, and John Smith may bring it to a broker to sell it; but if he hasn't done business there before, how's the broker to know that he really is the Smith named on the security?

Many husbands and wives prefer to open *joint accounts* with a broker, just as they may have joint checking accounts. In case one of them dies, the other can generally sell the securities without waiting for the courts to unsnarl the legal problems that are involved in settling any estate. Joint accounts are also used by individuals who are not related to each other but who have pooled their resources in a cooperative investment venture, often just for the sake of reducing commission costs on their trades.

People frequently want to open accounts for their own children or for the children of relatives, and historically this always presented a thorny problem, for in the absence of state legislation specifically authorizing such gifts to children, brokers incurred a measurable risk in selling stock that was registered in the name of a minor; a minor is not legally responsible for his acts, and if brokerage transactions were carried on in the name of a minor, he could, on coming of age, repudiate them, and the broker would have no redress.

Beginning in 1955, the various states began enacting laws permitting an adult, acting as a custodian without court appointment, to handle investments for a child. Such a custodian can buy stocks as a gift for a minor; he can sell them for a minor; and he can collect any dividends in the child's name. With the New York Stock Exchange and the entire brokerage fraternity plumping vigorously for the enactment of such laws, by 1961 all 50 states had laws permitting gifts of stock to minors. As a consequence, stock ownership among minors has increased more than in any other age group in recent years. In 1962, 450,000 minors owned stock; by 1965, the number had increased to 1,250,000.

Of course, it is still possible for parents or other relatives to buy stock for children by setting up trust funds and getting a court order appointing them as trustees so that they can legally buy or sell stock for the children. This is an expensive and cumbersome procedure, although it does permit wealthy people to realize important tax savings. It is generally much simpler for the parents or other relatives or friends to give stock to minors under the provisions of the states' laws.

If you want to open a *margin account* instead of a regular cash account, so that you can buy securities by paying only a portion of their purchase price, the broker will want to be especially certain about your financial solvency. After all, when you pay only part of the cost, the broker has to pay the balance, and that money may be on loan to you a long time.

Once you have opened an account — cash, joint, or margin — you can buy or sell whatever you want simply by phoning your representative — or writing or wiring him. Probably better than 80% of a broker's business comes to him by phone.

If you live outside New York and give an order for a Big Board stock to a registered representative, or a correspondent of some brokerage firm, that order is teletyped into the New York headquarters of the firm, where it is either switched automatically to that booth on the exchange floor nearest the post where it will be executed or it is phoned over to that booth. In either case the order is executed as promptly as possible by the floor broker. Then the process is put in reverse. The floor broker gives his clerk in the booth a report on the order and the price at which it was executed, and this information is transmitted by wire back to your representative.

The entire operation can literally be accomplished while you may still be on the phone talking to your representative about other matters. On a market order for immediate execution, the round trip from California to the exchange and back again, including the transaction on the floor, has been made in less than one minute. Actually five minutes or so is more like par for the course, and if the stock you are buying is one that doesn't trade frequently or if the whole market is very active and your broker's wires are flooded with traffic, it may take a lot longer.

In any event, once your order is executed, your representative will be glad to report to you. Whether you get the information by phone or not, you'll know the next day or so just what price you got on the order, because you will receive in the mail your broker's formal *confirmation* of the transaction.

If you have bought stock, this will be your bill. If you have sold stock, the confirmation will be a report on what you have realized, and the proceeds of that sale will automatically be credited to your account on the *settlement date,* five business days after the transaction.

Instead of having the proceeds credited to your account, you can, of course, ask that payment be made direct to you by check. In special circumstances, you may even be able to arrange for immediate payment, instead of waiting for settlement date, but brokers are extremely reluctant to make such advance payments because, after all, they don't get their money from the other broker till settlement date. Furthermore, advance payment can open the door to sharp practice by unscrupulous customers — a practice known as *free-riding.* A free-rider is a person who demands immediate payment on a sale and then uses that money to cover a purchase that he made, usually through another broker, and on which payment isn't due for five days — or even longer if he succeeds in persuading that broker to give him a further extension of credit. Meanwhile, throughout that whole period, the customer is using the broker's money, interest-free, to finance his stock purchase. He is, in effect, getting a free ride.

Some brokers pay interest on cash funds that accumulate in a customer's account in excess of a given figure, such as $500. This interest, perhaps 1% a year, becomes payable when the money is used to buy other securities at some later date.

Since Monthly Investment Plan customers pay in advance of purchase, the confirmation they receive is in effect a receipt and in no sense of the word a bill. An M.I.P. confirmation shows exactly how many full and fractional shares of the selected stock were bought with your payment and the total number of full and fractional shares accumulated in the account to that date.

Of course, if you sell stock in a regular cash account, you must see that the stocks are delivered to the broker. Since you have an account with him, he will know what stocks you own, and he will sell any of them for you on instruction, even if he does not have the certificates actually in hand. But he expects you to deliver the certificates, properly endorsed, as soon as possible after a sale, because he in turn must settle within five days with the broker who bought the stock.

So they won't have to bother with delivery problems, many security owners find it advisable just to leave their stock certificates or bonds with their broker. They are right there then when the owner wants to sell. Such securities are carried in the customer's account just as cash might be, and every month he gets a statement showing just exactly what securities and what funds are credited to him.

On stocks that are left with him, the broker will collect all the dividends that are due and credit them as cash to the customer's account. Similarly, on bonds he will see that the interest is paid, clipping the coupons, if it's that kind of bond, and he will credit the payments to the customer's account. Further, brokers will mail to the customer the regular financial reports on those companies whose securities he owns as well as all proxies and official notices of meetings, dividends, stock rights and conversion privileges, as those materials are supplied to him by the individual companies.

When a customer leaves his securities with his broker, the actual shares of stock are sometimes segregated and kept in his individual account, very much as they might be if he rented a safe-deposit box. As a general rule, however, this kind of custodian service is available only to those who own large amounts of securities. In all other cases, if a customer leaves his securities with his broker, they are held in *"street name."* This means that all the shares of a given security owned by all that broker's customers are lumped together and held in the broker's name; he keeps his own records of just what each individual customer owns. Thus, a broker might hold 100,000 shares of U.S. Steel for 2000 or 3000 individual customers. The shares would be made out in the broker's name, but he would send each customer a monthly statement showing just how many of those shares were his.

There is one big advantage to leaving your stocks with

your broker in street name: If you want to sell any of them, all you have to do is phone him and give him instructions. You don't have to bother with the delivery or endorsing of the certificates.

But is it safe to leave your securities with your broker, as you might leave cash with your banker?

The answer is that it's probably safer to leave them with a broker than it is to try to take care of them yourself. They are stored in his vault, and he carries insurance on them. When they are left with him, they can't be lost or misplaced, and the risk of loss by fire or theft is probably much less than it would be if you kept them in your own home or office.

Furthermore, the broker cannot borrow money on those securities nor can he sell or lend any of them except on express authorization. Those securities belong to his customers. He is only the custodian. The surprise *audits* which are sprung on all member firms once a year by the New York Stock Exchange further help to make sure that the broker is faithful to his trust.

But what if a broker goes under, despite all the regulations of the stock exchange and the Securities & Exchange Commission?

For years, an adequate answer to that was that brokers don't go bankrupt. Despite 1929, member firms of the New York Stock Exchange boast a solvency record over a 50-year period that is around 99% — better than the solvency record of state and national banks.

But in 1963, an event took place that shook the brokerage fraternity's confidence in its financial stability to the very foundations. In November of that year, one of Wall Street's most respected houses, Ira Haupt & Co., did go under to the tune of almost ten million dollars, and a second firm, J. R. Williston & Beane, was bailed out in the nick of time and absorbed by another firm.

The Haupt bankruptcy was brought on by inability of Anthony De Angelis, a big speculator in soybean oil and president of the now-defunct Allied Crude Vegetable Oil Refining Co., to meet an obligation to the Haupt firm in the amount of $18,000,000, and its doom was sealed when it was discovered that warehouse receipts which De Angelis had given Haupt as security were fraudulent. The receipts presumably were evidence that Haupt had millions of gallons of soybean oil stored in tanks in New Jersey, but the tanks were empty.

Ironically, Haupt's relations with its securities customers conformed impeccably to all requirements of the law and of the exchange, and these were the people — people who were in no way involved in Haupt's commodity mess — who stood to get hurt, because Haupt could obviously not meet its own loans from the banks.

To save those customers in particular and to preserve investor confidence in general — confidence the exchange had fought so hard to win for thirty years — the exchange devised a plan over one critical weekend which obligated all members to make good Haupt's loss. All told, after the liquidation of Haupt's assets, the bill, which was shared by members in proportion to the amount of their exchange business, came to $9,600,000.

In 1964, the exchange took one further step to protect investors against any possible recurrence of the Haupt debacle. It established a $25,000,000 fund, assessing all members on a pro rata basis over a three-year period, to cover the possible insolvency of any member firm, caused by anything short of fraud. To protect against fraud, the exchange has for many years carried a $10,000,000 *fidelity bond,* covering all members, and individual member firms carry their own fidelity bonds in addition.

Needless to say, as a result of the Haupt case, member firms that are involved in the commodities as well as securities business have taken steps to tighten up their operation and to make sure that no commodity customer overextends himself.

The Haupt case also added extra impetus to the *incorporation* of stock exchange firms as a means of building capital and improving financial strength. Time was when virtually all members of the New York Stock Exchange were *partnerships.* As a matter of fact, under the rules of the exchange they had to be partnerships until May 1, 1953, when the regulation was amended to permit firms to incorporate if they wished to. The advantage of incorporation lies in the fact that the maximum federal tax on a corporation is 52%, while individual partners in a firm frequently find themselves in substantially higher income tax brackets. Thus, by incorporation the owners of a firm are able to retain as capital a considerably greater proportion of its earnings. The amendment admitting corporations to membership also meant that the large nonmember dealers, operating as corporations rather than partnerships, could buy exchange seats if they wanted to. The legal complexities of changing a partnership into a corporation are such that brokers cannot easily make the changeover, but by the end of 1965, there were 152 corporations among the 651 member firms of the exchange, most of them having previously operated as partnerships. With steadily expanding business, as stock ownership spreads, brokers find themselves in need of steadily increased amounts of operating capital. That explains why many incorporated firms have been agitating for a change in New York Stock Exchange regulations that will permit them to offer their shares to the public—and why the public would probably be eager to buy those shares.

CHAPTER 20

What It Means
to Speculate

SPECULATING is an inevitable part of the business of buying securities. But then speculating is an inevitable part of just living.

Whenever you are confronted with an unavoidable risk — as indeed you are in many of your actions every day — you must speculate. You must meet the risk; you must take your chances. Often you are presented with a choice of risks; when you make up your mind about which one you will take, weighing the good and the bad features of each, you arrive at a speculative decision.

The Boston businessman who *must* be in Washington the next morning can fly or go by rail. He can figure on getting there faster if he flies, but there's always the possibility of bad weather, mechanical failure, even disaster. Those hazards may be somewhat reduced if he takes the train, but on the other hand, family or business circumstances may be such that it is desirable for him to make the trip in the shortest possible time. Faced with that kind of choice, the man must inevitably speculate.

The retailer who decides to stock up on a lot of goods is speculating on a price rise. He figures he can buy those goods cheaper now than he can some months later — and that he can sell them.

The manufacturer who must pick Jones or Smith for a key job must speculate on which will be the more able man.

And the farmer's whole operation is one vast speculation. When he puts the seed in the ground, he is speculating on his ability to grow a crop and sell it at a profit, despite weather, pests, blight, and changing market prices.

When a man takes a risk he cannot avoid, he is speculating. But when he takes a risk that he doesn't have to take, he gambles.

That is one distinction between speculation and gambling, and there is another. Speculation involves an exercise of reason, while gambling involves nothing but chance. The man who speculates can make an intelligent forecast of the hazards of his course. The gambler stands or falls on the flip of a coin or the draw of a card.

In the purchase of any stock or bond, even a government bond, there is an element of speculation, because the risk that it might decline in value cannot be avoided. For that matter, there is a risk just in having money — the risk that it won't buy as much sometime in the future when you want to spend it as it will if you spend it today.

But when a man buys securities, he doesn't have to operate on the basis of chance. He can make a fairly intelligent estimate of just how much risk he assumes on the basis of the record. And he has a wide range to choose from — all the way from a government bond to the penny stocks of those companies whose assets may be made up principally of hope.

The word "investments" is technically applied only to government bonds, municipal bonds, and first-quality corporate bonds. To an ultra-conservative buyer of securities for a bank or an insurance company, all stocks are considered too risky to be classed strictly as investments, despite the fact that some stocks have proved safer than many corporate bonds, particularly the debentures and secondary bonds of weak companies.

But because most preferred stocks and a good number of common stocks have shown themselves to be so stable, even the conservatives refer to them nowadays as "investment-type" securities. These are apt to be the stocks of utilities or food firms or banks or chain stores — industries that have shown themselves to be comparatively steady earners, come boom or depression.

Of course, what is one man's speculation is very often another man's investment, and below the level of topflight securities is a vast assortment of stocks which many men of sound judgment consider good investments primarily because of the liberal dividends they pay.

Often these are the stocks of companies whose fortunes rise and fall more sharply with the business cycle — companies in the automobile, steel, construction, or clothing industries. When business is good, they pay excellent dividends, and when it slumps, those dividends may be reduced or eliminated.

As a rough — very rough — rule of thumb, the degree of risk which you assume in buying one of those middle-quality *"cyclical" stocks* can be measured by the liberality of the dividend. The larger the dividend as a percentage of the selling price, the greater the risk.

Then there are other stocks — thousands and thousands of them — that must be frankly classified as speculations. But even here there is a wide range of quality. At the top of the list are those stocks that might be described as "good *growth* situations." They are the stocks of companies, often paying little or no dividend, which are regarded as attractive because of future prospects. Thirty years or so ago, many of the automobile and radio stocks might have been so classified. More recently, chemical, electronic, aluminum, office equipment, cosmetic, publishing, and pharmaceutical stocks have often been placed in this category. In recent years, these growth stocks have been the darlings of the investing public. Such has been the demand for these glamour stocks that prices were pushed up to a point where some stocks were selling at 30 or 40 or 50 times current earnings.

Some speculative securities are attractive, not because the future is so glowing, but simply because it looks a lot better than the past. A company may have had to pass some dividends or miss interest payments during a difficult period of reorganization, but once it starts to hit the comeback trail, its securities are apt to take on new life. Many a sizable fortune has been made out of buying bonds that were severely depressed in price because the company had to default on bond interest payments for a period. And that's also true of many preferred-stock issues on which dividend payments have accumulated for a number of years and ultimately been paid off. But these are strictly long shots and must be so regarded.

The most popular kind of speculative stock is apt to be issued by an aggressive small company, operating in one of the growth fields. Characteristically, these are over-the-counter stocks selling at relatively modest prices, unseasoned securities issued by companies that are so new they have no record of consistent earnings. They are long on hopes, short on cash. Rank speculations though they be, they attract interest because everyone knows that Xerox and Polaroid and

IBM — and Rod & Reel — were just such stocks once not so many years ago.

Finally, there are the outright penny stocks. A few of these may be the listed securities of old-line companies that have fallen on evil days. Their business has declined steadily, and their stock seems virtually worthless. But by all odds, the great majority of these low-priced stocks, selling at 50¢, $1, $2, maybe as high as $5, are issued by new ventures — stocks in questionable oil or mining companies that are peddled by high-pressure salesmen who expect to make as much as 50¢ on every dollar's worth they sell. Often by direct mail and even long-distance phone, the prospect is told that a block of 100 or 300 shares has been reserved in his name at a special bargain price, but he must buy within 24 hours or lose this chance of a lifetime. People who have charge accounts at expensive stores and professional people, such as doctors and lawyers, are particular targets for this kind of promotion, because their names and addresses are so easily available from direct-mail firms.

The most devastating thing is that these glamorous sales stories often have an element of truth about them. The men who put their money in the oil property "right next to our land" may actually have made 1000% on their investment already, but the fact remains that anyone who takes a flyer on this kind of deal is much more apt to lose everything he puts into it than he is to make a whopping profit.

Although there is an obvious difference between this kind of rank speculation and the solid investment which a government bond represents, it is also true that the distinction between investing and speculating frequently gets hazy as soon as you move away from either of these two extremes. Actually, the difference between investing and speculating is not to be measured so much in terms of the individual security as it is in terms of the motive of the buyer.

The investor is a man who puts his money to work in a company in the expectation of earning a reasonable and regular return on it, both in dividends and price appreciation, over the long pull. The speculator takes a short-term view. He is not interested in dividends; he is interested in making a quick profit on his money and selling out while he can get it. Often he takes a big risk in the process, but if he hits it right, he stands to make a lot of money.

Furthermore, under present federal tax laws he will probably be able to keep more of that money than he would if he made the same amount of money in dividends, salary, or other income.

Risk capital — the money that a man puts at risk when he buys or sells almost any kind of property — has played such an important role in building this country that Congress for more than a quarter of a century has always given favored tax treatment to profits realized in such ventures. These are called *capital gains,* and they include the profits realized on the purchase and sale of securities.

Tax rates often change from year to year, but in 1966 the law provided that a man who made a capital gain on any security that he owned for more than six months — a *long-term* capital gain — would not have to pay a tax on more than 25% of that profit. That was the absolute maximum. Actually, the tax might be considerably less, for instead of paying 25% on the entire gain, he could, if he chose, pay a straight income tax on only half the gain at whatever regular income-tax rate applied in his case. Thus, if a stockholder's maximum tax bracket was only 40% on regular income, the effective rate he would pay on a long-term capital gain would be only 20%.

In contrast, *short-term* capital gains — those realized on securities owned for less than six months — were, under the law in 1966, taxed at full regular income-tax rates.

Wealthy men are apt to find stock speculation particularly attractive, because they have to pay taxes in high-income brackets, ranging up to 70% in 1966 and as high as 91% in earlier years, and that 25% maximum tax on long-term capital gains appeals to them

Furthermore, the law offers them other special advantages. If a speculator has a capital gain of $5000 and a capital loss of $4000, he pays the gains tax on only $1000. If his losses exceed his gains, he can carry the losses over for several years and use them to reduce whatever tax he might have to pay on future capital gains. Finally, he is even permitted to deduct capital losses to a maximum of $1000 from his other income and thus reduce his regular tax.

Favorable as this treatment may appear to be, many businessmen and some economists argue that it is not favorable enough. They contend that new-venture capital — speculative capital — should be made much more freely available to business. This could be accomplished by reducing the tax on long-term capital gains or by permitting the taxpayer to classify his profit as a long-term gain after a period of, say,

three months instead of six. In 1966, Canada still had no
capital-gains tax, and that is one reason, it is argued, why
Canadian business was able to attract so much new capital
in the years immediately after World War II.

It is obviously only good sense for a stockholder to consider this matter of taxes on long-term and short-term capital
gains (or losses) in deciding whether or not to sell. Thus, it
would be ridiculous for a man in a high-income tax bracket
— say, 50% or 60% — to sell a stock on which he had a
substantial profit if he had owned that stock just a few
days less than six months. Obviously, by waiting those few
additional days, he could establish his profit as a long-term
capital gain, and he would be liable for a maximum tax of
only 25% on the profit. Only in the most unusual circumstance would his risk of loss in those few days be likely
to outweigh the extra tax liability he would incur by selling
his stock and taking a short-term capital gain, taxable as
regular income at the full 50% or 60% rate.

On the other hand, a too great concern about taxes on
capital gains can seriously warp investment judgment. Many
a stockowner has refused to sell and take a profit because
he didn't want to pay even a long-term capital-gains tax,
and while he complains about being *"locked in,"* his profit
dwindles away in a declining market. One stock market authority calls this "taxation rigor mortis," and he contends
that it costs stockholders a good deal more every year than
all the dubious new issues of penny stocks and other outright swindles. The man with a 100% profit in a stock will
complain bitterly about the 25% tax, forgetting that when he
bought the stock he would have been more than satisfied
with a 25% net profit, much less one of 75%.

If you have a profit in a stock, you might as well reconcile
yourself to paying a capital-gains tax on it and rule it out
of all future investment considerations. You can, of course,
hold on to the stock — and the profit, if you are lucky —
till you die, but even then your executors and your heirs
are going to have to worry about inheritance taxes.

Of course, you sidestep the tax by using your capital gain
to offset a capital loss. This provision has served to stimulate
a fair amount of speculation. A man with a capital gain
will very often figure that he can afford a much greater
measure of risk than he ordinarily would take, because if he
loses, Uncle Sam will, in effect, cover his losses up to 25%
of that capital gain.

The capital-gains tax constitutes the biggest paradox in the stock market. It stimulates speculation in the sense that it offers the high-income man a chance to build up capital at bargain rates — a tax of only 25% instead of 50% or 60% or more — but it simultaneously acts as a deterrent on speculation, particularly among the amateurs, because it is human nature to resist the payment of any tax and to postpone that evil day as long as possible.

Curiously enough, the professional speculator does not so often try to make a profit — a capital gain — by putting his money into a really speculative growth stock as he does by speculating in the 50 or 60 active stocks — many of them topflight investments — that usually account for most of the transactions on the Big Board.

There is a reason for this. At any given time, the price of a stock or the price of all stocks represents the combined judgments of all the people who are buying and selling. Most times a speculator is staking his judgment against the public judgment.

He may study the stock of a company in minute detail, and on the basis of that intensive analysis, he may feel that he knows better than the public what it's really worth — or, rather, what the public will sooner or later take as its real worth.

Again, he may think that he has a better feel of the market as a whole, knows better than the public does whether stock prices generally will advance steadily upward in what is called a *bull market* or decline for a period of time in a *bear market*. If he is right, the leading stocks — those that enjoy the widest public following — will probably provide the earliest confirmation of his judgment and hence provide the best opportunity for a quick profit.

On the assumption that his judgment is right, the speculator seeks to augment his profits — or protect them once they are made — by using various techniques of trading.

He may buy on margin.

He may pyramid profits.

He may sell short.

He may buy puts or calls.

And let it be noted that none of these techniques constitutes in itself unfair or dishonest manipulation of the market. On the contrary, all these techniques make for greater trading activity and a more liquid market. Very often, the investor might find it difficult to sell some stock if it were not for a speculator willing to assume the risk that the investor wanted to get rid of.

Periodically, there is public clamor about the ill-gotten gains of market speculators. People are apt to say "there ought to be a law" to curb them. In 1905, Oliver Wendell Holmes, Justice of the United States Supreme Court, in one of his famous opinions delivered the definitive reply to all such critics. Said Justice Holmes: "Speculation . . . is the self-adjustment of society to the probable. Its value is well known, as a means of avoiding or mitigating catastrophes, equalizing prices and providing for periods of want. It is true that the success of the strong induces imitation by the weak, and that incompetent persons bring themselves to ruin by undertaking to speculate in their turn. But legislatures and courts generally have recognized that the natural evolutions of a complex society are to be touched only with a very cautious hand . . ."

CHAPTER 21

How You Buy Stocks
on Margin

ONCE a security buyer has assured a broker of his financial responsibility and opened a margin account, he can buy stocks just by making a down payment on them. How big that down payment must be is governed by various rules.

First, the New York Stock Exchange says that no one can buy its securities on margin unless the down payment is at least $2000. Until April 1966, it was only $1000, and so when the Exchange doubled the minimum, it made it applicable only to new accounts opened afterwards.

Then there are the special requirements set by individual brokers. Some, for instance, will not permit a customer to buy any stock on margin unless it sells above $2 or $3 a share; others require a greater down payment than the Exchange.

Finally, and most important of all, there is the regulation exercised by the Federal Reserve Board, which has been empowered by Congress to say, in effect, just what the minimum *margin requirements* must be. Since 1934, when the board began to exercise its authority, it has set that minimum by saying that the down payment must represent a certain percentage of the total value of the stock that is being bought on margin. The percentage is changed from time to time, depending on how worried the board is about inflation and about the amount of stock trading that is done on margin.

The lowest figure which the board has ever set is 40%, and that figure prevailed for eight years, from 1937 to 1945. The highest figure has been 100%, and while that was in effect from January 1946 to February 1947, nobody could buy on margin, for the minimum down payment required by the board was equal to the full purchase price. In recent years, the figure has been 50%, 70%, or 90% at

various times with the higher percentages prevailing most of
the time. The board did reduce the figure to 50%, a few
weeks after the market break in May 1962, but it jacked
the rate back up to 70% in November 1963, where it still
stood in mid-1966.

Suppose the requirement at a given time is 50%. This
means that you can buy $10,000 worth of some listed stock
with $5000 (unlisted stocks are not sold on margin), and the
broker lends you the other $5000. Naturally, when he does
that, he charges you interest on the money he lends. How
much interest depends on how much money he in turn may
have to pay a bank — whatever the prevailing interest rate
is on brokers' loans — if he had to borrow the $5000 there,
as he often does, to lend it to you. He'll charge you that
prevailing interest rate plus, according to stock exchange practice, at least ½ of 1% for himself, sometimes more. The
total charge the broker makes may run anywhere from 3%
to 4½% in ordinary times, and up to 6% or 7% or even
more, when money is "tight," as in 1966. To many a broker
the interest he earns on *margin loans* constitutes an important source of revenue.

It may occur to you that you could get a better deal elsewhere than you can from your broker — not be required
to put up so much money in order to buy stocks on
margin. That's not true. Banks are not permitted to lend
any more on stock purchases than brokers can lend. It is
true that you can borrow a greater proportion of the down
payment, up to 90%, from unregulated lenders — so-called
"*factors*," but you will pay as much as 1% or 2% interest
a month, and any broker or registered representative who
helped you arrange such a loan would run afoul of the
S.E.C.

When a broker borrows money at the bank to lend you
so that you can buy stocks on margin, he has to give the
bank some security on the loan. That security may be the
very stock that you buy on margin. Hence, when you open
a margin account, you must agree to leave your margined
stocks with the broker and to let him *hypothecate* them,
or pledge them as security for whatever bank loan he may
need in order to carry your margin account or those of his
other customers.

If you were to buy $10,000 worth of stock on margin, you
would naturally pay all commissions and taxes on the full
$10,000 worth of stock. But you would also be entitled to

receive all the dividends on those shares, and this alone is sufficient to interest many a man in buying stocks on margin, when stocks are paying liberal dividends and margin interest rates are low.

For instance, when stocks are paying 6% and 7% dividends and margin interest rates are around 4%, the stock buyer stands to make a little extra profit just on his dividends if he buys on margin. Thus, by putting up only $5000 he might earn 6½% on $10,000, or $650, still assuming, of course, that the margin requirement is 50%. Meanwhile, his costs would amount to only $298 — $200 on a $5000 loan at 4% plus a $49 commission to buy the stock and another $49 to sell it. If he sold the stock at the same price that he paid for it, having neither a gain nor a loss there, he would have made a net profit, exclusive of transfer taxes, of $352.

In contrast, if he had used his $5000 to buy the stock outright, he would have had only half as many shares and received only half as much in dividends, or $325. Meanwhile, his commission costs on buying and selling would have amounted to $88, leaving him a net profit, exclusive of taxes, of only $237. In other words, on the same amount of capital, he could have made an extra $115, or about 49% more, in dividends by buying on margin.

Comparatively few people use margin this way. Ninety-nine times out of a hundred, the margin customer is interested in margin for the sake of the extra speculative profit he hopes to make.

For margin is the speculator's Number 1 tool.

Suppose a man has picked out a stock selling at $50 a share which he thinks will go up. Under a 50% margin rule, he can buy 200 shares of that stock, instead of just 100 shares, with his $5000. If it goes up five points, he makes $1000 instead of just $500, a 20% profit instead of 10%. That kind of profit can make even a 6% interest charge which he may pay on his loan look cheap.

But suppose the stock goes down in price? There's the rub.

It's then that he may receive a *margin call* from his broker, a call on him to put up more margin — that is, to increase his down payment. If he can't put up more money, the broker has the right to sell his stock — as much of it as may be necessary — to raise the required cash. This presents no problem to the broker, because all margined stock must be left on deposit with him.

How much more money may a margin buyer have to put

up if his stocks decline? The answer to this is governed by the *margin maintenance* rules of the New York Stock Exchange and those of the individual broker. The Federal Reserve Board isn't in the picture at all after the original purchase; if a buyer meets its margin requirements then — say, of 50% cash — he is never compelled by the Board to put up any more margin, even if the Board raises its requirements to 75% or more.

Under the New York Stock Exchange rule, however, a broker must call on a customer for more margin whenever the amount that the customer would have left if he sold his stocks and paid off the broker's loan represents less than 25% of the current value of the stocks. (It should be noted that some brokers have margin maintenance requirements that are higher than the minimums set by the New York Stock Exchange.)

To illustrate: Suppose a margin customer bought 100 shares of a stock selling at $60 a share at a time when the Federal Reserve Board required only 50% margin. In that case he would put up $3000 and he would borrow $3000 from his broker. Now suppose the stock dropped from $60 to $40 a share. If he were to sell out now, he would realize only $4000 on his holdings, and after he paid his broker $3000, he would have only $1000 left, which would be exactly 25% of the current value ($4000) of his stock.

If the stock fell below $40 in this instance, the broker would have to ask for more margin money so that the 25% ratio would be restored. Actually, he'd probably ask for a bit more so that he wouldn't have to make another margin call so soon again in case the stock continued to decline.

If a stock is bought on a 50% margin basis, it is evident that it can drop a full third in price — from 60 to 40, as in the example above — before a broker must call for more margin.

If the Federal Reserve Board's margin requirement was 75% instead of 50%, the stock could decline two-thirds in value before the customer would have to put up more money. Here's how that works: The customer buys 100 shares of stock at $60 a share and puts up 75% margin, or $4500. He borrows only $1500 from the broker. If the stock drops to $20, his holdings are worth $2000. At that point, he could sell out, pay the broker $1500 and still have $500 left, which would represent 25% of the current market value of his stocks ($2000).

The Federal Reserve Board's requirement governing the initial margin payment and the stock exchange rule on maintenance of margin explain why margin calls are comparatively infrequent today, except in very sharp market dips as in 1962 and 1966.

Finally, the exchange has put a brake on the heavy trader who might move in and out of a given stock several times during one day's trading. Brokers are now required to see that such *day traders,* if they are operating on margin, as most of them do, have enough capital in their accounts to cover the initial margin requirement on the maximum position they held at any time in the day's trading — not just their position at the end of the day.

Not only have the regulations resulted in fewer margin calls than there were at the time of the 1929 crash, but they have also greatly reduced the proportion of margin accounts in relation to all accounts. In 1929 it is estimated that margin customers represented 40% of all customers, but they accounted for a considerably larger proportion of a broker's total business. Just how large a proportion no one knows exactly, but as the market boiled upward in the late twenties, the margin customers were always the big buyers, the people who kept *pyramiding* their *paper profits* and buying more and more stock.

Here's how pyramiding worked in those days: Suppose a man bought 200 shares of a $50 stock. Under the lax margin regulations which prevailed then, he might have had to put up only $2000 of the $10,000 cost — maybe even less if he was a favored customer.

Now let's assume that his stock advanced to $75 a share. His total holdings would now be worth $15,000. If he sold at that price and paid off the $8000 loan from his broker, he would have $7000 cash; and on a 20% margin basis, this would enable him to buy $35,000 worth of stock. Actually, of course, he rarely had to go through the mechanics of selling out and buying afresh. The broker recognized the expanded value of his original holdings and accepted that added value as collateral on the additional purchases.

In this instance, the customer would have been able to own $35,000 worth of securities on a cash margin of only $2000, thanks to that 50% increase in the value of his original 200 shares. If he continued to be that lucky, he could run his paper profits to a hundred thousand dollars, a half million dollars, a million dollars, many millions of dollars, all on just $2000 cash.

And in the twenties many people did exactly that. But when prices started to decline and the margin calls came, many of them couldn't raise even a few thousand dollars cash, except by selling securities. And when they sold, that very act of selling depressed prices further and resulted in more margin calls. Again they had to sell. And so the vicious circle kept swirling downward into the great abyss.

There's nothing illegal about pyramiding — even today under the Federal Reserve Board rules brokers can accept securities as well as cash on the required margin payment — but it just can't work very effectively when you have to put up a margin of 50%, 70%, or 90% instead of 20%. Only a substantial increase in the price of your stock will yield you big enough paper profits to permit a significant increase in your holdings.

And that's another reason why margin accounts aren't as popular as they used to be. By the end of the war, they had declined to less than 10% of their number in 1929. In recent years there has been some increase, but margin buyers still represent only 10% or 15% of all the people who buy listed securities on the New York Exchange, even though they may account for 20% or 25% of all public transactions.

So few is their number and so well protected are their margin accounts that even if there were a serious decline in the market, it is unlikely that it could ever be turned into the kind of rout that made 1929 the debacle it was.

CHAPTER 22

What It Means
to Sell Short

WHEN a man opens a margin account with a broker, he is asked to sign an agreement giving the broker authority to lend his margined stocks to others. It is this lending or hypothecation agreement which makes it possible in most cases for other customers to sell stocks short.

Short selling normally accounts for only 5% or 6% of all the transactions on the New York Stock Exchange, and yet probably no other market technique excites so much public interest — or is so widely misunderstood.

A short sale is nothing but the reverse of the usual market transaction. Instead of buying a stock and then selling it, the short trader sells it first and then buys it back at what he hopes will be a lower price.

If it is legitimate to buy a stock because you think it's going to go up, why isn't it just as legitimate to sell it because you think it's going to go down? Why shouldn't you be able to try to make a profit in either direction? It can be fairly argued that the right of a bear to sell *short* is just as vital to a completely free market as the right of a bull to buy stocks, or go *long*.

Regardless of the logic of the situation, most people think it just isn't morally right to sell something you don't have.

What about the magazine publisher who sells you a three-year advance subscription to his publication?

Or what about the farmer who may sell his whole crop to a grain elevator or to a miller when the seed hasn't even sprouted yet?

Both of them sell something they haven't got just on the strength of a promise to deliver. And that's all a short seller does.

Furthermore, it isn't really true that he sells something he doesn't have. He has to *borrow* the stock that he sells, and he has to give it back. This he hopes to be able to do by *covering,* or buying it back at a price less than he sold it for.

Where does he borrow his stock? From his broker.

Where does the broker get the stock to lend? Usually from his margin customers who signed the lending agreement when they opened their accounts. If a broker doesn't have among his margin accounts the particular stock that a man wants to sell short, he will borrow it from another broker or from some individual stockowner who makes a business of lending his stock. But the broker *cannot* borrow stock from the account of any of his regular cash customers without specific authorization.

Why should one broker lend stock to another? Because he gets paid for it — an amount equal to the value of the borrowed stock — and he has free use of this cash until the stock is returned. Sometimes if the stock is in demand, the borrowing broker will even pay a premium to borrow it. Any such premium payment is, of course, charged to the short seller. If the value of a stock on loan increases significantly, the lending broker will expect more money; if it drops, the borrowing broker will expect a proportionate refund.

A short seller operates under essentially the same rules that govern margin buying. If the Federal Reserve Board has a 50% margin rule in effect, the seller must put up cash equal to 50% of the market value of the stock that he borrows and sells. Under stock exchange rules, the minimum margin cannot be less than $2000.

Suppose a man wanted to go short 100 shares of a stock selling at 60. If the Federal Reserve Board requirement was 50% at the time, he would have to put up $3000 cash. If the stock dropped to 50, he could buy it back, cover his short position by returning the stock, and make a profit of $10 a share, or $1000, less taxes and commissions.

But perhaps when the stock hits 50, he thought it would go lower. He could make more money if it did, but he wouldn't want to lose the profit he already had. In such a situation he might place a *stop order to buy* at 52. This is the exact counterpart of a stop order that a man who owns stocks may use to protect himself when he's afraid the market will drop. In this case, the short wants to protect himself against a rising market. If the stock does go up to 52, his stop order becomes a market order to buy at once.

If he buys back in at that price, he will still have a profit of $800, exclusive of all brokerage commissions and taxes.

Additionally, he will also be liable for whatever dividends may have accrued on the stock during the operation, because the lender obviously was entitled to get them during the time his stock was on loan.

This is one big reason why the short seller under the stock exchange rules has to maintain a margin of 30%, while the margin buyer is required to meet only that minimum figure of 25%.

The 30% maintenance-of-margin requirement means that the broker will call for more money whenever the amount of the margin that the short seller would have left if he bought the stock back and covered his short position would total only 30% of its current market price.

Suppose a man sells short 100 shares of a stock at 60. If the initial margin requirement were 50%, he would have to put up $3000. Now, instead of declining to 50, suppose the price of the stock goes up to 70. If he were to cover at that point, he would owe $7000 or $1000 more than he sold the stock for originally. That means he would have only $2000 margin left in his account ($3000 minus $1000) or just about 30% of the current value of the stock ($7000 times .30 equals $2100). At that point, unless he decided to take his loss and close out the transaction, he would be perilously close to getting a call for more margin.

Sometimes a short sale can be prudently used to protect a profit in a stock at a time when the buyer doesn't want to sell it and take his profit. Suppose, for instance, you had bought 100 shares of a stock and that it ran up twenty points in three months. If you were to sell and take your $2000 profit, you would have to pay a short-term capital gains tax on that profit. If you were in a 50% tax bracket, you would have to pay out $1000 in taxes, even more if you were in a higher tax bracket. So you want to hold on for another three months until your profit or capital gain can be reported as income in another tax year when you expect you will be in a lower tax bracket.

But suppose the stock were to drop during that three-month waiting period and you were to lose a substantial part of the $2000 profit? You don't want that to happen. And you're perfectly willing to forego the prospect of further price appreciation, a bigger profit, just to protect yourself against the risk of loss. A short sale of 100 shares of the same stock offers you just that kind of insurance. When you are both long and short the same number of shares of the same stock, your position is stabilized. If the stock rises, you make money on your long position and lose an equal amount on your short position. If it goes down, you make money on the short side and lose an offsetting amount on the long side. Your capital gains and losses cancel each other. When you stabilize this way, you don't change the tax status of your profit as it was when you went short; you simply decide in what year you pay the tax.

Another good thing about this kind of transaction, known as *"selling short against the box,"* is that you don't worry about any margin requirements, since they will always be amply met by your long position in the stock. As far as your margin position is concerned on both accounts, you are always in balance, for a loss in one is offset by a gain in the other.

While it is obvious that there is a legitimate place for short selling in a free and orderly securities market, it cannot be denied on the other hand that short selling has often been used for illegitimate purposes, and these abuses have frequently led to demands that short selling be outlawed. From the time 350 years ago when buyers and sellers first began to trade in the stock of the Dutch East India Company, the history of short selling has not been a pretty one. And it contributed some gaudy chapters to the history of the New York Stock Exchange, particularly in the nineteenth century, when short selling was a favorite tool of such famous market manipulators as Commodore Vanderbilt, Daniel Drew, Jay Gould, Jesse Livermore, and Jim Fisk.

In many battles, these men tried to catch each other in market corners. A market *corner* is created when one man or group succeeds in getting such complete control of a particular stock that others who may have sold it short cannot cover their purchases by buying the stock back, as they have to do, except on terms dictated by the controlling group.

One of the classic corners is that which involved the old Harlem Railroad, a predecessor of the New York Central. Vanderbilt got control of the Harlem and then proceeded to extend the road down Manhattan Island. Drew, who was also a stockholder in the road and had realized a handsome profit as the stock advanced in price, now saw an opportunity to make a much larger profit. He induced the New York City Council to repeal the franchise which had been granted for the extension of the road on the assumption that this bad news would depress the price of the stock. Simultaneously, he sold the stock short.

His maneuver did succeed in driving the price of the stock down, but as Drew sold, the Commodore bought. In the end, Drew and some of the members of the City Council who were associated with him in this notorious exploit found that they had sold short more stock than actually existed. They could not cover their short positions except on terms dictated by Vanderbilt — and the terms were ruinous. That is probably when the famous couplet, credited to Drew, came into our literature: *"He who sells what isn't his'n/Must buy it back or go to prison."*

Even when nothing so titanic as an attempted corner was involved, short selling proved an effective manipulative device for *pool* operators, who would join forces to bid the price of a stock up and then sell it short in order to make a big speculative profit.

Often such pool operators would risk very little of their own capital in the operation. They would stimulate public interest in a particular stock by adroit publicity and creation of considerable activity in the market for that stock. That activity was usually more apparent than real, because it would be generated by *wash sales*. A wash sale, now outlawed by the S.E.C., simply involved the simultaneous purchase and sale of large blocks, say, 1000 or 10,000 shares. Such big volume would attract the public, which inevitably seems to buy whenever there is a lot of activity in a stock. As the public bought and as demand forced the price up, pool operators would wait for the strategic moment when they thought the stock was about as high as it could get, and then they would begin selling it short, hammering the price down to a level where they could buy it back at a handsome profit.

One of the most important reforms introduced by the Securities & Exchange Commission is the regulation which now effectively prevents this abuse of the right to sell short. The S.E.C. accomplished this objective years ago by a simple regulation which essentially provides that a stock can be sold short only on a rising market.

Technically the regulation, now rigorously enforced not only by the S.E.C. but by all stock exchanges, works this way: If a customer places an order to sell short, that order as it goes to the floor must be clearly marked as a short sale, and the floor broker is forbidden to execute that order.

except at what is, in effect, a higher price. Thus, if a stock were last sold at 50, the broker could not sell that stock short except at a price of 50⅛ or higher; in this case he would be selling on an up tick.

There is one exception to this: The broker may sell the stock at 50, the same price as prevailed on the last sale, provided the *last previous* change in the price had been upward. In other words, there might have been one or two or six transactions that had taken place at that same price of 50, but a short sale could still be made at 50, provided the last *different* price was 49⅞ or lower. This is called selling on an *even tick*.

These regulations explain why the volume of short selling has dwindled so. Nevertheless, on some of the leading stocks which may on an occasion have been bid up too high in price, short sales can account for a substantial proportion of all transactions, perhaps as much as 20% or more on a given day. But this is comparatively rare.

Most of the short selling which is done nowadays comes not from the public but from members of the exchange. Does this mean that brokers are still up to their old manipulative tricks? Not at all.

Probably most of the short sales are made by the specialists, and they very often have to make these sales if they are to fulfill their obligations to conduct fair and orderly markets in the stocks they handle. Thus, if a broker wants to execute a buy market order for a customer and there are no other offers to sell, except perhaps at a price that is wholly out of line — perhaps as much as a full point higher — the specialist is expected to sell the stock at a better price, even if he doesn't have it in his inventory and has to go short in order to complete the transaction.

Floor traders and other floor brokers occasionally engage in short selling for their own personal accounts. When they do, it is not because they are trading on inside knowledge, usually it's just because they are cynical about the public's perpetual bullishness.

The public always wants the market to go up. The public always thinks it will — and so buyers act accordingly. In this kind of situation, who would deny an old bear the right to bet that the bulls are wrong again?

CHAPTER 23

Puts and Calls,
Plain and Fancy

In addition to margin buying, pyramiding, and short selling, the speculator can execute still one other market maneuver which is especially useful if he wants to protect a profit he has already made or insure himself against loss. He can buy a *put* or a *call* on any listed stock through any one of about two dozen dealers who specialize in this business.

If he buys a put, he buys the right to sell 100 shares of a particular stock — if he wants to — within a given period of time at a specific price which is fixed in the contract.

A call is the exact opposite. The speculator pays for the right to buy 100 shares of a certain stock at a set price within a given period of time.

Both puts and calls are called *options,* since the buyer has the option of deciding whether he will exercise a put or a call after he has bought it.

If he buys a call on a stock, he doesn't have to exercise it, doesn't have to buy the stock, but if the stock goes up enough to cover the cost of his option any time within the contract period, he can obviously realize a profit by calling on the dealer to sell him the stock at the stipulated lower price. If he buys a call and the stock goes down, he loses whatever he had to pay for the call, because there would then be no advantage in exercising it. A put works precisely the same way, except in reverse. If the stock drops below the set level, the buyer makes money by exercising his put and selling the stock at the higher price stipulated in the contract.

The prices and terms at which put-and-call dealers will sell options are pretty well standardized. The most common types of options are the 30-day, 60-day, and 90-day contracts, but some are sold for longer periods such as six months or a year.

On a 30-day put or call, the price that is set in the contract is usually the current market price, and the cost of the option will vary with the price of the stock and the dealer's estimate of how volatile or stable it is. Typically, a 30-day option on a stock selling at a price of 40 would be about $250. Thus, on a call, the stock would have to advance to 42½ before the buyer could show a profit, not counting the brokerage commission. But if there were any advance at all above 40, again not counting the brokerage commission, the buyer would want to exercise his call and at least save something out of the $250 he paid for his option. On a put, the stock would have to drop below 37½ for the option buyer to make a profit by selling the stock at 40, but he might well want to exercise the option at any price below 40, after allowing for the brokerage commission. Typically, 60-day and 90-day options on a $40 stock might cost about $325 and $400 respectively.

Occasionally, a speculator will buy both a put and a call on the same stock and thus put himself in a position to jump either way should the market take a decided turn either up or down at any time during the life of his contract. This is called a *straddle*.

Sometimes if a man has a long-term straddle, he can be lucky enough to make money on both sides of it. Perhaps the market rises sharply — in which case he can make a profit by exercising his call — and then drops sharply, enabling him to make money on his put, or vice versa.

Puts and calls are not traded on any exchange. If you want to buy one, you can arrange for its purchase through your regular broker. This costs you nothing, because he is compensated for the order by the put-and-call dealer. But in addition to the premium that you pay the dealer for your contract, you will, if you are buying a call, have to pay New York State transfer taxes; no taxes are levied on a put.

If you decide to exercise an option — either to buy the stock or to sell it at the price fixed in the contract — the purchase or sale will be handled by your regular broker, who will earn a standard commission on the transaction.

Although your contract for a put or call will be negotiated with one of the regular dealers, he is not as a rule the one who really carries the risk. If he writes a 30-day call for you on a stock at 40, he finds somebody else who will guarantee to deliver the stock at that price within 30 days and sells him the $250 contract for $225.

Who is this "somebody else"? It might be a wealthy individual, but more times than not it's likely to be an insurance company, a large trust, or a foundation — some agency with lots of capital and a big inventory of securities. These agencies find that they can earn a good short-term return on their money with negligible risk in the long run by taking over the put-and-call dealer's risk, but as far as many institutions are concerned, such operations are forbidden either by their charters or the securities law of the state in which they operate.

Of the $25 spread which the dealer would realize on your call ($250 less $225), he keeps $12.50 and splits the other $12.50 between your broker and the broker representing whoever takes the contract off the dealer's hands. Regardless of the duration of the option — 30, 60, or 90 days — the spread is generally the same and the $25 is divided in the same fashion.

The direct speculative uses of a put or a call are fairly obvious. Their uses for protective purposes are not always so clear, but if a man has a substantial profit in a stock he owns and wants to protect it for a special period, he can buy a put and accomplish the same objective as he would by selling short against the box. Or if he is a short seller, he can buy a call to protect himself against a rising market.

He could, of course, achieve the same objective without spending any money by placing a stop order to sell or a stop order to buy, but this device might not be elastic enough for him. For instance, if a man had bought a stock at 60 and it was now selling at 70, he might buy a 60-day put at 70 for $200 or so. But if he placed a stop order on the same stock, he would have to pick a precise price at which he wanted to sell.

If, for instance, he placed a stop order at 68, it might happen that a brisk sell-off would hit the market and the stock would drop at 68, at which point he would be sold out. Then after the market recovered, perhaps only a few days later, the stock might be selling above 70 again, but he would no longer own it.

Instead of buying a put, he might sell his stock at 70 and buy a six-month call at 70 for perhaps $250 or $300. If the stock dropped, the most he could lose would be the cost of the call. But if it continued rising, he would be in exactly the same position as if he still owned the stock except for the price of the call. The speculator's tax position — short-term vs. long-term capital gains — plays an obviously important role in his use of puts and calls.

Options have another distinct advantage to the speculator. A man can buy a call on a stock without tying up his money as he would have to do if he bought the same stock on margin. The same thing is true with respect to short selling. His actual out-of-pocket costs may be higher operating on a put-and-call rather than a margin basis, but if there is a significant price movement in the stock, his profit may make the cost look incidental. Under any circumstances, the most he can lose, if his judgment proves wrong, is the cost of the option.

The juggling of these various speculative devices, weighing the risks and the costs of each against the other, makes the business of professional speculation a highly complicated one. This alone can explain why it is probably true that more people who speculate lose money than make money.

But an even more important reason lies in the inclination of many a speculator to act on the basis of a tip or hunch — his unwillingness to study thoroughly all the facts about a company before he buys or sells its stock. Bernard M. Baruch, probably America's most successful speculator, made it an inviolable rule never to become involved in a speculative venture until he had mastered all the facts about it. As he once explained, successful speculation demands not only courage, persistence, and a judgment unclouded by emotion, but above all things it requires an infinite capacity for taking pains — the pains to analyze all available facts.

CHAPTER 24

How to Tell
What the Market Is Doing

WHEN most people buy securities for the first time, they are apt to do it for the wrong reasons. They will buy a stock because they've heard other people, their friends or business associates, talk about it.

It seems to be human nature to believe that the other fellow always knows a good thing, that he has reliable inside information on how a company is doing.

Is there such a thing as *inside information?*

Of course there is.

The officers and directors of a company know more about that firm and its prospects than anybody else could possibly know. And they have friends with whom they discuss their company's situation. In effect, those friends do have what appears to be privileged information — the real "inside." And because they do, the S.E.C. has long encircled their stock-trading operations with a set of rigid regulations that it polices vigorously. The commission wants no recurrence of the pre-1929 situation when many company officials or directors considered the privilege of trading in their company's stock on the basis of their own inside information simply part of their compensation.

Today, any such "insider" is required to report to the S.E.C. every purchase or sale he makes of his own company's stock, and the list of such transactions is published monthly. He is never permitted to sell his own company's stock short. Further, if an insider realizes any profit from buying and selling his company's stock within a six-month period, that profit is recoverable by the company, whether or not it can be demonstrated that he had used inside information. And if it can be shown that he masked his transaction in the name of his wife or some other relative or friend, he is just as liable as if he had traded in his own name.

Inside information is, of course, no longer inside when it has been made public, but when can such information be said to have become public? This was the key question in a test case initiated by the S.E.C. in May 1966. The case involved a dozen directors and officials of the Texas Gulf Sulphur Co., which in 1963 discovered valuable deposits of lead, zinc, and copper on its properties at Timmins, Ontario, in Canada. The company acquired adjacent properties and resumed drilling operations in March 1964. On April 16, Texas Gulf announced its discoveries at a press conference. The S.E.C. in its suit alleged that various officials profited from their inside knowledge by buying stock in the company, and it even went so far as to charge one director with a violation, although his purchase of 3000 shares was not made until an hour after news of the ore discovery was released at the press conference and published on a financial news service in virtually every major bank and brokerage office in the country. This particular charge was dismissed when the first verdict was returned in a federal district court, and all but two of the defendants were exonerated. But the S.E.C., unwilling to accept any such rebuff, made it clear that it would fight the case all the way to the U.S. Supreme Court. Actually, whether the commission won or lost its case was almost immaterial; industry had been put emphatically on notice that the S.E.C. intended to be more vigilant than ever in supervising transactions by company officials and other "insiders."

Yes, indeed, there is inside information about a company, but the really important inside information is usually so closely guarded that neither you nor any other investor is likely to hear it until it becomes generally available to all investors. Leaks of reliable information are few and far between, and that's why anyone who invests his money on what he believes to be an inside tip is apt to be seriously misled.

How, then, should a man set about investing?

If he doesn't know anything at all about the market or the stocks of various companies, where can he turn for information?

Probably the first and most obvious answer to that is the newspaper — one of the big metropolitan daily newspapers that carries complete stock market quotations and has a well-rounded coverage of financial news, or one of the various regional editions of the *Wall Street Journal*.

If he is not already familiar with the *stock tables,* probably his first step should be to study them regularly for a period of time. If he reads a morning paper, he will find the stocks traded during the preceding day on the New York Stock Exchange, listed in alphabetical order. The late edition of the evening paper provides that information for the stocks traded that same day.

If our Rod & Reel, Inc., were sold on the exchange, a complete entry for one day, with the appropriate column heads, might look like this:

Year to Date		Stock &	Sales in					Net
High	Low	Dividend	100s	Open	High	Low	Close	Change
42½	38¾	Rod & Reel 2	17	39¾	40¼	39⅝	40¼	+¾

The column heads make much of the information self-explanatory. Obviously, the stock has been traded in a fairly narrow range, having fluctuated only between a low of 38¾ and a high of 42½ all year. A comparison of this price range with the range recorded by other stocks will give you some general idea of whether Rod & Reel might be classified as an investment-type stock or a speculation. As a very rough rule of thumb, the greater the price fluctuation, the lower the investment caliber of the stock.

The dividend gives you another clue to the quality of the stock. With an annual dividend rate of $2 and a current price of $40, Rod & Reel is yielding exactly 5%. Very often after the dividend figure there will appear a small letter which will refer to a footnote. These footnotes can be very important, because they may indicate that the dividend figure includes extra dividends, or that this was the dividend paid last year, or that it represents only the total paid so far this year for a stock not on a regular dividend basis.

The figure for the number of shares traded simply shows how Rod & Reel stacks up alongside others as far as market interest is concerned. Sales volume of a stock in which there is considerable speculative interest will very often exceed that of some of the better-grade market leaders.

The open, high, low, and close figures give you a complete picture of how Rod & Reel moved during the trading day. Obviously in this case, it sold off ⅛ after opening at 39¾ and then recovered to close at the day's high of 40¼. On any given day, the pattern of price movement will not be the same for all stocks, but this profile on Rod & Reel will show you whether its market performance is generally in line with that for the market as a whole. If Rod & Reel had opened at its low for the day and marched steadily along to close at its high, while the market as a whole declined from the open to the close, you could conclude that Rod & Reel had demonstrated a good deal of strength, because it ran counter to the downward trend.

The *net change* figure (+¾) shows the difference between the closing price for one day (40¼) and the closing price of the *preceding day* (obviously 39½) — not the difference between the opening and closing prices for the day. Yesterday's close may have been either higher or lower than today's opening.

Occasionally, you may notice that the price of a stock is down from the preceding day, but the net-change figure doesn't show a corresponding drop. That's because the stock is being sold *ex dividend*.

Suppose Rod & Reel pays its quarterly dividend of 50¢ to stockholders on its books as of the close of business on Friday, September 15. Beginning Tuesday, September 12, and running through Friday, the stock will be worth 50¢ less, because anyone who buys it during that period will not be eligible for the dividend. This is so because it takes four business days to make delivery of stock and only those people who own the stock on Monday, September 11, will be on the company's records Friday, September 15. On the day a stock is sold ex dividend, its price is expected to decline by the amount of the dividend, and if that is exactly what happens, the net-change figure will show no gain or loss.

This four-day delivery interval is also important when a stock goes *ex rights*. Thus, a company with a new issue of additional stock might announce that stockholders as of Friday, September 15, would have the right to buy new stock in proportion to their present holdings at a price somewhat below the market. But obviously only those people who bought the stock on or before Monday, September 11, would appear on the company's records four days later, and anybody who bought the stock after that date wouldn't get the rights. Whenever a stock goes ex rights, it usually sells at a price that is lower by an amount roughly equal to the value of the rights. During the time that the rights can be exercised, they are bought and sold separately, and often quoted separately in the stock tables.

Obviously, it would be a mistake to draw any positive

conclusions about a stock on the basis of one day's trading pattern. But if you watch a stock over a period of time and compare it closely with a dozen or so others, particularly those in the same or a related field, you will begin to get an idea of how that stock is regarded by all the thousands of people whose transactions from day to day make the market.

In addition to the tables of prices on stocks traded that day, a few big-city newspapers also publish the bid-and-asked quotations on those stocks which are inactive. Even on an active day there are likely to be no trades at all in as many as a quarter of the 1200 stocks listed on the Big Board. The bid-and-asked quotations enable an owner to keep an eye on the price opinions about his stock even though it isn't traded.

Not all newspapers publish anything like this complete information on Big Board stocks. In the smaller cities, the daily newspapers may list only 100 or so stocks and give only opening and closing prices on these, plus maybe the net change from the preceding day.

The American Stock Exchange stocks don't get nearly as much play as those of the Big Board, and stocks listed on the other exchanges are likely to get press notice only in the areas where there is some public interest in them. Much the same standard determines just how many unlisted stocks are published and which ones, from the national and regional quotations supplied by the National Association of Securities Dealers.

Prices reported in the newspapers for bonds are apt to seem a little confusing. Although bonds are usually sold in $1000 units, their prices are quoted as though they had a $100 denomination. Thus a quotation of 98 would indicate an actual price of $980, and one of 98⅜ would be $983.75.

Since government bonds sold on the open market are traded not in eighths or quarters but in thirty-seconds, a special price-reporting formula has been developed for them. Thus, a printed quotation of 99.16 actually means a price of $995. Here's how you arrive at that: The point in the quote isn't a decimal point; it is only a device for separating the round figure from the fraction. Hence the quotation really stands for 99 16/32, or 99½, or $995. Sometimes Treasuries are sold on a price change of just 1/64 rather than 1/32. If a plus sign appears after the published quotation for a government bond, this means that 1/64 should be added to the published price.

In addition to prices on individual security issues, almost every daily paper publishes some report on the average movement of New York Stock Exchange prices.

There are a number of these *averages* which are supposed to serve as barometers of the business. The best known of them is the Dow-Jones average.

Actually, the Dow-Jones average isn't one average but four — one for industrials, one for rails, one for utilities, and a composite one which is supposed to reflect conditions in all divisions of the market. These averages are computed constantly and are instantaneously available as of that minute on desk-model quotation machines, but they are officially announced by Dow Jones only at half-hour intervals throughout the trading day.

The utility index is an average of prices for 15 utilities; the rail index covers 20 railroads; the industrial average is based on the stocks of 30 leading manufacturers and distributors; and the composite index includes all 65.

Over the years, these averages, which date back to 1896, have come to be accepted as the Bible of the business, partly because Dow Jones & Company, which originated them, publishes the country's leading financial newspaper, the *Wall Street Journal*, and operates the ticker news service, known as the *"broad tape,"* which can be found in virtually every major bank and brokerage office.

But in recent years the suspicion has grown that this Bible is not divinely inspired, that the Dow-Jones averages are not an infallible measure of the market. This criticism has been aimed especially at the Dow-Jones industrial average, probably the most important of them all, and it is based on two counts.

In the first place, it is argued that the 30 stocks which make up the index are not truly representative of all the industrials listed on the Big Board. Too many of them classify as "blue chips" — stocks such as General Motors, American Telephone, Standard Oil of New Jersey, Du Pont, Allied Chemical, F. W. Woolworth, Eastman Kodak, Sears Roebuck, American Tobacco, General Electric, and General Foods.

In the second place, over the years many of these stocks have been split several times, and with each split the price of the stock has dropped proportionately. Thus, if the split were two for one, the price of the stock could be expected to decline about 50%; on a four-for-one split it would decline about 75%.

Since the Dow-Jones averages are arrived at by adding the prices of all the stocks together and dividing by their number, it is obvious that the price reductions resulting from such splits could throw the average seriously out of kilter. Dow Jones has sought to correct such distortions by a mathematical adjustment, but this hasn't worked out too well. Those companies that have never split their stock still exert a stronger influence in the average than they should. (Thus General Foods exerts more influence than American Telephone & Telegraph, despite the fact that the total value of all its outstanding stock is only a small fraction of American Telephone & Telegraph.)

As a result of its mathematical imperfections, the Dow-Jones industrial average can go up while the aggregate value of all the shares of the stocks that comprise it goes down. This actually happens on occasion. For instance, on one particular day the Dow-Jones average showed an increase of about ½ of 1%, but on that same day the actual value of all the shares of the 30 companies dropped from 26½ to 25½ billion. The apparent gain was all accounted for by a rise in the price of a few stocks that didn't have nearly as many shares outstanding as those companies whose stocks declined.

In recent years, the premier position of the Dow-Jones industrial average has been seriously challenged by the 500-stock index of Standard & Poor's Corporation, the nation's largest securities research organization. For many years, Standard & Poor's had published other indexes — a 90-stock index and a 425-stock index — but it wasn't until 1957, when high-speed computers made more comprehensive indexes possible on an hourly basis, that Standard & Poor's decided really to lock horns with Dow Jones.

The 500-stock index, covering stocks that account for 86% of the total value of all Big Board stocks, is unquestionably a more scientifically constructed index and provides a much more accurate picture of what is happening in the market. This is true because it is computed by multiplying the price of each stock by the number of shares outstanding, thus giving proper weight to the bigger and more influential companies like A.T.&T. and General Motors — and IBM, which isn't even in the Dow-Jones average.

Despite the fact that the Dow-Jones industrial average has statistical shortcomings and the 500-stock index is definitely more scientific, the two indexes do move together with surprisingly little disparity. It's a rare day indeed when one ends up showing a plus and the other a minus, a situation that can exist only on a day when the market has had no clear-cut movement in either direction. On major swings, they move pretty much together, although one or the other may boast that its index gave the first indication of such a move. On balance, the Dow-Jones is apt to be more sensitive to short-term movements, and the 500-stock index provides a more reliable long-term perspective.

Although Standard & Poor's is proud of the fact that its index is used by the Federal Reserve Board and the Department of Commerce, as well as many other federal officials and business economists, Dow Jones — by virtue of its age and its popularity with financial editors of press, radio, and TV — continues to have an iron-bound grip on the public mind, particularly that public which frequents brokerage offices.

There is one significant difference between the two indexes, and that lies in the magnitude of the numbers they use. When the Dow-Jones industrials stand at 900, the 500-stock index stands at about 93, and that relationship holds pretty true right up and down the line: The Dow figure is almost ten times greater than Standard & Poor's. This results from the calculated effort by Standard & Poor's in 1957 to devise a computation process that would yield an index figure more nearly comparable to the average dollar price of all stocks traded on the New York Stock Exchange than the outrageous Dow figures.

For years the New York Stock Exchange attempted to persuade Dow Jones to divide its index by 10 or devise another formula that would yield an index figure only a fraction of the present level. But Dow Jones, which regards its averages as sacrosanct, despite the many changes brought about by substituting one company for another over the years, has turned a deaf ear to all such suggestions.

The reason why the exchange would like to see the Dow-Jones average fractioned is perfectly obvious: It worries about the effect on the public of front-page headlines or news announcements that proclaim the stock market dropped 10 points, 15 points, or even 20 points, as it has in a single day, according to Dow Jones. It isn't much happier when the headlines say that the market went up 10 points, 15 points, or 20 points. The big figures, up or down, give the public an entirely wrong impression of the volatility of the market. No matter how you attempt to explain the situation, people will go on confusing Dow-Jones points with actual dollars, and there is no relationship between the two. On a day when the Dow moves 20 points, the aggregate dollar value of all stocks listed on the exchange will change by less than 2%.

Dissatisfaction with the Dow-Jones average was certainly one of the key reasons why the New York Stock Exchange decided in 1966 to begin publishing its own official index — an index covering all 1200 common stocks on the exchange, computed continuously and publicly announced on the exchange ticker every half hour. Nor did it surprise anyone that the computation process used in this "official" index yielded a starting figure close to the $50 average price of all shares on the exchange. To be sure that the exchange is never embarrassed by its own index, it also announced that the index would be split 2-for-1 if it ever reached 100. In addition to its composite, the exchange also initiated four group indexes — industrials, transportation, utilities, and finance.

Another new index also made its debut in 1966: the first index of American Stock Exchange securities — devised, computed, and published hourly by the exchange itself. In addition to this "price-level" index, which reflects the actual average price of all listed stocks and warrants, the exchange reports daily on the breadth of the market — the number of issues that moved up or down by ⅛, ¼, ⅜, and so on — and it issues a monthly index showing the average *price-earnings ratio* of all stocks on the exchange. The price-earnings ratio of a stock is computed by dividing the price of the stock by its actual or indicated annual earnings per share. Thus, a stock selling at 30 with earnings of $2.00 a share would be said to have a price-earnings ratio of 15.

Wall Street's new computers are, indeed, beginning to earn their keep.

CHAPTER 25

How to Read
the Financial News

ONCE a man starts following stock prices and averages, it isn't long until he is reading the rest of the *financial section* of his newspaper.

Here, obviously, he will find much important information both about business in general and about individual companies — their plans for expansion, their new products, their sales and earning records. Some of these news stories dealing with individual companies may be a little on the optimistic side, since they are often based on publicity releases furnished by the companies themselves, but every responsible newspaper today makes an effort to be as objective as possible in the handling of such news.

A standard feature of the financial section in every big-city newspaper is the daily column in which the action of the stock market is reported and often analyzed in terms of various technical factors — the primary trend, the secondary movement, the resistance levels, and so on.

While it may be true that there are technical factors in the market that do affect its direction over short periods of time — because many people believe there are, if for no other reason — these are conditions which are apt to be of far greater importance to the professional trader or speculator than to the average investor, especially the newcomer who may be understandably confused by some reference to a "double top" or "head and shoulders."

Nevertheless, the market columns can make interesting reading after one gets used to the jargon, and soon even the neophyte finds himself acquiring some familiarity with such phrases as "technically strong" or "technically weak," the "short interest" and "the Dow theory."

The phrases *technically strong* or *technically weak* have fairly precise meanings. Suppose stock prices have been moving more or less steadily upward over a long period of time. Inevitably in such a bull-market movement, there are price advances and price reactions, ups and downs in the market. If the volume of sales is heavy when stocks go up and light when they go down during a bull movement, the market can be described as technically strong. Conversely, if volume is heavy on the down side and light on the rallies, the market is technically weak. This interpretation is based on the theory that sales volume always shows the dominant trend. That is why many newspapers regularly report the number of stocks that made new lows and the number that made new highs.

The term *short interest,* as applied most usually to the New York Stock Exchange, refers to the total number of shares of Big Board stocks that all the sellers are short; they have sold the stock but must still buy it back to cover their positions. No short sale, of course, can be made without a broker's knowledge, and hence a broker always knows the total number of shares that his customers are short in every stock. Once a month, member firms report these figures to the exchange, and the exchange makes a public report on the short interest in every stock where it is an item of consequence. Following its big study of the stock market, the S.E.C. made it clear in 1964 that it felt computers should make possible more detailed and more frequent analyses of the short interest. Although nothing had happened two years later, it seemed likely that the commission would ultimately have its way.

While the short interest at any given time may approximate a good single day's trading volume, anywhere from 3 or 4 million to 10 or 12 million shares, this still represents at the most only about 1/10 of 1% of all the shares listed on the Big Board.

Nevertheless, when there is a sizable short interest, the market is generally considered to be in a strong position. This may seem strange, but the fact of the matter is that that short interest does represent a cushion of buy orders. Those men who are short stock are ultimately going to have to buy, and their buying will help stabilize the market, maybe even force it up.

The *Dow theory* is at once the most celebrated, complicated, and least-understood interpretation of market action, probably because neither Charles Dow, who founded the Dow Jones Company, nor any of his various disciples has ever defined the theory precisely.

In essence, the Dow theorists hold that there is a primary movement in the market at all times — a kind of basic tidal action. Then there's a secondary movement which might be likened to waves. And finally there are the ripples on the surface that represent the daily movement of prices. They contend that it is possible to tell when either the primary or secondary direction changes by comparing the actions of the industrial and rail averages — Dow-Jones averages, of course. When both of them move in the same direction for a given period of time, either notably up or down, they are supposed to indicate a significant change in the direction of the market which will hold good until the two averages "confirm" each other again in an opposite direction.

This is what the learned market experts are talking about when they say "the rails confirmed the industrials" — or when they worry publicly about the failure of one to confirm the other.

Dow theorists contend that by their somewhat nebulous formula they have been able to forecast almost every significant movement in the market for many years. Other analysts, looking at the same set of facts, dispute the Dow theory's record. They say it can only be made to look good when the forecasting has become history. Nevertheless, many financial editors continue to expound the Dow theory, and various Dow disciples appear in the advertising columns from time to time, offering a letter service — usually short-lived — to explain the market action in Dow terms.

Very often in the reading of his newspaper, the new investor will encounter what appears to be a striking contradiction between the news and the market reaction to that news.

A company declares a special dividend — and its stock drops in price.

Sales of automobiles show surprising strength for some months — but motor stocks remain sluggish all through this period.

Congress enacts a new tax bill which lightens the tax burden on business — and the day it is passed, stocks sell off.

There is one simple explanation for these paradoxes: The stock market has *"discounted" the news*. The big traders, the people supposedly in the know, were sure that a special dividend was coming, because the company's profits had been increasing spectacularly. The strong demand for new automobiles didn't surprise them; they had been expecting it. And as for the tax legislation favorable to business, they would have been surprised if Congress hadn't enacted it. They had already bought or sold in expectation of these developments, and when the actual news breaks attracted public interest in the market, the professionals seized their opportunity to realize profits — to sell when others bought.

Some people consider the market an infallible barometer of general business. They say that you can tell what's going to happen to business by the way the stock market acts over a period of time.

Actually, this theory doesn't stand the light of investigation, and those who hold to it have a tall job of explaining to do if they try to account for even a few of the most glaring exceptions.

For instance, business conditions began to look a little less than rosy in the late spring of 1929, but it was not until late October of that year that the market hit the big slide, with some popular stocks slumping 100 points or more in four successive trading sessions, during which more than 40,000,000 shares of stock changed hands.

More recently the stock market has performed little better as a guide to our economic health; since the end of World War II, it has missed the boat on several important turns in business.

Thus, in 1945, business was retarded by the necessity of reconverting from war to peace, but the stock market kept boiling happily along until mid-1946, then declined 21% in five months when business had already begun to improve. The economy continued steadily on the upgrade for several years, but the market didn't catch up with this postwar boom until early 1949.

The market did turn down before general business in late 1948, early 1953, and mid-1957, but it gave an utterly fallacious signal in the first six months of 1962 when stocks sold off 25%, while business generally continued to boom merrily along, unperturbed by the Wall Street Cassandras.

But if the stock market doesn't faithfully anticipate business, it must sooner or later fall into step with the basic business trends, because in the end, stock values are determined by our economic health. That's why the investor is well advised to keep his eye on some of the more basic *indexes* of business such as the Federal Reserve index of industrial production and various series on employment, steel output, electric power production, construction, carloadings, retail sales, unfilled orders, and prices, both for farm goods and industrial raw materials, as well as data on credit, bank deposits, and interest rates. These will tell him how much America is producing, how rapidly this output is moving into the channels of distribution, and what kind of consumer demand there is for it. In the long run, these are the vital factors that will determine the real values of the stock that you own in any company — how much the company is likely to earn and what kind of dividend it can pay.

Obviously, if he reads the financial pages of his newspaper, the investor will gain something of an insight into what's happening to business. But the daily reports often lack continuity. The reader is unable to see the forest for the trees.

Many an investor who wants to be sure that he has a solid and well-balanced view of the business scene finds it desirable to subscribe to some specialized publication, such as the daily *Wall Street Journal* ($26 a year) or *Business Week* ($8). And because political developments are increasingly important in the conduct of business affairs, the *Kiplinger Washington Letter* ($24) and the *Whaley-Eaton American Letter* ($50) are also widely read by investors.

Still others look to Washington for another reason: because various government publications provide the most authoritative data about business conditions, however dully, at the lowest cost. Most noteworthy of these are the Council of Economic Advisors' *Economic Indicators,* a monthly compilation of more than 200 basic economic measures (including charts), and the Commerce Department's *Survey of Current Business,* a monthly collection of several thousand statistical series originating both in government and in business. An even sharper focus on key indicators that often point the way in which our economic cycle is moving is provided by *Business Cycle Developments.* Issued monthly by the Commerce Department ($6 a year), this valuable publication covers about ninety principal statistical series with over three hundred components. The Federal Reserve Board's monthly *Bulletin* is another important and reliable source of information about our economic health.

In addition to general business publications there are, of course, the financial periodicals — *Barron's* ($15), *Financial World* ($24), *Forbes* ($7.50), and the *Magazine of Wall Street*

($25) — that undertake to appraise the business situation primarily in terms of stock market values.

Perhaps as helpful a publication as any in this business and financial field is the *Exchange*, which is published monthly by the New York Stock Exchange and costs subscribers only $2 a year. And for the investor with an interest in companies listed on the American Stock Exchange, that exchange makes available its very readable *American Investor* at a nominal price of $2 a year.

But all of these publications and services leave the investor, in the final analysis, to work out his own destiny. They give him basic information, but they can't tell him precisely what he should do about it.

CHAPTER 26

Financial Advice—
at a Price

Do you want help with your investment problem — information, advice, recommendations?

You can get it — at a price. Whether it's worth the price you pay is something else again.

Maybe you want something more than advice. Maybe you don't want to worry about your investment problem at all. If that's the case — and if you have about $100,000 to invest, preferably a good deal more — you can turn the whole matter over to some topflight *investment counselor* whose sole business is that of guiding the investment destiny of his clients — making all the buying and selling decisions for them and seeing that they are properly executed by a brokerage firm. There are more than 100 of these counseling firms that spend their full time investing other people's money — for a sizable fee, of course — in New York City alone, and there are many others in all the major cities, from coast to coast.

In the main, these investment counselors do a sound job for their clients, including many institutions, but their services are obviously beyond the reach of the average investor.

Many big-city banks will be glad to take your investment problem off your hands — but again, only at a price that most investors can't afford. One kind of service these banks offer is the *investment advisory account* for which they charge an annual management fee, usually ½ of 1%. That wouldn't be too bad, except that they expect a minimum annual fee of at least $500, often much more. So again, unless you have at least $100,000 to invest, preferably more, such service is not for you, unless some unusual circumstance, such as a long-term absence from the country, would seem to justify payment of the bank's supervision fee.

Another kind of service that many banks offer is the

common trust fund. In operating such a fund, the bank takes
the aggregate money in the individual trusts and pools it
for investment purposes, with each trust sharing in the results on a pro rata basis. This is generally not a convenient
tool for the average investor to use. He has to have sufficient
capital to justify the establishment of a trust, and he has
to be willing to accept the restrictive provision that such a
trust imposes.

Well aware of the fact that there was a demand for a kind
of pooled investment service less expensive and less cumbersome than that now generally offered by banks, the First
National City Bank of New York obtained S.E.C. approval
in 1966 for a wholly new kind of *commingled investment
account,* open to the individual investor with an initial participation of as little as $10,000 and with additional par-
ticipation units set at $1000. Under this plan, the funds of
all participants would be pooled and invested by the bank
for a management fee of ½ of 1%. Each participant, of
course, would share in the investment results of the fund
in relation to the amount of money that he put into it.
Before this commingled investment account became operative
in June 1966, it was subjected to attack in the courts
by other Wall Street interests who are competing for the
investor's dollar on much the same basis.

Is there anyone else to whom the average investor might
look for help?

Indeed yes. There are dozens of *investment advisory services,* all only too willing to help him, and they offer him a
bewildering array of publications and services. Some are simply compilations of statistical information. Some undertake
to review business conditions as they affect the investment
outlook. Some provide recommendations about hundreds
of different securities — what to buy, what to sell, what to
hold. Some, believing that good investment advice can't be
turned out on a mass-production basis, undertake to provide
a kind of tailor-made service; they offer to answer inquiries
and to permit occasional consultation with their experts. And
some even offer a reasonably well-rounded counseling service
available at a negotiated fee to the smaller investor, perhaps
the man with only $25,000 to invest in securities.

Some of the financial advisory organizations have for sale
all of these different kinds of services, while others offer
only one kind or another.

Most controversial of all the services are those that undertake to give advice about the market, usually in a weekly letter, sold on a subscription basis. Many of these publications have their own rating service covering hundreds of different stocks that tell the subscriber whether to buy or sell, and most of them maintain *supervised lists* of those investments that they consider particularly attractive. In effect, these supervised lists are supposed to represent model investment programs.

Most of these services are more concerned about the short-term outlook — what the market is likely to do in the next couple of months — than they are with the problem of long-term investment. A few of them even limit themselves almost exclusively to a discussion of technical factors in the market.

There is one other common characteristic which these services share: They will all tell you how successful they've been in calling the turns in the market and in recommending good buys and good sells at just the strategic moment.

Technically, the S.E.C. has regulatory authority over these services as far as their advertising and public communications are concerned, but there are those who feel that this is one area in which the S.E.C. hasn't done the housecleaning job it might. In the financial section of almost every big Sunday newspaper, you can find many of these services advertising all kinds of pie-in-the-sky — "20 stocks that are good buys today" . . . "50 stocks that lag behind the market" . . . "120 stocks to protect you in a bear market."

In bringing these services to heel, the commission is admittedly handicapped by not having an industry organization like the New York Stock Exchange to share the regulatory responsibility. It has tried to induce the advisory services to organize some kind of an organization, but the services, realizing how much easier it would then be for the S.E.C. to bring pressure to bear on them, have turned a deaf ear. Then too, such highly ethical and responsible organizations as Standard & Poor's and Moody's Investors Service have an understandable reluctance to be associated on any basis whatsoever with the obvious quacks in the business.

In the absence of an industry organization to pursue a program of self-regulation, the S.E.C. can accomplish its housecleaning job on a piecemeal basis by bringing legal action against palpable offenders. This course is not only time-consuming and expensive, but the commission is discouraged about its effectiveness as a result of an unexpected setback it received in the action it brought against the Capital Gains Research Bureau. In this action, the S.E.C. alleged that officers of the Bureau were guilty of price manipulation by buying stock, touting it, then selling out when the price advanced. The S.E.C. failed to make its charge stick in court, and loss of the case put a crimp in its regulatory work as far as the advisory services are concerned.

Actually, how good is the advice these services provide?

There's no answer to that, because there is no way to compute and compare their batting averages. Some make flat-footed recommendations, and some hedge their suggestions with all kinds of qualifications. However, one stock market analyst who did keep check on sixteen services for a period of years found that if an investor had followed all their 7500 different recommendations, he would have ended up just 1.43% worse than the market averages.

Here are some of the best-known services:

Companies rendering a comprehensive research and advisory service:

The biggest firms in the financial research business are:

STANDARD & POOR'S CORPORATION, 345 HUDSON STREET, NEW YORK, NEW YORK 10014

MOODY'S INVESTORS SERVICE, 99 CHURCH STREET, NEW YORK, NEW YORK 10007

Known primarily as publishers of financial data, these two firms supply the entire investment business, including all the other advisory services, with the basic facts and figures on all securities sold in the public market and on the companies that issue them. Many of their publications, such as those dealing exclusively with bonds, are too specialized to be of significance to the average investor, but both he and his broker would be utterly lost if it were not for the complete and detailed information which these organizations supply on stocks, both listed and unlisted.

Much of the research material supplied by one firm is also supplied by the other, but they use different methods of organizing and publishing the material.

Most fundamental of all the reference books are Standard

& Poor's *Corporation Records* and Moody's *Manuals.* In these massive volumes, running into tens of thousands of pages, you'll find a brief history of virtually every publicly owned company in the United States and full financial data running from the present back over a period of years — figures on assets, income, earnings, dividends, and stock prices.

Standard & Poor's *Corporation Records* consist of six loose-leaf volumes in which reports on nearly 7000 individual companies are arranged in alphabetical order. These reports, providing all the basic financial data, are revised whenever new annual reports are issued or other important developments alter the outlook for a company; daily supplements are issued every two months summarizing news bulletins on a company-by-company basis. Standard & Poor's also has a special service reviewing conditions industry by industry. These industry surveys, supplemented by a monthly *Trends and Projections Bulletin,* cover developments in 44 industries with 1000 different companies. It is also the publisher of the authoritative daily *Dividend Record.*

Moody's presents its financial information on publicly owned securities in five twice-weekly publications covering municipal bonds, banks and finance, industrials, public utilities, and transportation. Subscribers to each of these publications receive an annual bound volume containing basic descriptions of these companies and investment situations at no extra cost.

These services, keeping abreast of all corporate facts and figures, are far too costly for most individuals. Nor is it necessary for a man to spend several hundred dollars a year on them, since he can usually refer to them in his broker's office, or his registered representative can get for him the information he wants on any company.

Both of the agencies, for instance, have a bulletin or report service on all the leading companies. In these bulletins, all the essential facts about a company are condensed on a single sheet, and all of them give some sort of opinion or evaluation of the company's stock. Most brokers subscribe to one or both of these services and make the data freely available to their customers or prospective customers.

Even more condensed information is provided in the *Stock Guide,* a pocket-size manual published by Standard & Poor's. Here in tabular form the investor can find the high-and-low prices over the past few years, current data on as-

sets, earnings, and dividends, figures on institutional holdings, and Standard & Poor's own quality ratings for 4750
common and preferred stocks, listed and unlisted. A new
edition of the *Stock Guide,* complete with lists of stocks
recommended for different objectives, is issued monthly, and
the service is priced at $24 a year. Many brokers give occa-
sional free copies of this manual to their customers and
prospects.

For the individual investor, both Standard & Poor's and
Moody's have special services and letters that comment on
business developments as they affect the outlook for individual stocks and industries. Standard & Poor's has its weekly
Outlook, a twelve-page weekly market letter ($65 a year);
a daily *Facts and Forecast Service* ($150); an *Investment
Advisory Survey* ($65), which consists of an eight-page con-
fidential bulletin featuring a supervised list of recommended
investments; and a *Portfolio Review Service* ($100), which
offers analysis of a subscriber's holdings and full inquiry
privilege, specific recommendations on what to buy or sell,
plus the *Outlook* or *Investment Advisory Survey.*

Moody's *Stock Survey,* a weekly letter of eight to ten
pages, reviews market conditions and analyzes various investment opportunities. Subscribers also receive a quarterly
handbook of common stocks, containing charts and data on
hundreds of different companies, and they are entitled to
review, inquiry, and consultation privileges ($144 a year).
In addition, Moody's offers its *Investors Advisory Service,*
consisting of the stock survey plus individual advisory reports, kept constantly up to date, on subscriber's holdings
($180 on ten securities, $3 for each additional security).

Finally, each of the services — Standard & Poor's and
Moody's — offer an individual investment counseling service at an annual retainer fee.

Chart and statistical services:

M. C. HORSEY & CO., 37 WALL STREET, NEW YORK,
NEW YORK 10005

Horsey's *Stock Picture,* issued bimonthly, provides price
charts on more than 1600 stocks for periods of time ranging
from 5 to 15 years. The cost of an annual subscription is
$60; the price of a single copy is $11. Included free with
an annual subscription is a copy of the *25-Year Picture,*

a compilation of charts on 239 companies covering a period of at least 25 years; if purchased separately, the cost
is $11. Charts in both publications show earnings, dividends,
and present capitalization.

F. W. STEPHENS CO., P. O. BOX A, NEWFOUNDLAND,
NEW JERSEY 07435

Stephens's *Graphic Stocks* contains charts on 1524 listed
stocks covering the most recent eleven-year period, complete
with data on earnings, dividends, and trading volume. It is
published bimonthly at an annual cost of $70 or a single-
copy price of $15. As a supplement to this service, the com-
pany also publishes *A Long Look at the Market* containing
charts on 85 companies back through 1929 (cost $10) and a
special edition of *Graphic Stocks* containing 744 charts for
the period 1924-1935 (cost $25). Stephens will also make
charts on individual listed stocks to order for any period of
time.

TRENDLINE CORP., 345 HUDSON STREET, NEW YORK,
NEW YORK 10014

Trendline, which is owned by Standard & Poor's but
functions as an independent division, publishes three major
stock market chart services. *Daily Basis Stock Charts,* covering 578 companies and 14 market indicators, is published
weekly. Each company chart shows the daily high, low,
close, volume, and 200-day moving average for the past
seven months, as well as a yearly range chart for 10 years.
Earnings figures with comparisons for eight quarters, dividends, and capitalization data are also provided. (The
cost is $225 a year or $5 a copy.) *Current Market Per-
spectives,* published monthly, includes charts of 960 individual companies showing the weekly high, low, close, and
volume for the last four years; along with historical price-
earnings ratios. The cost is $72 a year or $10 a copy.
Trendline also publishes the bimonthly *OTC Chart Manual*
which includes charts of over 840 leading over-the-counter
stocks and mutual funds. Each chart includes weekly high,
low, and closing bid prices for two years, annual price ranges
for eight years, and an earnings-dividend record for six years.
The cost is $75 for 6 issues or $15 a copy.

STUDLEY, SHUPERT STATISTICS, INC., 155 BERKELEY
STREET, BOSTON, MASSACHUSETTS 02116

Studley, Shupert's *Industrial Service* provides data running
back to 1929 on over 380 companies. All balance sheet
and income statement figures are included along with pertinent ratios, as well as the compound rate of growth for
both five-year and ten-year periods on sales, earnings per
share, and dividends per share. It is published annually
and is supplemented throughout the subscription year with
current data. Studley, Shupert also publishes the *Public
Utility Service* which provides data back to 1929 on about
170 utilities and telephone companies. It is published annually and supplemented throughout the year. The cost is
$400. The *Industry Composite Service* provides factual data
on 21 industries. It is published annually and dovetailed
with the company's *Industrial Service*. Data are presented
in a manner to facilitate a ready comparison of a company's
performance with that of any other company in the same
industry or with the composite performance of the group.
The cost of the *Industrial Service*, including the *Industry
Composite Service*, is $600 a year. The *Industry Composite
Service* alone costs $500.

*Companies offering business and investment advisory
services:*

ALEXANDER HAMILTON INSTITUTE, INC., 235 EAST 42 STREET,
NEW YORK, NEW YORK 10017

The Business Conditions Service offered by this well-
known organization is built primarily around its *Weekly
Newsletter of Management Principles,* a report on the latest
business practices and management techniques. This letter
also contains a weekly review of the economy. Additionally,
subscribers receive a *Weekly Investment Bulletin* which, in
addition to the usual market comments, maintains continuous
supervision over some 35 bonds, 15 preferreds, and 50 common stocks and gives special recommendations to buy, hold,
or sell. Two or three noteworthy stocks are discussed in
greater detail. The service includes other monthly bulletins
entitled *Business Progress, Personal Management,* and *Tax
Review*. The subscriber is also entitled to advice and information on his personal investment and business problems,

on request. The annual single-payment fee for the Business Conditions Service is $61.

AMERICAN INSTITUTE FOR ECONOMIC RESEARCH, GREAT BARRINGTON, MASSACHUSETTS

This independent scientific and educational organization undertakes to make the results of its fundamental research in economics available to the average man through the financial assistance provided by the annual sustaining members of the Institute. Its weekly *Research Reports* review in chart and text the most basic factors affecting supply, demand, and prices. The Institute also publishes basic studies in inflation, life insurance, investment trusts, social security, and the like, usually at $1 each. (A sustaining membership, including all publications, is $35 a year.) In order to retain its tax exemption, the Institute transferred to American Institute Counselors, Incorporated, its investment advisory services, including the *Investment Bulletin*, which covers three typical investment plans, designed for different objectives, and recommends specific securities for each plan. These plans are for long-term investment; no attempt is made to forecast short swings or technical movements. The cost of the *Investment Bulletin* is $10 a year, and all after-tax profits are turned over to the Institute.

AMERICAN INVESTORS SERVICE, 88 FIELD POINT ROAD, GREENWICH, CONNECTICUT 06830

On the assumption that most market moves are generated by conditions within the market itself rather than by economic factors, the weekly *Market Trend Analysis* and *Stock Selection Reports* of this service focus primarily on matters of timing and selection as influenced by technical conditions. However involved these considerations may be, the service reduces them all to a series of specific recommendations about what stocks to buy; thereafter these are marked hold, until a specific sell recommendation is made. (The price is $129 a year; $10 for a ten-week trial.) American Investors also renders an Account Management Service under which it assumes complete responsibility as to placing orders for a client's portfolio. Costs begin at ½ of 1% a quarter on the first $100,000 of holdings and are graduated down to ¼ of 1% on holdings in excess of $200,000. The minimum quarterly fee is $500.

BABSON'S REPORTS, INC., WELLESLEY HILLS, MASSACHUSETTS 02181

The Babson organization, founded in 1904 by Roger W. Babson, offers investors three different advisory services — a consultation service at $156 a year, a quarterly portfolio appraisal and review service at $384 a year (includes four complete reviews of the client's portfolio each year), and a complete investment management service at $1200 a year. The three service rates are fixed fees. No additional charges are made based on portfolio value or income. The company's *Investment and Barometer Letter* is supplied as a supplement to all three services.

INTERNATIONAL STATISTICAL BUREAU, 350 FIFTH AVENUE, NEW YORK, NEW YORK 10001

In the publication of its twice-weekly *Selected Securities Guide,* the Bureau draws on the business information which it gathers for its other specialized services covering such fields as metals, textiles, housing, distribution. In addition to reports on individual securities, the *Guide,* priced at $100 a year, makes specific recommendations on what to buy or sell and when to do it. Ratings on individual stocks indicate prices at which they may be considered cheap or over-valued for either long-term or short-term holdings. The Bureau also publishes a *Business and Investment Service* which provides more basic information on business and market trends, and the subscriber to this service gets the Bureau's other services — the *Guide,* and the monthly *Trend of Distribution* — at a price of $125 a year.

FORBES INVESTORS ADVISORY INSTITUTE, INC., 60 FIFTH AVENUE, NEW YORK, NEW YORK 10011

Owned by the publisher of *Forbes* magazine, the Institute provides a variety of investment services. *The Forbes Investor* is a weekly eight-page advisory publication containing specific recommendations on one or more stocks and current opinion on those previously recommended; its cost is $65 a year. *The Forbes Special Situation Survey* provides twelve reports a year at an annual cost of $150, each report covering one "high-potential" situation for those able to assume the risk, and all such situations are kept under review while still recommended. The Institute's *Portfolio Management Program* consists of a quarterly manual which recommends four different portfolios, consisting of ten stocks each; these portfolios are designed for growth, speculation, income, and a combination of growth and income. Cost of the program is $35 a year. Finally, Forbes offers its *Guide to Common Stock Profits,* a manual covering 40 stocks in seven investment categories. The cost of the manual is $15, but for an additional $25 the subscriber receives for two years reports at least quarterly on all stocks covered.

UNITED BUSINESS AND INVESTMENT SERVICE,
210 NEWBERRY STREET, BOSTON, MASSACHUSETTS 02116

Each issue of its comprehensive *Weekly Report* contains a review of the business outlook, a report on Washington developments, a forecast of commodity prices, an appraisal of the stock market, and specific recommendations for buying or selling different stocks. Regular reports are made on all stocks that are kept on supervised lists. Periodic features include analyses of individual stocks and groups of stocks, a report on bonds, various statistical indexes of business and a summary of the opinions and recommendations of other leading advisory services. The total cost is $72 a year, $38 for six months, and a subscription also includes personal consultation.

ARTHUR WIESENBERGER & CO., 61 BROADWAY,
NEW YORK, NEW YORK 10006

This stock exchange member firm draws on its direct contact with the market and with substantial institutional investors in publishing the semi-monthly *Wiesenberger Investment Report* ($75 a year). The *Report* picks out a relatively few stocks for intensive analysis and follows them up regularly. In each issue, it also appraises market trends and recommends investment policy. Another Wiesenberger publication is *Findings & Forecasts,* which examines the stock market and individual stocks from the point of view of timing and investor psychology; its cost is $500 or — for the firm's clients — $1500 in commission costs. Particularly outstanding is Wiesenberger's annual edition of *Investment Companies*, a compilation of the essential facts about all leading investment trusts, closed-end and open-end. This standard reference work is invaluable to the investor who may feel that he wants to buy a mutual fund for the protection it affords him but who doesn't know which one to buy or where to get the facts and figures that will enable him to come to an intelligent decision. Its price is $40.

CHAPTER 27

How Your Broker
Can Help You

In the last analysis, the best answer that any investor can find to the problem of what stocks to buy is likely to be the answer that he works out for himself through study and investigation.

But where, you ask, can the average man who is willing to do his own investigating turn for the facts and the information he needs? The answer to that is — his broker, preferably a member firm of the New York Stock Exchange.

Perhaps you think this is dubious advice. After all, isn't a broker interested in selling securities? Yes, a broker is a salesman. But that doesn't mean that your interests and his are completely opposed. Quite the contrary. Any salesman of any product wants his customer to be satisfied, because that's the best way of building his own business. That's especially true of the broker.

Then, too, there's an important difference between him and other salesmen. The automobile salesman wants to sell you a particular car. The insurance salesman wants to sell you a policy in his company. The salesman for a financial advisory service wants to sell you that service and nothing else.

As far as his own commission is concerned, the broker, as a general rule, doesn't care which Big Board stocks you buy. He has essentially no ax to grind, at least as far as listed securities are concerned, because he stands to make just the same commission on the same total investment. When it comes to over-the-counter stocks, admittedly, he could have an ax to grind, but most brokers realize that such a self-seeking policy can prove to be bad business in the long run.

All this is not intended to imply that the brokerage business is wholly without sin. Any business has a certain number of sinners in it, and if that business happens to involve

the handling of money, large sums of money, as the brokerage business certainly does, it is likely to have an even
greater-than-average number of sinners, do what you will
to exorcise them.

Over the years, the brokerage business has done an un-
paralleled job of policing itself, or trying to rid itself of
any unprincipled and unscrupulous element, and in recent
years it has redoubled its efforts. That increased effort can
be traced directly to the publication in 1963 of the S.E.C.'s
final report to Congress on its study of the securities business and to the enactment of the Securities Exchange Act
of 1964.

The S.E.C. made it unmistakably clear then that it intended to extend its regulatory surveillance to all the branch
offices of all the member firms all over the country and to
every man in every office. Furthermore, the commission made
it equally clear that unless the exchange, which it accused
of treating disciplinary matters too tenderly, did a competent policing job, it would hold the exchange and the
member firms responsible. The result was that the exchange
quickly organized its own police force and scheduled surprise calls on branch offices all across the country, checking
customer trading records and registered representatives. And
a number of member firms followed suit.

What were these policemen — or compliance officers, as
they were euphemistically called — looking for? In general,
they were looking for any abuses of public confidence.

In particular, they were looking for evidence of *"churn-
ing,"* the overstimulation of customers' trading in order to
build commission revenues.

They were looking for high-pressure salesmanship — telephone calls at night, undue persuasion of widows, attempts
to prey on the unsophisticated and the unsuspecting.

They were looking for misrepresentation . . . "It's bound
to go up . . . you can't miss."

They were looking for abuses of the discretionary authority that a customer sometimes gives his broker to manage
his account, to buy or sell as he likes.

They were looking for margin trading by customers who
plainly lacked the resources to undertake the risks involved.

They were looking for the flagrant incompetence or the
willful malfeasance that could result in the recommendation
of a clearly unsuitable investment — a highly speculative

penny stock for a retired couple to whom safety of capital was paramount.

They were looking for situations in which securities firms, or even individual partners or salesmen, sought to further their own undisclosed interest in a stock by promoting its sale in order to enhance the value of their own holdings.

In summary, they were looking for any abuse of what has come to be known in Wall Street as the S.E.C. *"shingle theory"* — the theory that when a broker hangs out his shingle he guarantees to the world that he will deal fairly and honestly with his customers.

The S.E.C. had said that it would hold the home-office executives of member firms wholly responsible for supervising their branch offices, and if there was any doubt on that score, it quickly vanished when the S.E.C. and the N.A.S.D. instituted actions against several leading firms. Those actions resulted not only in the expulsion of individual employees and branch office managers, but in fines and suspensions levied against the firms' top officials in Wall Street.

The public furor stirred up by these headlined cases was actually disproportionate to the problem involved. Admittedly, there were some sharp operators, unethical and unscrupulous men, among the 25,000 registered representatives then employed. Admittedly, top management among the member firms had been lax in exercising supervisory responsibility. And admittedly, the exchange had been less than stern in its disciplinary actions.

Still the fact remains that the business as a whole adheres to a standard of ethics and a concern for the public good that few other businesses can match.

And still the fact also remains that the vast, vast majority of registered representatives are honest, are scrupulous, are trustworthy, and are sincerely concerned about the welfare of their customers.

But even if the reliability of your broker can be taken for granted, what about his ability? How competent is he likely to be when it comes to giving you sound advice about your money and how to invest it?

Obviously, that's a question to which there is no absolute answer. Nobody could possibly contend that all the thousands of men in the business are preeminently well qualified to give investment help. Some are and some aren't. But thanks to the training programs that many leading brokerage firms have been operating for years now — some for as long as two decades — the standards of professional ability have been steadily raised. Most of these programs are of six months' duration, and with half that time spent in the classroom, eight hours a day, the graduates can be considered to be pretty knowledgeable about the investment business, even before they start to work in it.

Certainly this much can be said: As a general rule, there isn't anybody to whom you can go who is apt to be nearly as well qualified — not your banker, not your lawyer, and certainly not just a business associate or the fellow in the club car.

After all, the registered representative works at the job of investing at least seven hours a day, five days a week, and he has been doing it for years. He has facts, figures, and information at his fingertips that nobody else can lay hold of easily. He has easy access to the basic reference works — Standard & Poor's *Corporation Records* or Moody's *Manuals* — and he can get detailed data on almost any publicly owned company in the United States.

"Investigate before you invest" is still one of the soundest pieces of advice anyone can give you. And you might start your investigating by thumbing through either Standard & Poor's monthly *Stock Summary* or the *Monthly Stock Digest,* published by Data Digests, Inc., which most member firms will supply on request without charge. Either of these two publications will at least give you an idea of the kind of information you should have about any stock before buying it. The *Stock Summary* is a 40-page condensation of Standard & Poor's *Stock Guide,* providing key data on all New York Stock Exchange stocks, 450 stocks listed on the American and regional exchanges, and more than 650 over-the-counter stocks. The *Stock Digest* covers a somewhat greater number of stocks and provides even more detailed data on the trend of earnings and dividends plus thumbnail charts to show the nine-month price trend of each stock.

If this preliminary investigation leads you to develop an interest in several specific stocks, most brokers will be glad to supply you — within reason, of course — with free reports on these companies, reports that they buy from accepted research services or reports that are prepared by their own *research departments*.

In the brokerage business today, research has become vitally important, for it is the one service that can give a firm a genuine competitive advantage. No member firm can buy a listed stock for you any cheaper than another firm. They all pay the same price for it on the exchange at any given moment, and they all charge the same commission. But not all firms can give you the same well-qualified advice about how good a particular listed stock — or an unlisted stock, for that matter — may be for you in your particular circumstances and with your particular investment objective.

That's why a decision about which brokerage firm to use can be as important as deciding which stock to buy. How can you form an opinion about which broker might best be able to help you? Well, you might visit three or four different ones and ask them about the same stock. That would give you some idea of how well-informed each one was, what kind of research service each one provided.

Or better yet, write a letter to several firms and solicit the advice of their research departments about what you ought to buy. Most brokers handle many, many such letters every year, and generally they make no charge. If they do charge, they'll tell you, and you can decide whether you want to pay the fee or not. On the basis of their replies, you can make a reasonably informed judgment about the quality of their research — provided, of course, that you have leveled with them and given them detailed information about how much money you have to invest, what your financial situation is, and what you most want out of your investments. The more complete the information you provide about your circumstances, the more pertinent the broker's recommendations are apt to be.

And you need not feel that you are imposing on a broker to ask for this service, for many of them freely advertise their willingness to set up a program for the new investor or to review the holdings of present shareowners, whether customers or not, and make suggestions about what to buy or what to sell — and why.

A good research department is staffed with analysts who spend their full time following developments in certain assigned industries. Through business and industrial publications and some of the more reliable financial advisory services, an analyst keeps up with the published information on his industries, including, of course, the reports of competitive brokers. He establishes and maintains close contact with key officials in all the major companies in the fields he covers and visits frequently with them. Over the years, such officials have come to respect the qualified securities analyst, and they level with him about new products or services, company development plans, and the projected trend of earnings and dividends. Frequently, in a very real sense of the word, the good analyst today does obtain inside information, and he does have a basis for evaluating that one vital factor affecting a company's destiny which always eludes exact measurement — the quality of its management.

It is the analyst's responsibility at all times to see that his firm's registered representatives are fully informed about all important developments affecting the companies he follows, and periodically he prepares reports on these companies for distribution to the firm's customers and the public. These research reports are a far cry from the old *"broker's letter,"* a catch-as-catch-can commentary on the stock market, liberally interspersed with tips on what to buy or what to sell. Today, the typical research report on a company, prepared and distributed by a member firm, is a substantial piece of work, factual and honest. So that the customer may allow for any possible bias, some firms even go so far as to disclose in such reports any special interest which the firm or its owners might have in the stock as a result of their own substantial holdings or representation on the company's board of directors or a long-standing underwriting relationship. And if the S.E.C. has its way, such disclosures will become much more commonplace.

In recent years securities analysts have found a valuable new tool to aid them in their complicated studies. That tool is the high-speed computer, including all the paraphernalia that goes with a complete electronic data-processing system. Since the early sixties, major brokerage firms have been equipped with sophisticated computers — their number increases steadily — and since that time Standard & Poor's Corporation has made available to them, as well as banks, mutual funds, and other big financial institutions, its *Compustat* service, which consists of reels of magnetic tape on which are recorded all the essential data — literally millions of figures from balance sheets and income statements — for about 900 major industrial corporations and 100 utilities. These data are on an annual basis from 1946 to 1961 and on a quarterly basis since then.

As a consequence, security analysts no longer have to work endless hours digging the figures they need out of old corporate reports and performing calculations of their own to arrive at a reliable statistical analysis of a company's performance as compared with its competitors. All the analysts have to do now is ask the computer for the answer.

And in 1966, Standard & Poor's announced a new development that combines its Compustat tapes, the computer, and video transmission. With this system, an analyst in a firm that subscribes to the service is able to sit at his desk, punch a few keys, and have projected on a nearby video screen all the endless statistical information that Compustat provides. He might, for instance, want a chart that would compare a company's price-earnings ratio with that of an industry group as a whole. If he does, it is right at his fingertips.

Although computer-oriented research can be regarded as still in its infancy, brokerage firms have already found the machine particularly useful in three areas — information retrieval, security selection, and portfolio management.

Several large firms have already set up systems so that representatives in their branch offices can have direct wire access to the computer and retrieve instantly from its vast "memory" the latest opinion of the firm's research department on four or five thousand different stocks. The individual registered representative could not be expected to have valid information and opinions on anything like that many stocks to satisfy a customer who wants to know what he thinks about this company or that one. Now, if he works for a firm with a computer-operated retrieval system, all he has to do is punch a few keys and instantly, no matter how far away he is — even Europe — he gets by teletype wire a printed summary of the analyst's latest thinking about the stock, complete with his projections for earnings, dividends, and future price range. It is, of course, the responsibility of the research department at headquarters to see that the information file in the computer is kept constantly up-to-date.

In the area of security selection, the vast capacity of the computer makes it possible to screen rapidly an almost unlimited number of securities in order to find those that will match some predetermined set of standards — stocks that have shown consistent growth of earnings over some specified period, or stocks whose price performance has exceeded some established yardstick by a significant margin, or stocks that match some particular standard for dividend-payout in relation to earnings. In using computers in this fashion, the analyst establishes the criteria and lets the machine survey the field to find those that meet his standards. The ultimate objective of this kind of computer research is to find stocks that are undervalued or overvalued in relation to the market as a whole or any specified segment of it.

Portfolio management by computer is really only a further development of the techniques used in stock selection. To find stocks suitable for the investor interested in liberal income, the computer is used to review a vast number of alternative investments — a far greater number than an individual analyst could review in months or years — and because of the computer's high speed, the job is done in a matter of minutes.

The technical market analyst who is interested in trying to predict short swings in the market on the basis of such factors as the volume of short selling, the ratio of odd-lot to round-lot transactions, cyclical and random variations in price movements, and other esoteric data finds in the computer the answer to an infinity of mathematical problems he has wrestled with for years.

The advent of the computer has had one interesting effect on the analyst himself. Accustomed over the years to generalizations about the probable price action of a stock — "although short-term prospects are not promising, there is appreciable potential for long-term growth" — the analyst now finds it necessary to express his opinion in specific figures if his projections are to be used in any kind of a computer program. He must say, for instance, that over the next three months he expects no more than a 1% increase in the price of a given stock, while over a five-year period he anticipates a 12% price appreciation. The necessity of replacing qualitative judgments with quantitative predictions has had the salutary effect of sharpening his evaluations and even improving his accuracy.

How much you lean on your broker for help is up to you. You can in special circumstances open a discretionary account and give him a power of attorney to make all buying and selling decisions for you, but most brokers are loath to accept such complete responsibility for an account because losses, no matter how small or infrequent, breed trouble and discontent. They prefer to act on your specific instructions. That's why some brokers won't even accept discretionary accounts. One thing you can be sure of: Lacking such instructions, no reputable broker, no member firm of the New York Stock Exchange, is going to "put you into" some stock or "sell you out" of it. As a general rule, the registered representative today wants you to assume responsibility for managing your own investments — with his help.

He'll be glad to get you the facts and figures you need and to help you to interpret them, but he prefers that the decisions about what to buy and what to sell be wholly your own. For one thing, you'll be less inclined to blame him for whatever might go wrong if you determine your own investment course. More important, he knows that in the long run you are going to be a better and more successful investor. You'll have a greater interest in the problem, and you'll be more willing to work at the job of investing.

Many new investors today are learning the ropes in this investment business on a cooperative basis through the medium of an *investment club*. Typically, an investment club will be composed of a dozen or more neighbors, business associates, fellow commuters, or brother lodge members who meet together once a month, put $10 or $20 apiece into a common pool, and then spend an hour or two discussing the best possible investment for their money. These are serious sessions in which the pros and cons of various stocks are ardently debated. The rise of the investment club has been little short of meteoric, and in 1966, it was conservatively estimated that there were at least 40,000 clubs with some 600,000 members. Information on how to start an investment club is available in the form of a kit costing $3 from the National Association of Investment Clubs (Washington Boulevard Bldg., Detroit, Michigan 48226).

Despite the bookkeeping problems and occasionally the legal complications which such club business creates, brokers' representatives are more than willing as a rule to provide the clubs with company reports and meet with them to answer questions and guide the discussions. The commission return is negligible, but the opportunity for valuable missionary work, for educating club members in the techniques of investing, is tremendous. And many a worthwhile individual account has been generated by participation in an investment club.

One thing is sure: investment club members get a good grounding in the investment facts of life. They learn, as every investor must, that it's a difference of opinion that makes the market.

If you as an investor can arrive at buying or selling decisions that are better grounded in fact than the other fellow's, you are going to be right more often than he is. It's just that simple — and that complex.

CHAPTER 28

Can You
"Beat the Market"?

Isn't there any system to "beat the market," any system that will protect you against price fluctuations and virtually guarantee you a profit over the long pull?

Yes, there are such systems, and some of them work pretty well. They are far from foolproof, but at least they do point out some important lessons about successful investing. They are called dollar cost averaging and formula investing.

Dollar cost averaging simply involves putting the same fixed amount of money — $200, $500, $1000 — into the same stock, regardless of its price movement, at regular intervals — say, every month or every six months or so — over a long period of time. The Monthly Investment Plan is built on precisely this basis.

Following a system of investing a fixed sum of money in the same stock at regular intervals, you could have made a profit on probably 90% of the stocks listed on the New York Stock Exchange over almost any period of fifteen or twenty years you might want to pick.

Dollar cost averaging works simply because you buy more shares of a stock with your fixed amount of money when the stock is low in price than you do when it is comparatively high, and when the stock rises again, you make a profit on the greater number of shares you got at low cost.

Suppose you bought $500 worth of a particular stock when it was selling at $10 a share, another $500 worth three months later when it was $9, another $500 worth at $8, and so on, while the stock fell to $5, then rose to $15, and settled back to $10. If you then sold out, you would be able to show a profit of about 10%, ignoring both dividends and commission costs, despite the fact that you had paid an average price of $10 and sold out at exactly that same price. You don't believe it?

Don't bother to figure it out, because here's the proof. To avoid the complication of fractional shares of stock, it is assumed that at every different price level the buyer would purchase whatever number of shares would yield a total cost nearest $500.

Price per Share	Number of Shares Purchased	Cost of Shares	Number of Shares Owned	Cumulative Cost of Shares	Total Value of Shares
$10	50	$500	50	$500	$500
9	56	504	106	1004	954
8	63	504	169	1508	1352
7	71	497	240	2005	1680
6	83	498	323	2503	1938
5	100	500	423	3003	2115
6	83	498	506	3501	3036
7	71	497	577	3998	4039
8	63	504	640	4502	5120
9	56	504	696	5006	6264
10	50	500	746	5506	7460
11	45	495	791	6006	8701
12	42	504	833	6505	9996
13	38	494	871	6999	11323
14	36	504	907	7503	12698
15	33	495	940	7998	14100
14	36	504	976	8502	13664
13	38	494	1014	8996	13182
12	42	504	1056	9500	12672
11	45	495	1101	9995	12111
10	50	500	1151	10495	11510

All told, you paid $10,495, and your holdings would be worth $11,510, a gain of $1015, or almost 10%.

Exactly the same results — again exclusive of all dividends and purchase costs—would be achieved if the stock first rose steadily from $10 to $15, then dropped to $5, then came back to $10. The figures on that are in the table on page 183.

There's only one significant difference between the two tables. Note that you are considerably better off all the way along the line if your stock drops first and then comes back. Thus, in the first table, after the stock had fallen to $5 and recovered to $10, you could have sold out and made a profit of $1954, or about 35%, on your money.

So if the stock you buy drops in price and you have the confidence to believe that it will come back, as stocks in general always have, you would do well to continue buying

Price per Share	Number of Shares Purchased	Cost of Shares	Number of Shares Owned	Cumulative Cost of Shares	Total Value of Shares
$10	50	$500	50	$500	$500
11	45	495	95	995	1045
12	42	504	137	1499	1644
13	38	494	175	1993	2275
14	36	504	211	2497	2954
15	33	495	244	2992	3660
14	36	504	280	3496	3920
13	38	494	318	3990	4134
12	42	504	360	4494	4320
11	45	495	405	4989	4455
10	50	500	455	5489	4550
9	56	504	511	5993	4599
8	63	504	574	6497	4592
7	71	497	645	6994	4515
6	83	498	728	7492	4368
5	100	500	828	7992	4140
6	83	498	911	8490	5466
7	71	497	982	8987	6874
8	63	504	1045	9491	8360
9	56	504	1101	9995	9909
10	50	500	1151	10495	11510

it as it slides on down. This is called *"averaging down,"* and it's a concept which the investor who thinks the market is "too high to buy right now" might well keep in mind.

While no stock could ever follow the precise pattern set in the tables, the examples do serve to demonstrate the validity of the dollar cost averaging principle.

There's only one big catch to this system of beating the market. You've got to have the cash — yes, and the courage, too — to buy the same dollar amount of the stock at whatever interval of time you've fixed on, be it every month or three months or a year.

And if it drops, you've got to keep right on buying, in order to pick up the low-cost shares on which you can later make your profit. Unfortunately, when the stock market is down, the average man's bank account is likely to be down too, and so he often can't afford to buy at just the time he should. If instead of buying, he should have to sell at such a time, he might have to take a loss. This will always be true if a person has to sell at a price lower than the average cost of the shares he owns. In such circumstances, the dollar cost averaging technique will have provided no protection. Most times, it works over the long pull because the long-term trend of the stock market has been upward.

If a dollar cost averaging plan had been applied for twenty years at an annual rate of $1,000 a year to the stocks in Standard & Poor's 500-stock index, and if all dividends paid on these stocks had been reinvested, an investor by the end of 1965 would have realized a return more than four times his out-of-pocket investment. He would have achieved this result despite the fact that the market in that period suffered seven declines ranging from 15% to 28%.

The stock of the Radio Corporation of America offers a classic example of the advantages of dollar cost averaging. Let's assume that back at the beginning of 1929 you had a lump sum of $19,000 and you decided to invest it all in RCA stock. RCA was a popular stock then, highly regarded for its growth possibilities — just as it still is — and it was selling early in 1929 in the price range of $375 to $380 per share. So for your $19,000 you would have been able to buy 50 shares. Over the years, thanks to splits in the stock, those shares would have increased to 891 and you would have received a total of almost $7000 in dividend payments. As of mid-1966, when RCA was selling around $50 a share, your stock would have been worth about $44,000. This means that, together with your dividends, you would have realized a net gain of about $32,000 on your $19,000 investment.

That's not too bad, but consider how much more you would have made if you had followed the dollar cost averaging plan and put that same amount of money in RCA stock at the rate of approximately $500 a year for the same 37½ years. Here again it is assumed that the number of shares purchased (at the opening of the market each year) would have been that number which you could have bought for an amount closest to $500 — sometimes a little less, sometimes a little more. By June 1966, you would have owned 5262 shares of RCA, and you would have had a net gain, after payment of all brokerage commissions on your purchases, of $280,000. Of this sum, the $40,000 you would have collected in dividends would have been more than twice the total cost of your investment.

This is an especially impressive record because of the dramatic drop in the price of RCA from its 1929 high and the opportunity you would have had to pick up RCA shares at bargain levels in ensuing years. It should also be noted, however, that we would have an entirely different story to tell if we had taken 1933 as our starting date instead of 1929; then it would have been decidedly more advantageous for you to have made a big lump-sum purchase of RCA than for you to have acquired RCA stock in units of $500 a year. If you had put $17,000 into RCA at the beginning of 1933, your investment would have been worth about $800,000 in mid-1966, counting both price appreciation and dividends, whereas if you had bought the stock at the rate of $500 a year throughout the thirty-four-year period, you would have realized just a little more than 33% of that figure — a little over $265,000. But because few people have large sums that they can put into one stock at a time, confident that it will go steadily on up, and because most stocks do fluctuate from time to time, it is generally more prudent and more profitable for an investor to follow the dollar cost averaging plan, which can make it possible for him to capitalize on price fluctuations, rather than to take one big plunge.

This is an impressive record, but it is not unlike that which can be shown for many other stocks. The table (page 186) shows how you would have made out by June 1966, if you had put roughly $500 a year, beginning in 1929, into several other stocks which have also proved popular with M.I.P. investors.

Of course, this is history, and no one can guarantee it is the kind of history which will repeat itself. But it does provide a convincing demonstration of the value of accumulating shares on a dollar cost averaging basis over a period of time, and this is one of the most persuasive features of the Monthly Investment Plan, which makes it possible for the small investor to follow precisely this course in buying most of the stocks listed on the New York Stock Exchange.

Formula investing is not so much a system for beating the market as it is a mechanical means for enforcing prudence and caution. There are many different formula plans — almost every expert has his own — but stripped of their technicalities, all of them can be reduced to the basic premise that an investment fund should be balanced between stocks and bonds, and that the ratio of one kind of security to the other should be changed as the market rises and falls. You buy bonds and sell stocks when the stock market gets high — on the assumption that the market becomes increasingly vulnerable as prices advance — and you reverse the procedure when the market drops.

The premise may be basically sound, but it's one that

$500-A-YEAR INVESTMENT PROGRAM
January 1929 — June 1966

In the Common Stock	Total Cost of Shares Purchased	Shares Owned	Market Value	Total Dividends Received	Total Dividends Plus Market Value of Stock	Net Gain
Aluminum Co. of America	$19,189	1450	$119,806	$30,005	$149,811	$130,622
American Tel. and Tel.	19,021	655	36,025	22,616	58,641	39,620
Caterpillar Tractor	19,271	9168	380,472	77,924	458,396	439,125
Consolidated Edison	19,258	1074	38,530	25,251	63,781	44,523
Dow Chemical	19,374	2748	181,368	65,849	247,217	227,843
DuPont (E.I.) de Nemours*	19,482	421	124,445	54,928	179,372	159,891
Eastman Kodak	19,269	2902	372,907	51,864	424,771	405,502
General Electric	19,104	1147	121,725	39,855	161,580	142,476
General Motors	19,116	1826	146,993	86,004	232,997	213,881
Goodyear Tire & Rubber	19,248	6198	315,323	87,931	403,254	384,006
Gulf Oil	19,182	2999	149,950	52,681	202,631	183,449
National Biscuit	19,363	1105	48,344	23,434	71,778	52,415
Pacific Gas & Electric	19,138	1537	46,879	29,158	76,037	56,899
Phillips Petroleum	19,148	2209	111,002	71,186	182,188	163,040
Radio Corp. of America	19,008	5262	259,811	40,481	300,292	281,284
Sears, Roebuck	19,298	4671	258,657	60,490	319,147	299,849
Standard Oil Co. (N.J.)	18,989	1645	113,094	62,092	175,186	156,197
Union Carbide	19,259	1159	68,091	37,309	105,400	86,141
United States Steel	19,110	1281	55,499	53,618	109,117	90,007
Westinghouse Electric	18,735	1408	73,674	31,451	105,125	86,385

* The last four columns include the market value ($45,402) of 564 shares of General Motors stock received as dividend between 1962 and 1965, and cash dividends of $7,028 since paid on those shares.

the average investor can't apply very effectively, since his investment fund is rarely large enough for a formula plan to operate without distortion. This is so because all formula plans assume that that portion of the fund which is invested in stocks will perform generally as the market average does. Obviously, the fewer stocks you can afford to own the less likely are they to perform in line with the general market; they may do significantly better or they may do significantly worse. Again, the only bonds that a small investor can generally afford are government E bonds, and he can't expect to achieve the same interest return on these bonds as he might earn on other government or corporate bonds, particularly since the return on E bonds is measurably less in the early years. Savings bank deposits can, of course, be substituted for bonds.

Basically, there are three kinds of formula plans — the constant-dollar plan, the constant-ratio plan, and the variable-ratio plan. The *constant-dollar plan* assumes that a fixed dollar amount of stocks will be held at all times. Thus, if you had $20,000, you might decide to keep $10,000 — no more or no less — invested in stocks. If the dollar value of your stock portfolio rose — say, to $11,000 — you would sell $1000 of stocks and put the proceeds into bonds. If your stocks declined $1000, you would sell $1000 of bonds and buy stocks. One objection to the plan is that over any long period of years stock prices are likely to advance — at least they have historically — and if your stock investments are frozen at any specified level, you won't keep up with the parade.

The *constant-ratio plan* works like the constant-dollar plan except that you determine to keep 50% of your investment fund in stocks at all time and 50% in bonds. You don't use fixed dollar amounts. The constant-ratio plan is obviously more flexible, can be adopted more readily to the shifting cycles of the stock market, and assures you of at least partial participation in the long-term growth of common stock values.

The *variable-ratio plan* operates like the constant-ratio plan, except that you decide to vary the ratio invested in common stocks as the market rises or falls. Thus, you might start out on a fifty-fifty basis, but decide to keep only 40% of your funds in common stocks whenever the market, as measured by one of the accepted averages, moved up 25%. When the market advanced 50%, you would cut back your common stock holdings to 30% of your total funds, and if it went up 75%, you would have only 20% invested in stocks. If the market fell, you would reverse the operation, buying stocks at the designated market levels and selling bonds. There are dozens and dozens of variations in the variable-ratio theme, many of them involving complicated mathematical formulas and using a variety of economic indexes as well as the market averages. They are designed to permit the investor to take maximum advantage of interim fluctuations in the market while simultaneously protecting his long-term position.

But they don't always work that way. Thus, anyone investing on a formula plan which called for reducing his commitments in common stocks as the market advanced would have lost out on the big bull market which began in 1950. That's why even many big, conservative institutions have either abandoned or modified extensively the formula plans that they initiated a decade or more ago.

While the average investor may not be able to apply any neatly devised mathematical formula to his own situation, he can profit by paying heed to the one basic precept of all these formulas: Keep an eye on those market averages, and as they rise, let them act as a brake on your buying enthusiasm. Remember, no bull-market movement lasts forever.

CHAPTER 29

Should You Buy
a Mutual Fund?

THINKING is always hard work. Thinking about an investment problem is doubly hard because it frequently involves dealing with words and ideas that are somewhat strange.

In a situation like that, it's a real temptation to let somebody else do your thinking for you.

And that's just what thousands of new investors have done in the last twenty years: They have turned to the *investment trust* — especially the *mutual fund* — as the answer to all their investment problems. But many of them have found it to be no panacea.

There's no special magic about an investment trust — nor anything mysterious about its operation. Suppose you and some of your friends — twenty of you, all told — each have $1000 to spare. Instead of each of you investing his own money, you might decide to pool it. Then instead of forming an investment club and arriving at collective investment decisions, you turn the whole sum over to one individual, or manager, to invest for you.

In that situation, the twenty of you would constitute an investment trust or *investment company* in miniature.

Now let's assume you're lucky and that at the end of the first year the manager of your little trust is able to report that he has made money for you. The value of the stocks which the trust owns has risen from $20,000 to $22,000. Each of your shares in that trust is now worth $1100 ($22,000 divided by 20).

You've been so successful, as a matter of fact, that some of your other friends would like to join your little trust. The twenty of you must now make one of two decisions.

You can decide that you're going to restrict the trust to just the original members and their original capital. If that's what you decide, you will, in effect, have converted

your organization into a *closed-end trust*. There will be no
new members or shareholders in your company, unless, of
course, one of the original twenty wants to sell his share
to somebody else for whatever he can get for it. That's a
right all of you always have.

The alternative plan would involve a decision to expand
your trust and take in new members. Since your own shares
are now worth $1100 apiece, you decide to allow them to
buy in on that basis — $1100 a share. When they put their
capital in, that new money will be invested as your original
capital was, and all of you, the new and the old owners,
will participate, share and share alike, in whatever profits
the fund may make from now on.

And if still other people decide they'd like to buy a share
in your trust at any future time, you decide to admit them
at a price representing the trust's *net asset value per share*.
This is determined by dividing the total value of the trust's
holdings by the number of shares already outstanding.

If you decide to operate on this pattern, you will have
transformed your company into an *open-end trust,* or what
is known more popularly today as a mutual fund.

This, in theory, is the essential difference between the
closed-end and open-end trusts. In actuality, there are other
differences.

Closed-end trusts are stock companies whose shares are
bought and sold just like other stocks. The business of these
trusts is investing, instead of manufacturing or merchandising, but they are operated just like any other company
by officers and directors responsible to the shareholders.

Some of these companies, like Lehman Corporation and
Tri-Continental Corporation, are listed on the New York
Stock Exchange. Their stock can be purchased through a
member broker at standard stock exchange commission rates,
anything from one share to hundreds of shares. Prices of
these stocks go up and down just as all other stocks do.
Their worth depends on what the buyer is willing to pay
and what the seller will accept in the light of the trust's
earnings and the trend of the market. Sometimes an investment trust stock will sell at a premium price, a price greater
than its net asset value per share, and sometimes it will
sell at a discount or below that value figure, which is usually
computed and published once a quarter.

In contrast, shares of an open-end trust are always bought
and sold on the basis of their exact net asset value, a figure

that changes constantly because the value of the trust's investments quite naturally is always changing. Consequently, mutual funds usually compute and announce the net asset values for their shares twice daily, and this determines the price dealers will charge a buyer, or what the owner will get if he sells.

The two kinds of trusts do much the same kind of business, but the difference in their setup makes for a difference in their operation. A closed-end trust cannot at will increase its original capital; an open-end trust not only can but usually wants to.

There are two or three hundred closed-end funds, but of these only 21 are big enough to qualify for listing on the New York Stock Exchange. In contrast, there are at least a dozen times that many big mutual funds — funds whose assets exceed $10,000,000 and which are sold generally throughout the country — and hundreds of smaller ones.

During the past quarter century, the growth of mutual funds has been little short of phenomenal. From a half billion dollars in 1941, to $3½ billion in 1951, to $23 billion in 1961, and to $35 billion at the beginning of 1966, when seven funds could each boast of assets in excess of one billion dollars. In all that quarter century, there was only one year in which net assets declined, and that was 1962, when the stock market break put a crimp in fund sales. The number of individual shareowners in mutual funds has increased correspondingly — from a comparative handful in 1941 to 3½ million in 1966.

The reason for this fantastic growth is not hard to find. It can be expressed in one phrase: sales incentive. For it can be truthfully said that most mutual fund shares aren't bought; they are sold — and sold by some pretty high-pressure sales methods. Included in the army of mutual fund salesmen are registered representatives of New York Stock Exchange firms, thousands and thousands of local security dealers, direct employees of fund sales organizations, and a whole host of part-time salesmen — insurance salesmen, filling station operators, mailmen, retired workers, and even that fabled character of *The New Yorker* magazine, the old lady from Dubuque. Regardless of their knowledge of securities — or their lack of knowledge — all of these salesmen respond to one incentive: the lure of high commissions.

The buyer of a mutual fund in 1966 was typically required to pay a commission or *loading charge* of 8%. Some charged 7½ % and some 8½ %, but none more than 9% because that is the maximum permitted by law. (True, there are some 40 *no-load funds* — Scudder, Stevens & Clark and Loomis-Sayles are probably the best known — which employ no salesmen and charge no commission. But the average investor, even if he knows about these no-load funds, often has a hard time purchasing their shares, and that serves to explain why no-load funds account for only about 5% of the industry's total assets and 3½ % of the total number of mutual fund owners.)

To realize just how great a sales incentive the typical 8% loading charge is, look at the situation from the point of view of a broker. Most funds permit the salesmen to retain 75% of the loading charge — 6% out of the 8%. That means that if a broker sells $1000 worth of mutual fund shares, his firm nets $60. In contrast, if he sells his customer a stock listed on the New York Stock Exchange, his firm gets only the standard commission of $17. Mutual funds, as a general rule, make no charge when the customer redeems or sells his shares, and so the broker doesn't stand to make anything more than that original $60 on the transaction. On the other hand, there's always a possibility that the buyer of the listed stock will sell it some day and the broker will have a chance to make another standard commission of $17, but that second transaction is purely theoretical, and anyway, two $17 commissions are still little more than half of $60. If larger purchases are involved, the profit differential in favor of the mutual fund is widened. Thus on a $5000 transaction, the broker would get $300 if the investor bought a mutual fund from him but only $44 if he bought a listed stock.

But that's not the whole incentive story. The most aggressively promoted and rapidly growing mutual funds in 1966 were the *front-end load funds,* and on these funds, the broker or salesman stands to make a considerably bigger profit right away. Front-end load plans are sold on a contract basis, and the customer agrees to buy stated amounts of the fund over a period of time, usually ten or twelve years. The chief attraction of these plans to the salesman or broker is that such contracts usually provide that one-half of the buyer's total payments in the first year shall be deducted for the salesman's commission and other selling expenses. Thus, if the customer signs up for a $50-a-month plan, he will pay $600 in the first year, and $300 will be taken out for the sales commission, with the broker or salesman getting his usual 75% split on the spot.

Over the life of a front-end contract, the sales cost averages out to the same 8% loading charge — with 6% for the broker — but the big advantage to the salesman is that he gets the lion's share of the total commission due over the whole life of the contract in the first year, and he doesn't have to keep reselling the mutual fund, as he does if the customer buys a *level-load* (or noncontractual) *plan.* Nor does he have to worry about his commissions in case the buyer cancels his contract in a year or two because the salesman has already collected most of his fee.

If the buyer of a front-end load fund wants to cancel his contract and redeem his shares, he can't normally expect to recover the sales cost and break even until he has been in the plan for about three years, unless there has been a spectacular increase in the value of the fund's shares. And if the stock market isn't robust, it might be five or six years — or never. Meanwhile, the salesman has his take, all tidily sewed up.

Mutual funds offer brokers still one other incentive to push their sales. As the funds grow, they are constantly buying additional stock, big blocks of stock. Furthermore, they keep changing their portfolios, selling five or ten thousand shares of this stock and buying five or ten thousand shares of that one. The funds understandably tend to give this highly lucrative commission business on block purchases and sales to those brokers or dealers who do the best job of selling their shares.

This is known as *reciprocal business,* and although the brokers are frequently asked to give up 50% or 60% of the commissions they earn on such business — to help the fund reward other salesmen, to cover research costs, to pay for special order wires, etc. — the cooperating brokers are usually more than happy with the portion of the commission that they are permitted to keep. Actually, the days may be numbered in which brokers are permitted to earn fat commissions on fund purchases and sales, because several funds have bought seats on various regional exchanges so they can execute their own orders and keep the full commission themselves.

While it may be true that mutual funds are sold rather than bought, that does not mean that they are not good things to buy. The one great investment virtue that all investment trusts, closed-end and open-end alike, have to offer is the protection afforded the investor by virtue of their diversified holdings in many different companies and usually many different industries. There is obviously less risk in owning an interest, however small, in 50 or 150 different companies than in owning stock in just one company. This is the great argument, the protection provided by diversification, on which mutual fund salesmen pound away, and it's an argument of unquestionable merit.

There is another argument that they frequently advance which doesn't hold up so well under scrutiny, and that is the argument that professional management, such as all investment trusts boast, can invest the customer's money more wisely than he can — so much more wisely that mutual funds feel justified in assessing all shares a *management fee* that generally comes to ½ of 1% a year. This fee is taken out of the fund's profits before any distribution is made to shareowners, and if there are no profits, it is taken right out of capital. Very often, the men who comprise the management company that the fund retains to guide its investment policy are the same men who guide its sales destiny, although the law provides that no more than 60% of a mutual fund's directors can be connected with its advisory or management company.

If professional management is worthwhile, if it's worth ½ of 1% a year, it might seem logical to assume that mutual funds as a whole would show a performance record over the years superior to that measured by one of the accepted indexes that reflect just the average action of the market. Have the funds beaten the averages?

There can be no clear-cut, categorical answer to that question, because the answer depends on what period of time you are measuring and what kinds of funds you are talking about. For there are many kinds of funds. There are *common stock funds* whose assets are wholly invested in a diversified list of common stocks, but some funds accent growth while others like the no-load funds aim at more conservative objectives. There are *balanced funds,* whose holdings include bonds or preferred stocks as well as common stocks. And there is a wide variety of special-purpose funds, funds that have their assets invested exclusively in the securities of a single industry or of companies that operate in specific geographical areas. There are even funds that operate in part on borrowed money because they think they can earn more on the securities they buy than they will have to pay out in interest, and since funds are forbidden by law to buy on margin, they seek to gain added leverage by borrowing.

Because of the diversity of funds, any comparison of their performance record with the market averages can be challenged, but in 1962 when the Wharton School of Finance and Commerce completed the most ambitious study of mutual funds ever undertaken, it reported as follows to the Securities & Exchange Commission: "With respect to the performance of mutual funds, it was found that, on the average, it did not differ appreciably from what would have been achieved by an unmanaged portfolio consisting of the same proportions of common stocks, corporate bonds, government securities, and other assets as the composite fund portfolios."

Every year *Forbes* magazine reports on the performance of virtually all of the widely held funds and contrasts their records with one of the accepted stock market indexes or averages. In general, these reports seem to bear out the Wharton School's conclusion that professional fund management doesn't yield superior results, that the funds perform about as the averages do. This is particularly true with respect to the largest funds, whose portfolios are necessarily so diversified that their holdings inevitably represent a cross-section of the whole market. Smaller, more aggressive funds that are fortunate enough to have bought good growth stocks at an early point in their development, as the Dreyfus Fund did with Polaroid, are apt to have more spectacular records, but their achievements are restricted by a legal requirement which provides that no fund may invest more than 5% of its assets in any one corporation, nor may it own more than 10% of any corporation's voting stock.

Furthermore, although the aggressive funds may outstrip the market in rising markets, they are apt to fall substantially behind in declining markets. The reverse of that situation, of course, prevails with respect to the more conservative balanced funds. That is the reason why mutual funds are likely to turn in surprisingly inconsistent results. This was demonstrated in a study by Professor Eugene Fama of the University of Chicago's Graduate School of Business which showed that no one of the 39 major funds he studied ranked in the top half of the group consistently over the ten-year period from 1951 through 1960.

Year in and year out, the investor who is interested in investment companies, closed-end or open-end, can get the most definitive information about their performance records from Wiesenberger's annual *Investment Companies* (page 169), which he can refer to in many brokerage offices and public libraries.

The mutual funds owe their great growth over the past quarter century wholly to the Investment Company Act of 1940, for that law gave specific sanction to all of the selling practices which have permitted the funds to prosper — and which, incidentally, have galled the Securities & Exchange Commission for years. At the time the Act was passed, mutual funds were almost unknown, and in approaching Congress with a request for legislation in the investment company field, the S.E.C. primarily had in mind a law that would enable it to regulate the closed-end investment trusts and outlaw the many practices which had permitted the trusts to enjoy an ill-starred boom as the market roared to its 1929 high.

In those days paeans of publicity about investment trusts led the little man to believe that he was going to get a bandwagon ride to the promised land of perpetual prosperity.

But many of the trusts abused his confidence. They played fast and loose with his money. Trust-fund managers paid themselves large fees and bonuses for their somewhat questionable services. They split commissions with accountants and legal counsel to line their own pockets. Enjoying almost complete freedom to invest trust funds as they saw fit, the managers placed themselves too willingly at the service of investment bankers anxious to market new and dubious stock issues. They resorted to all kinds of speculative practices. They bought on margin. They pyramided paper profits. And they used the trusts to obtain control of whole industrial empires, often with only a paltry outlay of actual cash — cash furnished, of course, by investors in the fund.

When the crash came in 1929, there were almost 700 investment trusts, and they boasted "assets" of $7 billion, assets that were scattered like a handful of dry leaves when the big wind came. One big trust which had reported assets of over $150,000,000 was so hard hit that it publicly stated in 1932 that there was no point in trying to appraise the value of what was left from the wreckage, because it knew that the cost of making an inventory of its assets would actually exceed those assets.

When the Securities & Exchange Commission in 1936 began a study of the investment trust business, it was solely interested in a law that would eliminate such practices as margin buying, require full and open disclosure, and drive the crooks and manipulators from the business. In the Investment Company Act of 1940, it got the authority it wanted to accomplish those objectives, but something funny happened on the way to enactment.

What happened is that industry lawyers in a five-week nonstop conference with the Securities & Exchange Commission, which was then under some Congressional pressure to compose its differences with the industry, wrested from the commission a broad new charter for the mutual funds, including statutory approval of loading charges, front-end load contracts, and management fees.

There was only one thing the funds would have liked to have and couldn't get and that was freedom to advertise. Since mutual funds are constantly issuing new stock, they necessarily fall under the prospectus provisions of the 1933 Act which applies to all new stock issues. This means that mutual fund advertising must be limited to the name of the fund, the offering of a prospectus, and a descriptive sentence or two about its objectives.

After the Wharton report and three special studies by its own staff, the Securities & Exchange Commission on December 2, 1966, finally asked Congress for legislation that would severely restrict many of the selling practices on which fund managers and salesmen have grown rich and successful. Skilled in political infighting and counting heavily on its Congressional allies, the industry was equally ready to fight any modification of the existing law. The prospect was for a long legislative battle and some ultimate compromise.

Among the many reforms that the Securities & Exchange Commission wanted, probably the most important was an outright ban on front-end load contracts. The S.E.C. has never been impressed with the industry's argument that the investors need some form of strong compulsion, such as threat of loss in the early years, to keep them saving and investing regularly. The S.E.C. points out that 20% of all those who enter into front-end contracts have been forced to sell at a loss and that these are the investors who can least afford such loss. Sold in units of as little as $10 or $20 a month, the front-end load plans have been pushed on lower-income people, people with less savings and less life insurance than buyers of level-load plans.

The Securities & Exchange Commission also sought a 5% ceiling on all loading charges on the grounds that higher charges were exorbitant and unjustified, and it asked that the mandatory character of the charge be modified in some way so that there might be some element of price competition introduced into the sale of mutual funds.

Further, the commission took dead aim at the standard ½ of 1% management fee. The S.E.C.'s contention has always been that these fees were justified neither by the results which such managements achieved nor by the actual costs incurred in providing such investment advisory service. On a billion dollar fund, the management fee will yield $5,000,000 a year, and if the handful of men who divide that money happen also to be a part of the fund's sales management, their take-home pay can be generous indeed. Pointing out that mutual fund management fees averaged seven times more than banks charged for a comparable investment advisory service, the S.E.C. asked Congress for a law, enforceable in the courts, which would guarantee that such charges would be "reasonable."

Other reforms of only slightly less significance which the Securities & Exchange Commission wanted include the following:

(1) A prohibition on the sale of shares in a fund's management company if such a sale affected the fund adversely.

(2) An outright ban on "super funds" whose holdings consisted solely of shares in other mutual funds.

(3) Measures to prevent fund managers from seeking to capitalize personally on their inside knowledge of the fund's purchases and sales.

(4) Further study of the trading activity of funds. In 1965 funds traded 25% of their portfolios, in contrast to a 16% turnover rate for all shares on the New York Stock Exchange.

Finally, the commission urged the exchanges to amend their rules and commission schedules so that mutual funds could not force brokers to give up a part of their commission on fund transactions as payment to other security dealers who sell fund shares. In attacking this reciprocal business, the commission urged the exchanges to lower commission rates on big transactions.

Back of all these demands for reform lies a concern which even the Securities & Exchange Commission is reluctant to express: What might happen if the market went into a real tailspin — a prolonged downturn. That's the time when people who owned shares in a mutual fund would be most tempted to cash them in, for that is when they, as individuals of generally modest means, would be most likely to need their savings. And yet that is precisely the time when it would be most difficult for a mutual fund to redeem its shares, because to raise cash, it would probably have to sell stocks from its portfolio.

Most funds, of course, have a cash reserve, because even in a good year redemptions may run as high as 30% or more of the value of all new shares sold. But if there was a heavy run on the trust, it would have to sell off sizable blocks of stock to raise cash and it might very well have to take a loss on those forced sales. Additionally, those very sales might further depress the market and make it even more awkward for the trust to meet the next round of redemptions.

It is true that the funds generally have performed creditably during all the recent market declines, but not even the 1962 break, when prices on the New York Stock Exchange dropped more than 25%, could be considered a really severe test, for the break was comparatively short-lived.

Many of the changes in the mutual fund industry that the Securities & Exchange Commission would like to see brought about may be achieved not by legislative enactment but by the abrasive effect of new competition. Attracted by the lure of high profits and anxious to diversify, a railroad, a rubber company, and several insurance companies have bought control of existing mutual funds in the past few years. Scudder, Stevens & Clark is managing a no-load fund for the giant American Farm Bureau Federation, and Loomis-Sayles is selling its no-load shares to New York State schoolteachers. And waiting in the wings in mid-1966 was the giant Sears, Roebuck & Co., which was readying its own mutual fund for sale to the public through its subsidiary Allstate Enterprises — at a cost which it was rumored would be substantially less than the usual loading charge.

But the biggest threat of all was unquestionably the First National City Bank's commingled investment account (page

160), which is, of course, really nothing but a no-load mutual fund. Even though banking regulations severely restrict the bank's promotion of the fund, which was cleared by the S.E.C. and first offered for sale in June 1966, the mutual fund industry was so worried that it had already instituted two legal actions to try to kill the fund before it really got rolling. Both suits, one brought by the N.A.S.D. and one by the Investment Company Institute, charged that a commingled investment account violated the Banking Act of 1933, which was aimed at divorcing commercial and investment functions. What distressed the mutual fund industry was the certainty that other big banks would follow First National City's lead, if the commingled investment account proved successful.

And still another form of worrisome competition is that now offered by the new *variable annuity* insurance policies which are now offered on a group basis by the Prudential Insurance Company and several others. Under the variable annuity plan, the premiums which are paid in are largely invested in common stocks, and when policies mature, monthly payments are determined by the value of the investment at that time. The courts forbade Prudential to offer these policies on an individual basis, but even on a group basis, variable annuities represent a sizable threat to mutual funds, since they offer much the same kind of diversified investment.

Yes, in 1966, regardless of how the mutual fund business might make out with the Securities & Exchange Commission and Congress, it began to look as though the industry would not enjoy much longer the advantages of a well-run cartel. And to the investor, interested in obtaining the advantages of a diversified portfolio at reasonable cost, that was nothing but good news.

CHAPTER 30

Why You Should Invest
—If You Can

WHY should a man who has extra money invest it in stocks? Here is the answer to that in one chart and one table.

Chart I (page 203) shows the movement of stock prices from 1915 into 1966, as measured by Standard & Poor's long-term index of industrial stocks.

The table below shows the average annual yield on the stocks included in Standard & Poor's industrial index back to 1926, which is as far back as this series of statistics goes:

1926	4.86	1936	3.39	1946	3.81	1956	3.95
1927	4.73	1937	4.83	1947	4.90	1957	4.18
1928	3.93	1938	4.96	1948	5.47	1958	3.87
1929	3.61	1939	3.87	1949	6.63	1959	3.11
1930	4.84	1940	5.51	1950	6.69	1960	3.36
1931	6.40	1941	6.62	1951	6.17	1961	2.90
1932	7.74	1942	7.04	1952	5.88	1962	3.32
1933	4.06	1943	4.76	1953	5.86	1963	3.12
1934	3.37	1944	4.69	1954	4.92	1964	2.96
1935	3.52	1945	4.13	1955	3.97	1965	2.94

A casual examination of this table might suggest that there was cause for concern in the steady downtrend in stock yields during the fifties and their failure to make any recovery in the early sixties, but it should be remembered that these yields are percentage figures arrived at by dividing dollar dividends by dollar prices for the stocks in the index.

Hence, any decline in the yield figure could be the result either of an actual decrease in the dollar dividends paid or an increase in the price of the stocks. The latter explanation is clearly the right one as far as the decade of the fifties is concerned. Yields may have dropped from 6.69% for the

201

year 1950 to 3.11% for 1959, but during this same decade, as Chart I shows, per-share prices rose from an average index number of about 20 to more than 60.

To illustrate what these figures really mean, suppose you had bought a stock at $20 a share in 1950 and received a representative dividend of 6.5% on it that year. On this basis, you would have received a dividend of $1.30. If that stock behaved like the average of all others, it would have been selling at about $60 a share at the end of 1959 and paying a yield of about 3%, which would mean that your actual dollar dividend would have increased to $1.80, or about 45% more than it was in 1950. Furthermore, it would mean that on your original investment, you would be earning a full 9%, since you would be getting a dividend of $1.80 on your $20 investment.

The yield that an investor realizes from a stock is not affected in any way by changes in its price *after* he buys it; it is affected only by a change in the dividend. Thus, if you pay $100 for a stock paying a $5 dividend, you realize 5% on your money, regardless of whether the stock drops to $80 or goes up to $120, as long as the $5 dividend is paid. If the dividend is increased to $6, you make 6%, and if it is reduced to $4, you make 4% — regardless of what happens to the price of the stock.

Now let's take another look at the chart. It shows that stock prices have moved generally upward for the past 50 years in a fairly well-defined path. One notable exception is that precipitous drop from the 1929 peak to the 1932 bottom.

Isn't that an alarming exception, in view of the present price level?

No, it isn't. The character of the market in recent years differs markedly from what it was in 1929. It has been essentially an investment market. Thanks to regulations of the government and the exchange, there has been virtually none of the speculative orgy which produced the big crash. Certainly, from time to time, glamour stocks like electronics or drugs have had a big play, but there has been no over-extension of credit, no pyramiding, and, most important, no manipulation of the market.

Why have people been investing?

Why have stock prices been going up over the years?

Because American business has grown steadily, and there is every reason to believe it will continue to grow — con-

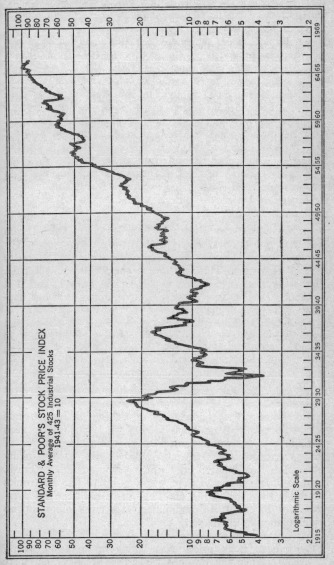

STANDARD & POOR'S STOCK PRICE INDEX
Monthly Average of 425 Industrial Stocks
1941-43 = 10

Logarithmic Scale

CHART I

tinue to develop new products, new industries, new markets, and continue to expand all along the line.

Figures compiled by the U.S. Department of Commerce on our *gross national product* — the total value of all goods and services produced in this country — tell the story of growth better than any others. In 1929, the first year for which such figures were compiled, gross national product was estimated at $103 billion. In the great depression, it fell to a low of $56 billion in 1933. Since then, growth has been steady — and little short of phenomenal. In 1960 gross national product was valued at $504 billion, and by 1965 it had advanced to $681 billion. And the National Industrial Conference Board confidently predicts that by 1975 gross national product will exceed a trillion dollars!

That's one good reason for investing — for owning a share in American business — but there's a second equally persuasive reason.

Take a look at Chart II. Something new has been added — a second line showing stock prices in terms of a dollar whose value, or purchasing power, does not fluctuate from year to year. This line is, in effect, a measure of the purchasing power of common stocks, since it shows how much stocks are worth in terms of a dollar whose value is adjusted to reflect changes in the *cost of living,* as compiled by the Bureau of Labor Statistics.

When the cost of living goes up and the country is in a period of *inflation,* stock prices tend to rise for one reason: Companies make and sell goods. When these goods are worth more in terms of dollars, the companies that make them are obviously also worth more in terms of dollars, and so are the shares of stock that represent the ownership of those companies. This is not true of all stocks, of course, but it is true of most stocks.

In periods of inflation, money that is invested in common stock or other property is not as likely to lose its purchasing power as money which is simply set aside in a savings bank or invested in bonds that have a relatively fixed value. Common stocks may not provide perfect protection against inflation, but they will do until something better comes along.

Certainly for the average man they are a better inflation hedge than real estate, for instance. Real estate prices usually rise too in a period of inflation, but it is not as easy to be a good judge of real estate as it is to be a good judge of stock values; the element of risk is much greater. Further-

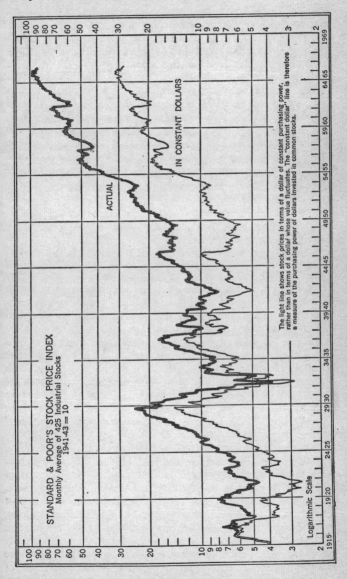

CHART II

more, it is never so easy to dispose of real estate, particularly in a period of depression, if you suddenly need to raise cash. Finally, with real estate you have to contend with a great many other problems, like taxes, repairs, zoning changes, and special assessments, whether or not it produces any income for you.

For all these reasons — for income, for a chance to see your capital grow, for the protection of its purchasing power — you may decide you want to invest in stocks.

But wait a minute. Maybe you shouldn't. Are you sure that those dollars you plan to put into the stock market are really extra dollars? Remember, there is an inescapable factor of risk in owning stocks, even the best of them. The averages may go up, but your stocks may go down. That is a risk worth taking for the man who isn't going to be seriously hurt in case he loses some of those dollars. But it's not a risk that a man should take if he's likely to need those dollars to meet some emergency.

What if there were a serious and expensive illness in the family? Are your savings adequate to meet that situation? What about the other expenses you may have to meet, such as the cost of a new car, house repairs, furniture, college expenses for your children? What about insurance? Have you got enough so that you are sure your family would be able to maintain a decent living standard if you were to die?

If you can answer yes to all these questions, you can and you probably should consider putting your extra dollars into common stocks.

CHAPTER 31

How Good
Are Common Stocks?

PROBABLY the most convincing evidence of the value of investing in common stocks is that supplied by two studies measuring the rate of return yielded by common stocks listed on the New York Stock Exchange, which were conducted by the Center for Research in Security Prices at the Graduate School of Business of the University of Chicago. The center has been sponsored since its inception by Merrill Lynch, Pierce, Fenner & Smith Inc., the world's largest brokerage firm, and the two studies that have been published on rates of return constitute the most definitive measurement of the stock market that has ever been made.

Basically, the question to which the center addressed itself in 1959 was this: Just how good are common stocks as investments? What average rate of return might an investor expect to realize if he simply selected a stock at random — without any professional guidance or research information — from those listed on the New York Stock Exchange, and what would be his average risk of loss?

Obviously, such a question could be answered only in terms of the historical record, and this the center set about compiling. It took five years and $250,000 to put all the essential data on computer tape because of the high standards of accuracy which were established. First, the center insisted on going back to January 1926, so that it could not be accused of ignoring the 1929 bull market or the consequent crash. It also insisted on covering all the 1715 stocks that had been listed at any time since 1926 on the exchange — not just a cross-section or sample but all the stocks, good, bad, and indifferent. Finally, the center wasn't satisfied to work with an annual or semiannual price but insisted on recording the price at each month end for 35 years for each listed stock, and since those prices had to be comparable throughout the whole period, it meant that they had to be adjusted to take account of every stock dividend, stock split, spin-off, merger, or other change in a company's financial structure. All told, more than 30,000 such adjustments had to be made in the price data. In addition, information on 100,000 dividend payments was put on the tapes.

The center's file of price and dividend data is unquestionably the most authoritative record that exists, guaranteed to be 99.44% accurate.

Because the compiling and recording job took almost five years, the two studies on rates of return tell the story of the market only through December 1960. The first of these studies by Professor James H. Lorie, director of the center, and Lawrence Fisher, associate director, shows that the average rate of return for all common stocks on the New York Stock Exchange from January 1926 through December 1960 — assuming reinvestment of all dividends and after payment of all commissions — was 9.0% per annum compounded annually. In other words, a dollar invested in January 1926 would have grown to $20 in December 1960.

Since the study covered all listed stocks, the 9% rate represents what an investor might have expected to realize on average by a purely random selection of any one stock — before taxes, of course.

If dividends were simply accumulated and not reinvested, the average rate of return for the same 35-year period would have been 6.9% per annum compounded annually.

The study reports rates of return for 22 different time periods, some of which involve the 1929 bull market high and some the 1932 depression low. Here are some of the key results (with dividends reinvested).

Period	Per cent per annum compounded annually
Sept. 1929 - June 1932	−48.8%
Sept. 1929 - Dec. 1940	−3.1%
Sept. 1929 - Dec. 1950	+4.8%
Sept. 1929 - Dec. 1960	+7.7%
June 1932 - Dec. 1940	+21.1%
June 1932 - Dec. 1950	+18.6%
June 1932 - Dec. 1960	+17.3%
Dec. 1950 - Dec. 1960	+14.7%
Dec. 1955 - Dec. 1960	+11.2%

As Professor Lorie points out, these rates of return on common stocks were higher than the returns in comparable periods on all other forms of investment — savings accounts, mortgages, corporate bonds, governments and municipals.

The second study by Professor Fisher answers the questions of how often and how much the investor might have gained or lost on the stocks listed on the exchange from 1926 to 1960.

To arrive at its conclusions, Professor Fisher computed results for every possible combination of month-end purchase and sales dates for every stock throughout the 35-year period. For any one stock, this would have represented 87,900 monthly combinations, and for all exchange stocks it meant tabulating results on 56,557,538 such possible transactions, a job that would have taken thousands of man-years without a computer.

Here is the key finding of this study: If one had picked a stock *at random* from the Big Board list, if he had then picked a purchase date *at random* between January 1926 and December 1960, and if he had picked *at random* any later sales date within the same period, he would have made money 78% of the time, and the median return, assuming reinvestment of all dividends and payment of brokerage commissions on purchase and sale, would have been 9.8% per annum compounded annually. At that rate of interest, money doubles in about seven years, and the study showed that the investor would have had a better than 50-50 chance of doing exactly that — doubling his money — with purely random selection. His risk of losing as much as 20% a year on his investment was only one in thirteen whereas his expectation of making as much as 20% per annum compounded annually was one in five.

The study demonstrated two other points of vital significance to any investor:

(1) If the investor had picked three or four stocks at random instead of just one, the risk of loss would have been considerably reduced and the probability of a larger profit considerably improved.

(2) If the investor had not been forced to sell during a period of economic recession — if he had been able to hold on for a year or two — his chance of making a profit and the amount of profit would have both been significantly increased.

PROFIT PROBABILITIES ON COMMON STOCKS
SALE PERIOD

Purchase Period		Jan. 26 Sept. 26	Oct. 26 Oct. 27	Nov. 27 July 29	Aug. 29 Feb. 33	Mar. 33 Apr. 37	May 37 May 38	June 38 Jan. 45
		U	D	U	D	U	D	U
Jan. 26-Sept. 26	U	.46 -4.2%	.60 8.3%	.77 18.2%	.37 -8.0%	.38 -4.6%	.44 -1.9%	.48 -0.5%
Oct. 26-Oct. 27	D		.58 10.0%	.75 21.0%	.32 -11.9%	.33 -6.7%	.40 -3.0%	.45 -1.5%
Nov. 27-July 29	U			.59 10.0%	.15 -29.7%	.21 -13.0%	.27 -7.4%	.35 -1.0%
Aug. 29-Feb. 33	D				.13 -45.6%	.56 4.3%	.59 3.9%	.62 3.9%
Mar. 33-Apr. 37	U					.69 21.0%	.49 -0.8%	.55 1.7%
May 37-May 38	D						.13 -59.6%	.55 2.3%
June 38-Jan. 45	U							.66 9.1%
Feb. 45-Sept. 45	D							
Oct. 45-Oct. 48	U							
Nov. 48-Sept. 49	D							
Oct. 49-June 53	U							
July 53-July 54	D							
Aug. 54-June 57	U							
July 57-Mar. 58	D							
Apr. 58-Apr. 60	U							
May 60-Dec. 60	D							

The value of long-term investing, the value of being able to hold on through a period of weakness in the market, is convincingly demonstrated by the table on pp. 212-3. It may look complicated, but it's well worth five minutes of study.

The table shows by economic periods from 1926 through 1960 how you would have made out if you had bought a stock at random from those traded on the New York Stock Exchange, reinvested your dividends, and sold that stock in the same period or at any later period. The bold-face decimal figures show you what percentage of the time you would have made money — thus, .46 means you would have made money 46% of the time, and the light-face italic figures

LISTED ON THE NEW YORK STOCK EXCHANGE, 1926–1960

SALE PERIOD

Feb. 45	Oct. 45	Nov. 48	Oct. 49	July 53	Aug. 54	July 57	Apr. 58	May 60
Sept. 45	Oct. 48	Sept. 49	June 53	July 54	June 57	Mar. 58	Apr. 60	Dec. 60
D	U	D	U	D	U	D	U	D
.72	.77	.71	.82	.84	.88	.89	.91	.90
4.1%	4.7%	3.9%	5.4%	5.8%	7.0%	6.6%	7.5%	7.3%
.70	.75	.69	.79	.82	.87	.88	.91	.90
3.7%	4.4%	3.5%	5.1%	5.4%	6.7%	6.3%	7.2%	7.1%
.62	.67	.62	.73	.77	.84	.85	.90	.89
1.9%	2.8%	2.1%	3.9%	4.3%	5.7%	5.3%	6.3%	6.2%
.84	.86	.83	.89	.90	.94	.93	.95	.95
8.6%	8.9%	7.3%	8.8%	8.8%	10.0%	9.4%	10.3%	10.0%
.90	.92	.86	.93	.94	.96	.95	.97	.96
9.0%	9.4%	6.4%	9.7%	9.4%	10.9%	10.0%	11.0%	10.6%
.93	.95	.90	.95	.96	.98	.97	.98	.98
11.6%	11.4%	8.5%	10.7%	10.5%	12.0%	10.9%	11.9%	11.4%
.98	.97	.92	.97	.97	.99	.98	.99	.99
24.0%	18.6%	11.5%	14.1%	13.1%	14.9%	13.1%	14.1%	13.4%
.65	.74	.60	.83	.85	.93	.92	.95	.94
16.6%	11.1%	2.8%	9.4%	9.5%	12.3%	10.7%	12.2%	11.6%
	.38	.36	.78	.83	.92	.90	.95	.94
	-7.0%	-5.2%	9.1%	9.3%	12.8%	10.7%	12.4%	11.5%
		.48	.93	.92	.96	.94	.98	.96
		-1.8%	21.7%	15.1%	18.2%	14.3%	15.9%	14.4%
			.73	.68	.91	.88	.95	.92
			11.9%	7.3%	15.8%	11.4%	14.0%	12.5%
				.70	.94	.88	.95	.93
				18.8%	24.8%	12.3%	15.6%	13.2%
					.64	.48	.79	.77
					7.6%	-0.9%	10.5%	8.6%
						.37	.88	.82
						-17.3%	25.6%	13.9%
							.64	.50
							11.8%	0.2%
								.40
								-11.0%

on each line below show you the median rate of return (per cent per year compounded annually) you might have expected to realize. The periods themselves are all of different lengths, but each one corresponds to a recognized upswing or downswing in business as defined by the National Bureau of Economic Research. The U identifies an upswing, and the D a downswing. The periods listed vertically are for purchases; those listed horizontally are for sales.

Here's how to read the table: Let's assume that you made your random purchase in the first period between January 1926 and September 1926 and then sold out in that same period. Your chance of making a profit would have been only 46%, and your average expectation of profit or loss would have been minus 4.2%. Now, assume that you bought in the same period, between January 1926 and September 1926, but did not sell until almost twenty years later—sometime in the period between February 1945 and September 1945. Now you would have had a 72% chance of making a profit, and the average profit would have been a plus 4.1%. Finally, if you had made your purchase in that first period and did not sell until the last period, between June and December 1960, your chance of making a profit would have been 90%, and your median profit expectation would have been equal to 7.3% compound interest for 35 years.

To see how the table proves the value of long-term investing, look at the bold-face figures diagonally down the table from upper left to lower right. These figures show your average chance of making money if you had bought and sold within the same period. Now contrast those figures with the bold-face ones in the last column to the right, reading straight down from top to bottom. These show your expectation of profit if you had held your stock and not sold it until the last period covered by this study.

Here's how the figures look when set down right together:

Buy and sell in same period	Buy and hold till last period
.46	.90
.58	.90
.59	.89
.13	.95
.69	.96
.13	.98
.66	.99
.65	.94
.38	.94
.48	.96
.73	.92
.70	.93
.64	.77
.37	.82
.64	.50
.40	.40

Obviously, the longer you hold the stock the greater your expectation of profit. What is true of your average chance of profit is equally true as regards the median profit or loss. Here's how the comparative figures read:

Buy and sell in same period	Buy and hold till last period
−4.2	7.3
10.0	7.1
10.0	6.2
−45.6	10.0
21.0	10.6
−59.6	11.4
9.1	13.4
16.6	11.6
−7.0	11.5
−1.8	14.4
11.9	12.5
18.8	13.2
7.6	8.6
−17.3	13.9
11.8	0.2
−11.0	−11.0

Neither of these studies guarantees anything about future investment success, but if you are willing to assume that the past is any kind of a guide to the future, their meaning is clear and unmistakable.

Since these two studies cover all the stocks listed on the New York Stock Exchange, the results they show are the results you might have expected on the average to achieve with the random selection of any one stock, and for this reason they exemplify what is called the *random walk* hypothesis. They have been accepted today in financial and academic circles as establishing the standard yardsticks against which anyone who has a technical theory of his own must measure performance if he wants to prove that he is better than average. The Center for Research in Security Prices expects to update these studies periodically.

The computer file of price and dividend data has now been taken over from the center by Standard & Poor's Corporation, and the tapes will be made available to universities

for further research work, such as the center itself is pur
suing steadily.

The entry of the scholars into the field of stock marke
research may not guarantee that someday the touchston
to investment success will be found, but it should go a long
way toward disabusing the public of its misplaced confidenc
in those who regularly advertise its easy availability in the
financial pages of our newspapers.

CHAPTER 32

How You Should Invest
—If You Can

THE stock you'd like to buy, of course, is the one that just doesn't exist. You'd like a stock that is completely safe, one that pays a liberal dividend, and one that's bound to go up.

There are a lot of good stocks that will probably satisfy you on any one of these counts, but none that will accomplish all three objectives.

If you want safety in a stock, you'll have to give up the hope that it will increase sensationally in value.

If you'd like to see your money grow, you have to be prepared to take a considerably greater measure of risk.

Sometimes it's possible to find either a fairly safe stock or one that seems likely to appreciate in price that will also yield you a better-than-average dividend. But even here, as a general rule, you can't have your cake and eat it too. If you get a liberal dividend, it will probably be at the expense of one of the other two factors.

Hence, the first step in solving your investment problem is to decide on the one objective you most want to attain by your investments. Is it safety of capital? Or liberal dividends? Or price appreciation?

When you start thinking about stocks that might best match any of these objectives, you should first take a look at various industries and their future prospects. Remember, the carriage industry was a thriving business at the turn of the century.

To see how these various factors might influence your own investment selections, consider how seven different people in widely varying circumstances might approach their investment problem.

Mr. Adams is twenty-four years old, unmarried, and, as far as he can see, likely to pursue his course of single blessedness for some time to come. Having received his college degree and completed his tour of duty in the Army, he now has a trainee's job as a chemist with a large food-manufacturing company. His income is $7000 a year, and thanks to the fact that he still lives at home, he can save at the rate of $2500 a year. With a $10,000 ordinary life insurance policy and a $5000 group policy issued by his company, he has made a start toward building an estate for himself.

With the savings which he accumulated while he was in the Army, he now has about $4500, very little of which has to be earmarked for emergencies as long as his responsibilities are as light as they are. Then too, if he really got in a serious jam, he knows he could count on his folks to help him out.

He wants to see his capital grow, and so he wants to invest in stocks that have good growth possibilities, even though such stocks may yield only a scant return in dividends now.

Such a young man can afford to take a considerable measure of risk, but before he starts eyeing some of the more speculative stocks, he probably ought to put out an anchor to windward. Marriage has a way of creeping up on a man when he least expects it.

He can probably afford to invest $4000, and of this at least $1000 ought to go into Series E government savings bonds. Another $1000 might be divided between two solid common stocks — stocks that might be described as defensive in character, because they have weathered many an economic storm in the past with little loss in value and with an unbroken record of dividend payments.

One of these might be a public utility like Pacific Gas & Electric or Consolidated Edison of New York. And the other one might be a stock like General Electric. Such a stock may fluctuate a little more when business expands or retracts, but it is still essentially stable, because the company makes so many different products for so many different markets.

Mr. Adams might then very properly put his remaining $2000 into stocks of a more speculative nature — stocks with good growth possibilities. Maybe automotive stock. Maybe something in electronics or guided missiles. But probably first of all, a chemical stock — a field in which he should know firsthand something about new and promising developments.

As for his future savings — that $2500 he expects to ac-

umulate each year — that money too can go largely into
rowth stocks as long as his present situation remains un-
hanged. But he probably ought to start a systematic savings
lan with his broker, or he won't have those funds for in-
estment.

Mr. Adams can accomplish that in one of two ways. He
an open a Monthly Investment Plan account and apply his
nonthly savings toward the regular purchase of some stock.
Or he can save his money, and when a sufficient sum has
ccumulated, he can buy additional shares on an odd-lot
asis at a lower commission cost than he would pay on an
M.I.P. account.

Consider now the case of Miss Baxter, a capable young
voman of thirty. As secretary in a large company, where she
as worked for ten years, she now makes $130 a week,
about as much as Mr. Adams. But age and sex can make a
lifference. She lives alone in a kitchenette apartment, re-
ponsible only to herself. She has no family to worry about,
and she doesn't expect her mother and father, who live in a
ittle town out West, ever to have to worry about her. She
tands on her own feet.

A thrifty person, she has managed over the years to put a
ittle away every month. Now and again she has supple-
nented these savings with a special bonus check. Currently,
he finds she is able to bank about $100 a month out of her
alary. All told, she too has about $3500, a large part of it
n E bonds, which yield 4.15%.

Now Miss Baxter has decided she wants to invest in stocks.
Why? Because every time she cashes a bond, the $100 she
gets for it seems to buy less than it did the last time — not
much more than what she could have bought seven or
eight years ago with the $75 she put into the bond. She
wants to put her money into some investment where its
purchasing power will be better protected and where she'll
still get a good return on her money. And if she's
ucky, maybe she'll make a profit on her stocks — a big
enough profit so that in five years she will be able to take
that trip to Europe which she has always promised herself.

But maybe stocks will go down, her stocks included. That's
a risk she has to take, and fortunately it's one she can afford to take. If stocks drop, she can probably wait for them
to come back without any serious jeopardy, because her job
offers her a good measure of security. Quite apart from her

own medical and hospital insurance, she knows the firm wil
help her over any rough spots. And as for protection in he
old age — well, the firm has an excellent pension program
and that plus federal old-age insurance should take care o
her quite handily.

What kind of stocks should Miss Baxter buy?

Obviously, she wants to be pretty conservative in her se
lections, but she probably doesn't have to make safety he
sole objective. She can afford to take what's called a "busi
nessman's risk," and she should look for stocks that pay
relatively liberal dividends.

Miss Baxter should put her money into a half dozen dif
ferent stocks, each of them a blue chip, each a leader in it
own industry — stocks like National Dairy, Sears, Roebuc
& Company, Eastman Kodak, Standard Oil of New Jersey
or Standard of California, General Electric, RCA, Genera
Motors, or Ford, plus one good utility.

She should put about $500 apiece into each of these half
dozen stocks. This means she will have to sell $3000 of he
E bonds. She should sell the most recent ones and keep
$500 worth of the oldest ones, because as those bonds ge
closer to their maturity dates, they pay a proportionately
higher rate of interest.

As for the $100 a month which she is able to save, Miss
Baxter might prudently keep half as an emergency fund
until it exceeded $1000. With the other $50 a month she too
might open a Monthly Investment Plan account and put this
sum regularly into buying additional shares of one of the
stocks she already owns. As a matter of fact, she might
open two or three M.I.P. accounts, putting her $50 into one
stock one month and into another stock a second month or
a regular, rotating basis.

Mr. and Mrs. Chandler face quite a different problem, de
spite the fact that Mr. Chandler's income as a skilled tool
maker in an auto-parts manufacturing plant is about $800C
a year. To begin with, they live on a very modest scale in a
small Ohio town. Still in their thirties, they have been able
to raise two children, now eight and ten, buy their own home
and still save a little bit.

They have only about $1000 in their bank account, but
from now on that's going to grow fast. Mr. Chandler was
made foreman just last month, and that means $15 a week
more in the pay envelope. Furthermore, in just a couple of

months, the mortgage will be paid off, and they will have another $50 a month free and clear.

What it all adds up to is that they've got $1000 now, and they figure on having at least $1000 a year to invest from now on.

What about protection for his family? Mr. Chandler has a $5000 insurance policy, and he considers that plenty, in view of the benefit program which his union sponsors for all members.

He has become sold on stocks; he wants to go ahead right now, buying stocks in order to build a little estate.

That's a program that makes sense, provided he handles it right. He hasn't a lot of money to put into the market, and to start with, he wants to be sure that money is well protected. What if one of his children has to be hospitalized for a long time with something like polio?

Where should he start? His local utility — the Ohio Edison Company — might be as good as any. The dividends will help pay his electric bill. That's an idea that has real appeal for Mr. and Mrs. Chandler.

After that, he might buy ten shares of a natural-gas company, a stock that offers assurance of a fairly stable price, plus some possibilities of growth as natural-gas consumption continues to grow.

His future investments for some time might be of much the same type — fairly stable stocks but ones that nevertheless offer some prospect of growth over the long pull; nothing as spectacular as television or electronics, which market technicians might call "aggressive-growth situations," but perhaps something like American Can Company, which stands to grow as our population and food consumption increase.

Mr. and Mrs. Davenport are much better off financially, but from an investment point of view they're not as well off as the Chandlers. As one of the younger officers in a big advertising agency, Mr. Davenport makes $22,000 a year, but his scale of living is such that after taxes, mortgage payments on his $50,000 house, and premiums on a $50,000 life insurance policy, there's not much left over at the end of the year — nothing more than he might need to pay an unexpected doctor's bill. His equity in the house — the unmortgaged part that he owns — and the cash value of his life insurance policy represent about all his savings.

But Mr. Davenport has struck it rich. He just got a special

$5000 bonus, because he brought a new account into the agency last year. And Mr. Davenport knows exactly what he's going to do with that $5000. He's going to buy common stocks in two companies he has just read about. One of them is a new small airline serving a growing resort area, and the other is a company that Mr. Davenport believes is going to lick the problem of desalting sea water economically.

Furthermore, the stocks of both these companies have high *leverage*. Mr. Davenport just learned about leverage, and what he knows about it makes both stocks look more promising in terms of quick profits.

A stock has high leverage if the company that issued it has a lot of bonds and preferred stock outstanding in relation to the amount of common stock. Here's how leverage works: Suppose the company has to pay $500,000 in bond interest and preferred dividends every year. If it customarily makes only $1,000,000 profit before the payment of such fixed charges, it has only $500,000 left for the common-stock holders. But if the company suddenly makes $3,000,000 instead of $1,000,000, it will have $2,500,000 available for dividends on the common. In this situation, the company's profits would have tripled, but the amount of those profits available for dividends to the common-stock holder or for reinvestment in the company would have been multiplied five times, since holders of the bonds and preferred stock would still get only their guaranteed half million.

With such an increase in profits, there might well be an extra dividend on the common stock, maybe even an increase in the annual rate of the dividend, and because of that prospect, the price of a high-leverage stock shoots rapidly ahead whenever its profit outlook is good. On the other hand, when the profit picture is bad, such a common stock drops more rapidly than do the more conservative stocks of companies that have no bonds or preferred stock outstanding.

When Mr. Davenport announces what he expects to do with his bonus, Mrs. Davenport puts her foot down. It sounds altogether too speculative for her. That money, she contends, should be set safely aside to assure a college education for their two children.

How should Mr. and Mrs. Davenport solve their problem? Probably $2000 of their $5000 ought to go into government bonds in case the family meets a real emergency. As for the balance, the stock of a closed-end investment trust like Lehman Corporation or Tri-Continental Corporation might represent a happy compromise between Mrs. Davenport's conservatism and Mr. Davenport's "all-or-nothing" impulse.

Ordinarily it would not be prudent for a man to put all his investment funds in a single security, but an investment trust is an obvious exception because of its diversified holdings. Furthermore, shares in a closed-end trust can be bought on the exchange at standard commission rates (no loading charge) and are frequently available at a substantial discount — that is, at a price below net asset value per share.

Then too, Mr. Davenport is still only in his early forties and looks like a comer — the kind of a man who will get a number of bonuses and salary increases. As time goes by, he will probably be buying other stocks, and to save on commission costs, he might just as well begin buying in good-sized units.

Mr. Edwards is a Nebraska wheat farmer. For fifteen years life has been good to him. He has had good crops and has got good prices for them. He is completely clear of debt on his farm and on his equipment, and all of it is in excellent condition. Insurance is no worry to him, because his boys, both of them in college now, could take over the farm and make a good living out of it if anything should happen to him.

He has $14,000 in extra capital, but he's beginning to wonder if he's doing the best he can with it. His older son started him thinking about that the last time he was home from college. Mr. Edwards has $4000 in savings bonds, $4000 in a local building and loan association, $3000 in a savings account, and about $3000 in his checking account.

Obviously, he has far more cash than he needs. One thousand dollars in his savings account and another thousand in his checking account should suffice, especially since that $4000 worth of E bonds is really the equivalent of cash and stands as an adequate backlog in case he has bad luck with his crops this year or has to make unexpected repairs to buildings or equipment.

Hence, he could prudently put $4000 cash into securities, and he probably ought to sell his $4000 worth of building and loan shares *and* invest that money in stocks too — a total of $8000. The building and loan shares yield him perhaps 5¼ %, but he can get a good return, plus growth potential, by investing it in common stocks. Furthermore, his building and loan shares really represent an investment in real estate, and since his principal asset, the farm, is also real estate, it would seem wise for him to diversify his investments.

Here is a man who can really afford to take a fair measure of risk with his money for the sake of getting a better-than-average growth potential, because he already has a substantial measure of protection — far more than most people have. In fact, he can afford to be a bit speculative in his selections.

First, it would be natural for him to invest in a good farm-machinery stock — something like International Harvester — but he ought not to put too large a share of his $8000 into such a stock, because if farmers suffer a reverse in their fortunes, as they did in 1954-1956, so usually do the machinery manufacturers.

He might also properly invest in a company like Pillsbury or General Mills that processes the grain he raises.

But he might be better advised to put his money in the stocks of companies that have no relationship to his own business of farming — perhaps natural-resource stocks like Anaconda Copper or American Natural Gas, or the automobile companies like General Motors or Ford, or chemical stocks like Du Pont, Monsanto, or Dow. Other stocks that might suit his situation would be Merck, Minnesota Mining & Manufacturing, or Honeywell or Carrier, because all these companies operate in fields that show great future promise.

Mr. and Mrs. Frank are a retired couple, both over sixty-five. Old-age pensions plus small benefits accruing from a company pension plan are sufficient to provide an income of about $200 a month. Their only other assets consist of a home, which they own free and clear, and $35,000 in savings, most of it realized on annuities and life insurance policies in which Mr. Frank thriftily invested through the years.

On the other hand, if their assets are limited, so are their liabilities. Their two children are both married, and their futures are as secure as those of any people with moderate incomes can be.

The first impulse of Mr. and Mrs. Frank is to conserve what they have — to invest it in government bonds. But even with a 4.15% return on E bonds, their income from all sources would still be only $3852.50, or a little less than $75 a week.

Maybe they should put their $35,000 into preferred stocks

that could pay them a 4½% or 5% dividend. That would mean at least a little more income.

But maybe Mr. and Mrs. Frank are placing too high a premium on safety by confining their selections to conservative investments that will yield only 4% or 5%. Just how happily could they live in their declining years on $75 or $80 a week? They could get by, of course, but there certainly wouldn't be much left for any little luxuries — nothing for an occasional trip to see the children and the grandchildren. And all their lives they had looked forward to a little traveling after they retired.

In a situation like that, might it not be better for them to take somewhat more risk with their money for the sake of an occasional profit on some stock? Maybe they could put as much as two-thirds or three-quarters of their money into the so-called "cyclical" stocks — stocks that follow the business cycle more closely. It would seem feasible for them to put $3000 into a good company in each of a half-dozen different fields — petroleum, merchandising, paper, automobiles, chemicals, maybe even metals or aircraft or airlines.

During a business decline, dividends might be reduced, and that could make things a little hard for them. But what if they did have to sell $500 or $1000 worth of stock in a bad year in order to make ends meet? At their age, they can afford to dip into capital if they have to without putting their lives in peril. And consider the rewards they might reap in a good year. Dividends at 8%, 10%, even 12% were not remarkable on cyclical stocks like General Motors and Kennecott Copper in the period of 1948 to 1952 and might return again. More important, price increases of 20%, 30%, and 50% were commonplace then, and there is reason to believe that they can be had today with careful selection of good growth stocks.

For rewards like these, Mr. and Mrs. Frank can afford a sizable measure of risk on the bulk of their capital.

Finally, consider the situation of Mrs. Gordon, the fifty-seven-year-old widow of a successful doctor. Her principal assets consist of the family home and $95,000 worth of life insurance. True, the doctor did leave an assortment of stocks, but they proved to have a cash value of only about $5000, because, like most medical men who have little contact with business and less time in which to study it, Dr. Gordon had bought only the most speculative of securities — Canadian oil shares, stock in a plastic airplane company, and some preferred stocks that must have looked attractive because of big accumulations of back dividends — dividends that were owed but unfortunately never paid.

Mrs. Gordon doesn't want to see her capital dissipated that way. She wants to live off the income but leave the principal intact, so that she can pass it along to her three children, all of them now well launched on substantial careers of their own.

Mrs. Gordon begins her calculations where every investor in such a situation must: "How much income do I have to have?" She figures she can manage on $5000 a year, which means, of course, that she must get a return of 5% on her $100,000.

Time was when an investor like Mrs. Gordon would have had to put at least half of her money into common stocks if she wanted to realize a return of 5%. Thus, in the early fifties, she could have expected to earn only about 3% on government bonds and 4% or so on corporate bonds and good-grade preferreds. To average out at 5%, she would have had to turn to common stocks, but she would have experienced no difficulty finding top-quality stocks that would have given her a dividend return of 6% to 8%.

The bull market in the last decade changed all that. The dramatic upsurge in common stocks meant that yields (dividends figured as a percentage of the purchase price) declined sharply. As a consequence, Mrs. Gordon would have a hard time finding good-quality stocks that would pay her a 6% dividend, and she would have to learn not to be dismayed at having to pay a price fifteen or twenty times earnings per share. As a matter of fact, if she were investing for growth instead of income, she might find some of the more attractive issues selling at 30, 40, and even 50 times earnings.

Luckily, however, for Mrs. Gordon, as the yield on common stocks declined, the interest yield on government and corporate bonds rose sharply. So did the yield on preferreds, though less dramatically.

As a matter of fact, Mrs. Gordon would have little difficulty getting her 5% return by confining her investments wholly to bonds and preferred stocks. But she would probably be well advised still to put a good part of her funds — perhaps as much as half — into top-grade common stocks, partly because she may need some price appreciation on her investments to offset continued inflation and partly because such investments would provide insurance against a reversal in the cycle. She may advisedly put some of her money into the common stocks of utilities, because the stability of their operations makes for stability of both income and value. Some may be bank stocks selected for similar reasons. But most of them will probably be industrials of the blue-chip variety — stocks that have paid dividends consistently for a long period of years and thus offer some compensation for any compromise she may be forced to make temporarily in the 5% income return that she feels she needs.

Half of those listed on the New York Stock Exchange can boast of such records running back at least 25 years, and many of these can also be classified as the "bluest of the blue," because they are also the stocks of companies that have no bonds outstanding, and little or no preferred. Hence, all earnings or virtually all earnings are available for dividends on the common; and this can be important in a period of bad business. These low-leverage stocks — stocks like J. C. Penney, Du Pont, Eastman Kodak, Merck — are especially attractive to any conservative investor.

As a general rule, Mrs. Gordon should not put more than 10% of the capital that she has for common-stock investments into any one industry or more than 5% into any one company.

No one of the programs outlined for these seven investors is likely to fit your own situation. But a consideration of their problems and the ways in which they might have been solved can serve to illustrate the kind of sober thinking that every investor must go through before he can hope to decide what stocks or bonds are right for him. Remember, there is no all-purpose security — no stock that fits ideally into every man's portfolio. Each man must work out his own investment salvation for himself.

That's why the best advice that was ever given is "Investigate before you invest." And the investigation should properly begin with your own financial situation.

CHAPTER 33

When Is
the Time to Sell?

THUS far we have been talking almost exclusively about buying stocks — about investing for the long pull.

But just because a convincing case can be made for the fact that it is a good idea to have extra dollars invested, it doesn't follow that it is a good idea to keep them invested in the same securities.

Change is the common denominator of all life, and change can and does vitally affect the value of investments.

The intelligent investor keeps in mind two broad kinds of changes — changes in his own situation and changes in investment opportunities.

As far as the first classification is concerned, it is perfectly obvious that the kind of investment program which is well suited to a young man with no great responsibilities to anyone except himself is not the kind of program he should pursue when he starts rearing a family. And investments which are geared to that period of life when he is carrying the heaviest load are not the kind he should carry when the kids are through school and he is able — at the peak period of his earning power — to branch out on his own again and try to build something of an estate for himself before he has to start thinking soberly about retirement.

It is, of course, always later than we think, and changes in a man's personal situation, in his financial circumstances, come usually so gradually that he is rarely shocked into an awareness of the fact that it is high time he sat down and took a personal inventory of his situation — where he stands now and where he is headed. Most of us are just too used to rolling with the punch or drifting with the tide.

This is peculiarly true as far as investments are concerned because of the strange, irrational attachment that most men

— and women too — seem to feel for the stocks or bonds they own. It's no overstatement to say that many a man becomes married to his stocks and is apt to talk a good deal more pridefully about them to his associates in the clubhouse or on the commuter train than he does about his wife.

Once a man buys stock in a company, he seems to feel some sort of compulsion to talk it up to others — sell it to them. Thus he seeks from others confirmation of his own good judgment. In such circumstances, sale of the stock is almost tantamount to treason.

There is another psychological reason why most people are loath to sell securities. Very often, the decision to buy — the selection of Stock A over B, C, or D — was so charged with emotional conflict that the buyer wants to shut the door on the whole episode. Certainly he doesn't relish the idea of fighting the issue out all over again and weighing the comparative values against E, F, and G.

Nevertheless, there is that inexorable fact that investment values do constantly change and what was a good buy last year may be an even better sale this year.

Every investor owes it to himself to take an objective look at his holdings — as objective as possible — at least once a year. And when he tackles that job, he should ask himself at least one simple question about every stock in his list: "If I had the money, would I buy this stock at today's prices?"

If the answer is no, if you own a stock you wouldn't enthusiastically want to buy, you should consider the advisability of selling it, even if you have to take a loss on it — or *especially* if you have to take a loss.

And if you don't want to make the decision yourself, you might at least ask your broker for his opinion. As a matter of fact, if you don't want to review your whole investment program once a year as you should, you should submit the problems with all pertinent data to your broker and ask him for his recommendations and suggestions. Brokers are used to such requests, and in the main, they do a remarkably conscientious job on them. They know that suggestions for changes that are advanced simply for the sake of building commissions for themselves are bound to backfire and result in the long run in the loss of customers.

Of course, there are some investors who approach the job of evaluating their securities with the kind of relish that all of us should bring to bear on the job. These are the stock-

holders who carefully read the annual reports that they get
from the companies whose stock they own and painstakingly
compare performance with results in other years and other
companies.

Only a trained accountant can get the real meat out of a
corporate report, but there are a few simple points that
every investor can check on easily and determine if there
are any danger flags which might suggest the desirability
of a switch to another stock.

If the dividend is cut, even the least sophisticated investor is apt to be properly concerned, but the dividend is
actually of less importance in evaluating a stock than the
earnings figure. If a company's earnings drop, the stockholder has a right to know why. Often there are legitimate
reasons. The company may have decided to retire some debt
that had been a constant drain on its resources over a period
of time, or it may have embarked on some new program of
expansion or development. Such decisions might cut sharply
into earnings for any given year, but they hold a promise of
expanded profits in years to come.

Again, there are times when business in general or any
given industry in particular may go through a period of
stress. Hence, a company's earnings record must always be
considered on a comparative basis. A bad earnings record
on your stock is in itself no substantial reason for a switch
in holdings if other companies are doing no better.

Any cut in dividends or drop in earnings is certain to be
fully elaborated in the company's annual report, and although
the management will place the most palatable construction
possible on such unpleasant facts, its explanations are apt to
be pretty trustworthy, for they must pass the scrutiny of
trained security analysts in brokerage offices and banks.

The price-earnings ratio of a stock, which can always be
computed from the reported figures, is actually a more reliable measure of investment values than straight earnings
per share, for it reflects something of how other investors
regard your stock. Suppose your stock sold last year at a price
fifteen times earnings per share but sells now at only ten
times earnings. A drop like that would reflect a serious loss
of investor confidence in your company, unless, of course,
stocks in general had been under pretty heavy selling pressure and price-earnings ratios had dropped all along the line.

A decline in the price-earnings ratio on your stock is
the kind of danger signal that suggests a more intensive

study of other figures in the annual report. You might, for instance, look at the *income statement* and see how net sales have fared. Have they fallen off to a disturbing degree? And what about operating costs? Have they risen unduly? Has there consequently been a serious squeeze on profit from operations — net sales less operating costs? How does the margin of profit, obtained by dividing operating costs by net sales, compare with the figure for earlier years? How does it compare with other companies in the same industry?

Next, you might take a look at some of the key figures shown in the company's *balance sheet*. You will especially want to look at the *current assets* and the *current liabilities*. On the asset side of the ledger you will want to see if there has been any big drop in the company's cash position or its holdings of government bonds. You might similarly be concerned about any undue increase in *accounts receivable* — what people owe your company — or in *inventories*. Any big increase in inventories is apt to prove risky, for a sharp drop in prices could cause heavy losses. Then too, a big inventory figure can mean that the company has a lot of unsalable merchandise on its hands.

As far as current liabilities are concerned, the most important item is apt to be *accounts payable*, for this represents the money your company owes for raw materials, supplies, insurance, and the like.

More important than the total figure for current assets or the total figure for current liabilities is the relationship between the two. Most security analysts figure that current assets should be twice as large as current liabilities, but that is only a rough rule of thumb. In industries like railroads where inventories are not a major problem and where accounts receivable can easily be collected, lower rates of assets to liabilities are acceptable. On the other hand, in industries like chemicals or tobacco, ratios of three to one or four to one are more commonly expected.

The difference between current assets and current liabilities represents a company's *net working capital* — the money it has to grow on — and this is the lifeblood of business. Any serious shrinkage from year to year in a company's working capital is something that might properly worry an investor and make him think seriously about selling his stock.

Of course, even if an investor takes the time and trouble to look at just a few of these key factors in his company's

annual report — and there is no question of the fact that he
should — he is still not likely to have a substantial basis
for deciding to buy or sell, for the figures for any given
year take on meaning only as they are compared with the
same figures for earlier years and for other companies in
the same field which may represent alternative investments.
Furthermore, the most important question of all — how good
is the management? — is one to which the investor can find
only an inferential answer in any annual report.

Here is where he has the right to look for help and
service from his broker. Within reason, at least, he can expect detailed and specific answers to his questions, reliable
data on the basis of which he can make up his own mind
whether to buy, sell, or hold.

While brokers are frequently accused of stimulating customers to switch from one stock to another for the simple
sake of building commissions, the blunt fact of the matter
is that they don't suggest enough sales to enough of their
customers, probably because they are afraid of that very
accusation. And the customer, left to his lethargic devices, goes along, year after year, holding on to the same
old stocks, blissfully ignoring his own self-interest. A few
years ago a New York Stock Exchange survey showed that
a third of all people who owned stock had never sold
any. They had just bought and held on.

This static attitude toward investments is reflected in figures showing the *"turnover rate"* on the New York Stock Exchange. The turnover rate shows the percentage of all the
shares listed on the exchange that are traded in any given year.
In 1915 to 1920 it was 117%, and although it dropped to
70% from 1920 to 1925, it rose to a peak of 132% in 1928.
From then on the trend was almost steadily downward to a
low of 9% in 1942. There has been some revival of trading
interest since then, but the average figure for 1950 to 1960
stood at only 15%. It dropped back to 12% in 1962 but
revived again to 16% in 1965 and was headed higher in
1966. Of course, the number of shares listed on the exchange has increased steadily over the years, so percentage
figures are somewhat misleading, but not until 1963 did the
volume of shares traded surpass the 1,124,800,000 shares
that changed hands in 1929.

The do-nothing attitude of many stockholders with substantial profits on their holdings is unquestionably explained
by their reluctance to pay a capital-gain tax on their profits.

This is certainly the least defensible of all reasons for failure to sell.

Because the long-term outlook for American business is a bright and promising one, no one wants to preach a doctrine of "sell . . . sell . . . sell." Nevertheless, if you think you can improve your investment position, it is ridiculous to go along comforted simply by the thought that inflation and an expanding economy will rescue you from your own faulty judgment.

It is a truism of the stock market that there is a sell order to match every buy order. There has to be. That's something worth remembering. The man who sells a stock — some stock you own — very often has done his homework a little more conscientiously than the buyer. He has a better reason for selling the stock than anybody has for buying it — or than you have for holding it.

CHAPTER 34

The Folklore
of the Market

THE cheapest commodity in the world is investment advice from people not equipped to give it.

Many a man who doesn't own a share of stock still fancies himself as something of an authority on the market, and he's ready and willing to deliver himself of an opinion about it on the slightest provocation. If he actually owns stock himself, chances are you won't have to ask his opinion. He'll tell you what to buy, what to sell, and what's going to happen to the market. And you can't stop him.

The more a man knows about the market, the less he is willing to commit himself about it. The wisest of them all, old J. P. Morgan, when asked his opinion of the market, always used to reply, "It will fluctuate." He wasn't just being canny. He knew that was the only provable statement that could be made about the market.

Nevertheless, over the years, a number of generalizations about the market and about investing have come to be accepted as gospel. Actually, these homespun axioms must be accepted as little more than folklore. And like most folklore, each of them has a certain element of truth about it — and a certain element of nontruth.

For instance:

"Buy 'em and put 'em away."

This would have been a fine piece of advice if you had happened to buy $1000 worth of General Motors stock in 1923. By mid-1966 that stock would have been worth more than $60,000, and you would have collected over $40,000 in dividends.

But in the early twenties the car everybody was talking about was the Stutz Bearcat, and there was a great deal of speculative market interest in Stutz stock. You might very well have decided to buy $1000 worth of that. How would you have made out on that purchase? The answer is that you would have lost all your money, and furthermore you would never have collected a penny in dividends.

Of course, there is a measure of sense in the axiom. If you start worrying about fluctuations of a point or two and try to buy and sell on every turn, you can pay out a lot of money in commissions needlessly and maybe end up with less profit than if you'd "bought 'em and put 'em away."

Nevertheless, it's only good sense to remember that securities are perishable. Values do change with the passage of time. Industries die, and new ones are born. Companies rise and fall. The wise investor will take a good look at all his securities at least once a year, and he could do worse than to ask his broker to review them with him then.

"You never go broke taking profit."

That's obviously true. But you can certainly get hurt badly.

Suppose you had put $50 into Sears, Roebuck in 1906. By 1940, the stock that you had bought would have been worth $1276 at its high. That would have been a nice profit — and you might have decided to take it.

But look what you would have lost if you had sold. By 1954, your same holdings in that stock would have been worth over $4300, and by mid-1966, that same stock was worth almost $20,000.

Or consider another classic case. In 1914, you could have bought 100 shares of stock in International Business Machines for $2750, and in just eleven short years you could have sold out for $6364. Certainly you can never go broke taking profits of nearly 250%.

But as far as IBM stock is concerned, you certainly would have taken a licking if you had sold in 1925. For by the middle of 1966, your original 100 shares would have grown to 28,409 and they would have had a market value of $9,900,000.

Of course, a profit *is* always a nice thing to have — in the pocket, not just on paper.

"Buy when others are selling. Sell when they buy."

This sounds like a neat trick, if you can do it.

Obviously, you can't make money if you consistently buck the trend of the market. Where, for instance, would you have been if you had been selling stock all through the bull market since 1950?

So the trick lies in anticipating the action of all the others — in buying just before the crowd decides to buy and selling just ahead of them. This is just exactly the trick that the exponents of various formula plans try to turn by hitching their buying and selling operations to some arbitrary decline or advance in the market.

Others, less scientific, simply try to sell at the tops and buy at the bottoms. But how do you know when the market hits bottom? How far down is down?

Make no mistake about it. Anyone who tries to practice this fine art is "playing the market" in the purest sense of the phrase. He's speculating; he's not investing.

"Don't sell on strike news."

There's some truth to the old adage. Nowadays, labor troubles in any big company or in any industry are apt to be pretty well publicized. Consequently, the market is likely to have discounted the possibility of a strike during the time it was brewing; the stock will already have gone down in price, and it may even advance when the strike news breaks.

Again, many people think that a strike doesn't really damage a company's long-term profit picture. They contend that while a strike is on, demand for the company's products is only deferred, and as soon as the strike is over, the company will enjoy better business than ever.

But such a theory is often little more than wishful thinking. After all, most strikes end with the company facing a higher labor bill. And many times the demand for its products which a company couldn't fill while its employees were on strike has been happily filled by a competitor.

"Don't overstay the market."

A fine piece of advice, but how do you know when to sell and take your profit — if that's what you're interested in?

Sometimes you can tell by watching those basic business indicators that show what's happening to production, distribution, and consumption of goods. But sometimes you can't, because the market doesn't seem to be paying too close attention to them. That was certainly true in the years after World War II, in 1962, and in 1966.

Nevertheless, if business appears to be on the skids, and the stock market is still boiling merrily upward, sooner or later there's going to be a reckoning.

"Always cut your losses quickly."

Nobody wants to ride all the way downhill with a stock if the company is headed for bankruptcy, but at the same time you don't want to be stampeded into a sale by a price decline that may have no relationship to the fundamental value of the stock.

Remember, the price of a stock at any time reflects the supply and demand for that stock, the opinions and attitudes of all the buyers and all the sellers. If a stock is closely held, if its *"floating supply"* — the amount usually available in the market — is limited, the price of that stock can be unduly depressed for quite a period if some large holder is selling a sizable block of it, just because he may need the cash and not because he thinks less of the stock.

The market on any given day is made by just a tiny handful of all the people who own stocks. On the exchange as a whole ten million shares may be traded in one day, but that still represents only 1/10 of 1% of all shares listed on the exchange. The 99.9% who aren't selling have some reason for holding on — or think they do.

Of course, there is much truth in the observation that unsophisticated investors do tend to sell a stock too readily when they have a profit in it and to hang onto a stock in which they have a loss, hoping that it will come back.

"An investor is just a disappointed speculator."

This cynical observation has a measure of truth in it. Every stock buyer hopes for a big fat profit, even if he won't admit it to himself. So when the market drops, he does the best he can to assuage his disappointment by assuring himself and everybody else that of course he never expected to make a killing — he was just investing on the basis of the fundamental stock values.

This is especially true of that congenital bull — the odd-lot buyer. As a class, the odd-lotters almost always buy more than they sell. And all too often, they finally decide to buy only when the market is already too high.

So often does this happen that some speculators gauge their own actions by the relation of odd-lot buying to odd-lot selling. When that ratio increases — when the proportion of odd-lot purchases rises — the speculators sell.

But in the long run, the small investor often has the last laugh. After all, the stock market has gone pretty steadily up for 50 years, hasn't it? And since the odd-lot man is a heavy buyer of the market leaders — the 100 stocks that usually account for two-thirds of the exchange volume — he has made out pretty well over the long pull.

On the other hand, many a big speculator, like Daniel Drew, has died broke.

"A bull can make money. A bear can make money. But a hog never can."

That's one to remember.

The desire to make money leads most people into the market. Call it ambition or greed, it remains the prime motivating force of our whole business system, including the stock market.

But greed is always dangerous. It's an engine without a governor.

So you made a killing once in the market. Good. You were lucky. Don't think you can make one every day.

If you own a good stock, one that's paying you a good return on your money and seems likely to go on doing so, hang on to it. Don't keep looking for greener pastures, bigger profits. And forget about the other fellow and the killing he made — or says he made. Maybe he can afford to speculate better than you can.

In short, if you're an investor, act like one.

CHAPTER 35

Who Owns Stock?

IF Wall Street didn't exist, it would be necessary to invent it. In fact, that's just exactly what our forefathers did.

Why must there be a Wall Street?

Because, in our economy, capital, like labor, must be free to work where it wants to. If you've got extra dollars, you've got the right in our society to say where you want to put them to work in order to make more dollars.

And that's a right which would be a pretty empty one if there weren't some means for you to transfer your funds from one enterprise to another when you wanted to.

Wall Street provides that means. It's a marketplace for money.

And in the past twenty years, it has played an increasingly important role in our economy. It has made it possible for millions of people to put their savings to work in American business. That has been good for them, good for business, and good for the whole country.

Time was when only the wealthy people owned stocks and bonds. That's not true any longer. For one thing, there aren't as many wealthy people as there used to be. The millionaire is the vanishing American.

If business is to have the money it needs to go on growing, somebody has to take the rich man's place. That somebody can only be the investor of moderate means — thousands of such small investors, because it takes 1000 of them with $1000 each to equal the $1,000,000 in capital that one wealthy man may have supplied yesteryear. And tomorrow it will take many, many more thousands of them, because business is constantly in need of more and more investment capital to build new plants and replace old equipment. From the turn of the century to the end of World War II, business put $218 billion into plant and equipment, but in the next ten years, expansion accelerated so rapidly that $232 billion of capital were needed — more than in all the preceding 46 years. And the rate at which industry invested in new plant and equipment continued to grow until in 1966 such expenditures exceeded $60 billion with a forecast by the National Industrial Conference Board of $89 billion by 1975.

Wall Street bears the primary responsibility for recruiting the new investors who must supply this capital, Wall Street and all its counterparts throughout America — La Salle Street in Chicago, Montgomery Street in San Francisco, and Main Street in many a Middletown.

Wall Street takes its responsibilities seriously. Every year it puts millions of dollars into booklets, pamphlets, and letters to explain securities. It uses educational advertising — newspapers, magazines, television, radio, even car cards and billboards. It has taken the story of stocks and bonds to country fairs, department stores, labor unions, and women's clubs. It has even put the story into movies that any group can show free of charge.

How well has Wall Street done with all this educational effort in stimulating new investor interest?

Better than you might think — but not nearly so well as it must.

Not until June 1952 did Wall Street know just how it stood on the job. Strange as it may seem, nobody could say how many stockholders there were in the country until the New York Stock Exchange got the Brookings Institution to find out. American Telephone & Telegraph knew it had 1,200,000 stockholders back then. And 30 other big companies knew they had more than 50,000 apiece. But nobody knew just what duplication there was in those stockholder lists. And nobody knew the grand total for all companies.

The Brookings Institution reported then that the total was 6,490,000, representing a little more than 4% of all individuals and just about 10% of all the families of the country. Disappointing as that total figure was when it was announced, Wall Street found encouragement in the fact that about one-fifth of the total had become stockholders in the preceding three years.

Four years after the Brookings study, the New York Stock Exchange retained Alfred Politz Research, Inc., to make another census of shareholders, and its findings were announced in July 1956. Politz reported a total of 8,630,000 stockholders in publicly owned corporations, an increase of 33% in four years.

Since then, the New York Stock Exchange has conducted similar censuses every three years, and each census has shown a steady increase in shareownership, until in 1965 the exchange was able to report that the total of individual stockholders had passed the twenty-million mark. Here are some of the highlights of the 1965 report:

More women than men own stock; 51% of all shareowners are women. However, since women outnumber men in the general population, the incidence of shareownership among men is greater; 17% of all adult males and 16% of all adult females own stock. The exchange census did not delve into the reasons why women outnumber men in the investment world, but since housewives account for more than a third of all shareownership, it seems reasonable to assume that many men have put their holdings in their wives' names for tax or estate reasons. Certainly men account for a considerably greater proportion of total stock trading, although no one can ignore the fact that women, especially business and professional women, have become increasingly active in the market.

The median household income of all shareowners was $9500, as compared with $8600 in 1962 and only $6200 in 1956. Although shareowners in the $10,000 to $15,000 income bracket have shown the largest increase, some 55% of all stockholders still report family incomes of less than $10,000. Included in this number, of course, are many retired people whose annual incomes are no index of their ability to own stocks; many of them depend to a considerable extent on dividends from stocks that they accumulated in their earlier, high-income years.

Half of the adult shareowners, ten million of them, have attended college, and of these, six million are college graduates.

People who own stocks listed on the New York Stock Exchange account for 62% of all shareowners, but in the period from 1962 to 1965 their number increased only 13%, while those who owned only over-the-counter issues or mutual funds or both increased 34% — with mutual funds accounting for most of that growth.

California, with 2,500,000 shareowners, took the lead in shareownership away from New York by a margin of 100,000, but the New England states still show the greatest proportion of shareowners in relation to population.

Between 1962 and 1965, the biggest increase in shareownership was in communities with populations between 2500 and

25,000. Nearly 30% of all the nation's shareholders live in towns of that size.

The median age of all new shareholders in 1965 was 41, compared with 39 in 1962, and 35 in 1959.

Despite the consistent gains in shareownership over the years, it is noteworthy that some fifteen million people with family incomes of $10,000 or more still in 1965 did not own any common stock. It is also significant — at least as far as brokers are concerned — that the majority of stockholders have few, if any, transactions during an entire year; the number who trade actively, buying or selling at least once a month, probably do not exceed 600,000, little more than 3% of the total.

Nevertheless, the New York Stock Exchange sees an ever-brighter future ahead. On the basis of our projected growth in gross national product, personal income, and corporate profits, the exchange in 1965 predicted that by 1975, shareownership would grow to thirty million, while daily trading volume would increase to an average of ten million shares.

Those rosy expectations may well be realized, but there are still some perplexing questions that trouble Wall Street.

Why is it that probably a third or more of the people who would appear able to invest don't actually own any stocks?

Why has the average age of *new* shareowners risen steadily over the years? Why did the proportion of shareowners in the 21-39 age bracket drop as it did — from 14.3% to 13.3% of the total between 1962 and 1965? Why aren't these younger people investing in greater numbers?

Why should shareowners represent only 16% of the population while 88% have savings accounts, 79% own their own homes, and 53% own U.S. savings bonds?

In short, why don't more people invest?

There's one clear-cut answer to that. Millions of people still don't understand stocks and bonds, and what people don't understand they are apt to be afraid of.

We may be the richest nation in the world, the very bulwark of a modern and enlightened capitalism, but the blunt fact of the matter is that we are as a nation financially illiterate.

Some years ago, the New York Stock Exchange undertook to find out just how much — or rather how little — America knew about securities. For the job, it retained the Public Opinion Research Corporation.

In this survey, people were asked just how they would

invest money if they had some extra cash, and to make the problem as easy as possible, the researchers suggested six different channels of investment — government bonds, corporate bonds, stock, life insurance, real estate, and savings banks. You could divide the money up any way you liked — all of it in one or a little in each.

Here are the kinds of investment and the proportion of the people who favored putting at least some money into each of them.

Government Bonds	83%
Life Insurance	67%
Savings Banks	43%
Real Estate	42%
Stocks	16%
Corporate Bonds	13%

To see just how much knowledge and understanding lay behind these selections, the researchers then told the people to assume that ten years of steadily rising prices lay ahead of them.

Would they, in that situation, the researchers asked, see any disadvantage to owning government bonds?

More than half of the people — 56% of them — blandly said no. They could see no disadvantage to having their money in an investment with a fixed-dollar value in a period of inflation!

Yes, ignorance is unquestionably the biggest deterrent to investing. But there's another factor in the picture too. Successful investing isn't simple. It means thinking your own investment problem through to a logical conclusion. It means being willing to study the facts about various securities. It means checking up on a stock before you buy it and after you buy it.

That's not easy, admittedly. But it's not beyond the capabilities of any of us. Not if Nicholas J. Harvalis could do it. Maybe you saw the story in the newspapers about him when he died in 1950 — the uneducated immigrant who worked all his life in restaurants for a wage that never exceeded $125 a month but who managed to leave an estate of $160,000.

Here is how he did it, as related by his counselor, Max D. Fromkin of Omaha:

Fromkin & Fromkin
Keeling Building
Omaha 2, Nebraska

February 13th, 1951

I give you now the story of Nicholas J. Harvalis, late of Omaha, Nebraska, who departed this life on the last day of the month and year of 1950, to wit, December 31, 1950, shortly after the close of the market for the year.

Nicholas was a friend of mine for over 25 years, and during that time I was his attorney and counselor.

Nicholas came to this country from Greece at the age of 15 years. He was without education and money, and he immediately went to work as a waiter in various cafés and restaurants operated by his countrymen in Omaha at wages which provided a bare living for him.

He was unmarried and lived the many years in Omaha alone in a modest room.

He was thrifty to a point of many times denying himself the comforts of life in order to save from his earnings sufficient to make investments for his security and old age. He employed his leisure hours reading and studying financial papers and books. He also spent many hours in the Public Library poring over history and philosophy.

On May 18, 1927, he became a citizen of the United States by naturalization. He was a firm and optimistic believer in the opportunities offered the common man in the United States, and he believed that the greatest return in investments was in common stocks of well-managed companies.

Thus, beginning about 1937, he started a systematic purchase of common stocks. His early investments were in National Distillers, Laclede Gas, General Motors, S. S. Kresge, Atlantic Refining, International Nickel, J. C. Penney, General Electric. He bought a few shares in each of these companies and added to them from time to time.

He kept meticulous records of all of his transactions, including dividends received. His dividends, which at first were modest, he would save and reinvest in these same stocks.

He subscribed to the *Wall Street Journal* and avidly read the paper from cover to cover. As a matter of fact, at the time of his death the only thing in his room apart from bare furnishings was a neat stack of issues of the *Wall Street Journal* for the last two years.

In 1943, he began selling stocks for long-term profits when he felt the market was high, and later he began a repurchasing program.

In 1943, his earnings from wages as a waiter and soda jerk in a local drugstore known as the Paxton Pharmacy at 15th & Harney

Streets in Omaha were $1,602.00, while his income from dividends of common stocks was $1,825.00.

In 1944, his earnings from wages were $1,525.00, and his dividends from common stocks rose to $2,285.00. In the same year he made from gains in the sale of stocks the sum of $2,600.00.

In 1945, his wages were the same, but dividends from stocks came to $2,785.60. Long-term profits in that year were $7,713.84.

In 1946, he began acquiring Cities Service stock.

In 1946, his dividends from stocks fell to $1,506.24, but his gains on the sale of stocks were very substantial.

In 1947, his dividends rose to $2,191.24.

In 1948, his dividends were $10,562.98.

In 1949, his dividends were $7,081.24.

In 1950, his dividends were $10,095.50.

During all these years he earned from wages as a soda jerk a sum not to exceed $1600 per year.

When he died on December 31, 1950, he was the owner of the following common stocks:

    1370 shares Cities Service common
     200 shares Boeing common
     300 shares Rock Island common
     100 shares General Electric common
     200 shares American Bank Note common
      40 shares Hearst Consolidated Publications 7% preferred
     200 shares Great Northern Iron Ore.

The above shares had an approximate value at the time of his death of $160,000.00.

Nicholas J. Harvalis kept perfect records and had in his room every statement from his broker of every transaction he had ever made. In addition he made accurate reports for income tax purposes and was proud to pay his government every cent of tax for the privilege of his citizenship and the opportunity that his government gave him.

In my association with him as his attorney I found him always to be a very polite, mild-mannered, and courteous individual. He was often asked for advice on the market and was always very cautious to mention only highly rated dividend-paying stocks.

Nicholas amassed this huge sum considering his limitations and in his death he leaves to his brother and sisters (11 of them) in Greece a substantial inheritance, which they will no doubt spend more freely and with less good judgment than the man who earned it.

Very truly yours,
MAX FROMKIN

Few of us would be willing to pay the price Mr. Harvalis did for his achievement. But then most of us would be willing to settle for just a small measure of that success — the success that can be achieved not by luck, not by "insid tips," not by speculation, but by prudent and intelligent ir vesting.

Appendix I

In any given year, about 90% of the 1200 stocks listed on the New York Stock Exchange can be expected to pay a cash dividend. Of course, it's not always the same 90%, but approximately half of the stocks haven't missed a dividend in at least a quarter of a century.

Stocks with long records of continuous dividends are generally regarded as very stable, even though in a bad year one or more of them may stumble and have to pass a dividend.

If stability is of primary concern to you in your investment program, you may be particularly interested in the following list, prepared by Standard & Poor's Corp., of stocks on the New York Stock Exchange that have paid quarterly dividends for 40 years or more through December 1965.

Stocks Paying Quarterly Dividends for Forty Years or More Through December 1965

Stock	Year Continuous Dividends Began	Stock	Year Continuous Dividends Began
Air Reduction Co.	1917	Boston Edison Co.	1892
Allied Chem. Corp.	1921	Brown Shoe Co.	1923
Amerada Petroleum	1922	Burroughs Corp.	1906
Amer. Brake Shoe	1904	Carolina Tel. & Tel.	1900
American Can Co.	1923	Carpenter Steel	1908
Amer. Elec. Pwr.	1910	Cent. Aguirre Sugar	1916
Amer. Home Prod.	1926	Cent. Hudson G.&E.	1903
Amer. Natural Gas	1904	Central Illinois Lt.	1921
American News Co.	1864	Chase Manh't'n. Bk.	1918
American Snuff Co.	1903	Chesebrough-Pond's	1919
Amer. Tel. & Tel.	1882	C.I.T. Financial	1924
American Tobacco	1921	Cleveland Elec. Ill.	1912
Associates Investing	1920	Clevite Corp.	1922
Balt. Gas & Elec.	1911	Coca-Cola Co.	1921
Beech-Nut Life Sav.	1903	Combustion Engr'g	1912
Borden Company	1924	Commonw'l. Edison	1890

Stock	Year Continuous Dividends Began
Con. Edison	1892
Continental Can	1923
Corn Products Co.	1919
Corning Glass Wks.	1922
Dentists' Sup. N.Y.	1923
Detroit Edison Co.	1909
Dome Mines, Ltd.	1920
Dow Chemical	1912
Duke Power	1926
DuPont (E.I.) Nem.	1905
Eastman Kodak Co.	1902
Elec. Storage Btry.	1901
Fafnir Bearing Co.	1913
Firestone Tire & Rub.	1924
First Nat'l. Stores	1914
Foxboro Company	1916
Garlock, Inc.	1906
General Electric	1899
General Foods	1922
General Motors	1923
Grant (W.T.) Co.	1917
Great Atl. & Pac.	1925
Great North. Paper	1910
Heime Products	1912
Heller (Walter E.)	1921
Hercules Powder	1913
Houston Ltg. & Pwr.	1922
Ingersoll-Rand Co.	1919
Interco, Inc.	1913
Int'l. Business Mach.	1916
Int'l. Harvester	1910
Iowa Power & Light	1916
Island Creek Coal	1912
Kroger Company	1910
Liggett & Myers Tob.	1912
Link Belt Co.	1913
McAndrews & Forbes	1908
May Dept. Stores	1911
McCall Corp.	1926
McIntyre Porc. Mines	1924
Melville Shoe	1917
Minn. Mng. & Mfg.	1916
National Biscuit	1899
Nat'l. Dairy Prod.	1924
Nat'l. Fuel Gas	1903
Nat'l. Lead	1906
Nat'l. Standard	1922
Nat'l. Steel	1908
New England T. & T.	1886
Norfolk & West'n Ry.	1901
Norwich Pharmacal.	1925
Olin Mathieson Ch.	1926
Orange & Rock Util.	1914

Stock	Year Continuous Dividends Began
Otis Elevator	1911
Owens-Illinois	1907
Pacific Gas & El.	1919
Pacific Lighting	1909
Pacific Tel. & Tel.	1925
Parke, Davis	1897
Pennsalt Chemicals	1913
Pennzoil Co.	1926
Phila. Electric	1913
Pitts. Plate Glass	1899
Potomac Electric	1920
Procter & Gamble	1898
Public Serv. E. & G.	1920
Pullman, Inc.	1867
Quaker Oats	1922
Raybestos-Manh't'n.	1898
Rex-Chainbelt	1922
Richardson-Merrell	1925
Riegel Paper	1897
San Diego Gas & El.	1909
Scott Paper Co.	1926
Shattuck (Frank G.)	1925
Sherwin-Williams	1922
Singer Company	1890
South'n. Cal. Ed.	1910
Stand. Oil Calif.	1912
Stand. Oil Ind.	1913
Stauffer Chemical	1915
Sterling Drug	1913
Sun Oil Co.	1912
Texaco, Inc.	1903
Texas Gulf Sulphur	1921
Texas Utilities	1919
Timken Roller Bear.	1921
Toledo Edison	1922
Torrington Co.	1898
Union Carbide	1918
Union Electric	1918
Union Oil Calif.	1916
Union Pacific R. R.	1907
Union Tank Car.	1919
United Eng. & Fdry.	1902
United Shoe Machy.	1899
U. S. Gypsum	1919
U. S. Pipe & Fdry.	1926
U. S. Playing Card	1896
U. S. Tobacco Co.	1918
Upjohn Company	1921
Washington Gas Lt.	1885
West Va. Pulp & Pap.	1892
Westinghouse Air Br.	1894
Woolworth (F. W.)	1912
Wrigley (Wm.) Jr.	1911

Appendix II

MANY investors, especially those who are conservatively inclined, are interested in knowing what stocks are most favored by the big institutional investors — pension funds, insurance companies, foundations, investment companies, colleges, and the like. They believe with some logic that the professional managers of such large funds are better able to judge long-term investment values than they are.

Below is a list of the Big Board institutional favorites, prepared by Standard & Poor's Corp. for the New York Stock Exchange as of April 15, 1966. Obviously, relative ranking on the list will change from time to time, but once a stock has been bought by several hundred institutions, it is not apt to be dislodged easily from its position of status.

STOCKS WHICH ARE INSTITUTIONAL FAVORITES

Stock	Number of Institutions Holding Stock	Number of Shares Owned (000 Omitted)
General Motors	1279	11096
Standard Oil (N.J.)	1179	12767
American Tel. & Tel.	1112	10097
Int'l. Business Mach.	1057	3669
General Electric	1005	5553
Texaco, Inc.	946	11860
DuPont (E.I.) Nem.	811	14729
Union Carbide Corp.	787	5636
Socony Mobil Oil	695	5075
Gulf Oil Corp.	647	9437
Eastman Kodak Co.	626	5898
Sears, Roebuck & Co.	619	4130
Monsanto Co.	573	3944
Ford Motor Co.	556	6775
Phillips Petroleum	521	2546
International Paper	507	6748

Stock	Number of Institutions Holding Stock	Number of Shares Owned (000 Omitted)
Standard Oil (Ind.)	492	4733
National Lead	480	1013
General Foods	475	1702
American Cyanamid	471	1215
Amer. Elec. Pwr.	462	6098
South'n Cal. Edison	445	4699
Dow Chemical	436	2358
Standard Oil of Cal.	435	5125
Texas Utilities	423	4517
Goodyear Tire & Rub.	420	4851
Gen'l. Tel. & Elec.	417	6639
Chase Manh't'n. Bk.	402	2247
Commonw. Edison	400	3360
Minn. Mng. & Mfg.	397	2940
Nat'l Dairy Prod.	393	489
Southern Company	385	7887

Stock	Number of Institutions Holding Stock	Number of Shares Owned (000 Omitted)	Stock	Number of Institutions Holding Stock	Number of Shares Owned (000 Omitted)
Allied Chem. Corp.......	379	3160	American Can Co.........	320	1707
Merck & Company........	375	4178	Honeywell, Inc. 320		2024
Penney (J. C.) Co.......	372	1467	Int'l. Harvester............	318	2053
			Procter & Gamble........	313	1212
Caterpillar Tractor........	371	6337			
Virginia Elec. & Pwr...	367	3476	U. S. Gypsum Co.........	310	1125
Pfizer (Chas.) & Co.....	362	2186	Scott Paper Co.............	308	2286
Pacific Gas & Elec.......	359	3435	U. S. Steel Corp.........	297	2205
Amer. Home Prod.........	356	1503	Kennecott Copper	294	1370
			Continental Can	290	1891
Continental Oil	345	4927			
Central & So. West.....	345	4225	Pub. Serv. El. & Gas..	289	3526
Westinghouse Elec.	338	4375	Nat'l. Cash Register....	287	1124
Int'l. Nickel of Can.....	336	3906	Reynolds (R.J.) Tob.....	281	3335
Consumers' Power........	335	2059	Royal Dutch Petro.......	280	7608
			Cons. Edison (N.Y.)......	278	2093
Corn Products Co.........	325	1052	Union Pacific R. R.....	275	2311

Appendix III

Savings banks in New York State are permitted to invest in common stocks that meet certain very high standards of investment quality. They are also authorized under law to invest in shares of an investment company owned by and operated exclusively for mutual savings banks of the state. For this purpose, Institutional Investors Mutual Fund, Inc., was set up and has been operating since May 1953.

As of March 31, 1966, this investment company, operated by the Savings Bank Trust Company, held in its portfolio shares of the following common stocks, listed by industry classification:

Shares		Per cent of Total
	AEROSPACE	
43,400	Cessna Aircraft Company	1.60
24,000	United Aircraft Corporation	1.55
		3.15
	AIRLINES	
24,100	American Airlines, Inc.	1.27
14,000	Northwest Airlines, Inc.	2.10
21,500	Pan American World Airways, Inc.	1.05
		4.42
	AUTOMOBILES AND ACCESSORIES	
10,600	General Motors Corporation	.75
	CHEMICALS	
22,338	Air Products & Chemicals, Inc.	1.32
14,500	American Cyanamid Company	.89
32,416	W. R. Grace & Co.	1.26
29,700	Hercules Powder Company	.83
24,900	Pennsalt Chemicals Corporation	.88
26,400	Union Carbide Corporation	1.26
		6.44

Shares		Per cent of Total
	COMMUNICATIONS	
41,000	General Telephone & Electronics Corporation	1.29
	ELECTRICAL EQUIPMENT AND ELECTRONICS	
33,400	AMP, Incorporated	1.40
24,250	General Cable Corporation	1.31
21,000	General Electric Company	1.73
11,400	Magnavox Company	.95
43,000	McGraw-Edison Co.	1.03
27,367	Sunbeam Corporation	1.11
12,200	Zenith Radio Corporation	1.43
		8.96
	ELECTRIC UTILITIES	
38,400	American Electric Power Company	1.11
21,000	Baltimore Gas & Electric Company	.58
22,700	Central and South West Corporation	.77
22,538	Commonwealth Edison Company	.85
23,300	Kansas City Power & Light Company	.69
17,600	Kansas Gas & Electric Company	.42
30,300	Louisville Gas & Electric Company	.75
29,400	Middle South Utilities, Inc.	.50
14,600	Northern Indiana Public Service Company	.68
47,930	Oklahoma Gas & Electric Company	.97
28,600	Public Service Company of Indiana, Inc.	.94
35,200	Public Service Electric & Gas Company	.97
28,200	Southern California Edison Company	.78
28,400	The Southern Company	.64
21,300	Tampa Electric Company	.43
14,500	Texas Utilities Company	.63
17,300	Toledo Edison Company	.49
		12.20
	INDUSTRIAL MACHINERY	
30,300	Allis-Chalmers Manufacturing Company	.81
26,400	The Black & Decker Manufacturing Co.	1.20
25,200	Worthington Corporation	.77
		2.78
	INSURANCE	
17,000	Continental Casualty Company	.64
28,900	Hartford Fire Insurance Company	1.47
44,005.5	United States Fidelity and Guaranty Company	1.75
		3.86

Shares		Per cent of Total
	MEDICINE AND HEALTH	
39,000	The Kendall Company	1.35
40,214	Max Factor & Company	1.08
39,000	Merck & Co., Inc.	2.27
30,600	Miles Laboratories, Inc.	.89
4,100	The Norwich Pharmacal Company	.17
38,161	Rexall Drug and Chemical Company	1.23
22,700	G. D. Searle & Co.	1.05
		8.04
	MISCELLANEOUS	
23,100	Essex Wire Corporation	.66
43,900	Harris-Intertype Corporation	1.12
35,400	Textron, Inc.	1.13
		2.91
	NATURAL GAS	
15,000	Arkansas Louisiana Gas Company	.44
15,300	Consolidated Natural Gas Company	.76
27,150	Peoples Gas Light & Coke Company	.81
		2.01
	NONFERROUS METALS	
17,000	Aluminum Company of America	1.10
	OFFICE EQUIPMENT	
18,000	Addressograph-Multigraph Corporation	.93
9,150	International Business Machines Corporation	3.55
23,000	Xerox Corporation	4.26
		8.74
	PAPER	
23,100	Hammermill Paper Company	1.04
38,600	Rayonier, Incorporated	1.13
22,000	Union Bag-Camp Paper Corporation	.79
		2.96
	PETROLEUM	
23,500	Continental Oil Company	1.10
30,500	Kerr-McGee Corporation	1.67
26,700	Socony Mobil Oil Company	1.85
28,400	Standard Oil Company (New Jersey)	1.57
25,300	Texaco, Inc.	1.40
45,000	Union Oil Company of California	1.84
		9.43

Shares		Per cent of Total
	PRINTING AND PUBLISHING	
16,900	Scott, Foresman & Co.	.84
10,500	The Times Mirror Company	.47
		1.31
	RECREATION	
19,200	Eastman Kodak Company	1.77
22,800	Polaroid Corporation	2.51
		4.28
	RETAIL TRADE	
10,000	S. S. Kresge Company	.55
27,000	The Kroger Company	.64
18,700	Sears, Roebuck & Co.	.80
		1.99
	STEEL	
18,300	The Cleveland-Cliffs Iron Company	1.10
35,400	Copperweld Steel Company	.72
		1.82
	TEXTILE AND APPAREL	
30,500	American Enka Corporation	.86
27,600	Burlington Industries, Inc.	.94
31,500	Celanese Corporation of America	1.80
24,500	Cluett, Peabody & Co., Inc.	1.47
		5.07
	TRANSPORTATION	
43,000	General American Transportation Corporation	1.29
29,000	United States Freight Company	1.23
34,900	Westinghouse Air Brake Company	1.06
		3.58
2,218,219.5	Total Common Stock	97.09

Index

253

If you think this book was good, wait 'til you see what *else* we've got in store for you!

Send for your FREE catalog of Bantam Bestsellers today!

This money-saving catalog lists hundreds of bestsellers originally priced from $3.75 to $15.00—yours now in Bantam paperback editions for just 50¢ to $1.75! Here is a great opportunity to read the good books you've missed and add to your private library at huge savings! The catalog is FREE! So don't delay—send for yours today!

Ready for Mailing Now
— — — — — — Send for your FREE copy today — — — — —

BANTAM BOOKS, INC.
Dept. GA3, 414 East Golf Road, Des Plaines, Ill.

I'm tired of paying high prices for good books. Please send me your latest free catalog of Bantam Books.

Name_____

Address_____

City_____ State_____ Zip_____

Please allow about four weeks for delivery

GA3—2/69